How Can We Know What God Means?

How Can We Know
What God Means? ❧

The Interpretation of Revelation

Jorge J. E. Gracia

palgrave

HOW CAN WE KNOW WHAT GOD MEANS?
© Jorge J. E. Gracia, 2001

First published 2001 by PALGRAVE™
175 Fifth Avenue, New York, N.Y.10010 and
Houndmills, Basingstoke, Hampshire RG21 6XS.
Companies and representatives throughout the world

PALGRAVE is the new global publishing imprint of St. Martin's Press LLC
Scholarly and Reference Division and Palgrave Publishers Ltd (formerly
Macmillan Press Ltd).

ISBN 0–312–24025–2 hardback
ISBN 0–312–24028–7 paperback

Library of Congress Cataloging-in-Publication Data
Gracia, Jorge J. E.
How can we know what God means? : the interpretation of revelation /
Jorge J. E. Gracia.
    p.   cm.
    Includes bibliographical references and index.
    ISBN 0–312–24025–2 – ISBN 0–312–24028–7 (pbk.)
    1. Revelation.   I. Title.
BL475.5.G73   2001
212'.6—dc21   2001032753

A catalogue record for this book is available from the British Library.

Design by Letra Libre, Inc.

First edition: September 2001
10 9 8 7 6 5 4 3 2 1

Printed in the United States of America.

Fides quaerens intellectum.
Anselm

Contents

Preface

Why should anyone bother to ask how we can know what God means? The reasons are many. Religion is undergoing a renaissance of sorts throughout the world today, but there are both serious conflicts between religious groups and strong disagreements as to the correct way of interpreting divine revelation even within the same religion. In spite of the growth of secularization, technology, and science, statistics tell us that religious conversions are on the rise, and the number of people who take religion and divine revelation seriously is at an all-time high.[1] This phenomenon, however, has increased rather than decreased conflicts among members of different religions and even within the same religion. Protestants fight Catholics in Northern Ireland, Serbian Greek Orthodox fight with Kosovo Muslims in Yugoslavia, Muslims fight with Jews in Palestine, Hindus fight with Muslims in India, and so on. These conflicts demoralize thoughtful believers and lend support to those who wish to attack religion. Religious communities find difficulty explaining how their faiths, whose aims are often associated with spiritual fulfillment, blessedness, and enlightenment, can give rise to frustration, wretchedness, and confusion. A source of clarity turns into a cause of obfuscation, and an instrument of peace and justice becomes the arm of violence and abuse. Those who lack faith, then, are confirmed in their view that religions are no more than irrational superstitions, or ideological instruments used for the exploitation of others, and should be eradicated from the face of the Earth.

Religious disagreements become particularly bitter when it comes to the appropriate ways of understanding and dealing with revelation, even within the same religious traditions and with regard to the same scriptures. Liberal Christians reject the literal interpretation of the Christian scriptures favored by Evangelicals; many Protestant groups do not accept the role of tradition in interpretation that Roman Catholics consider essential; Orthodox Jews strictly follow eating regulations presented in the Torah, but Reform Jews take these in a different sense; and so on. The sources of these disagreements vary considerably. Some are rooted in historical events and traditions, but quite often they signal deep confusions concerning the interpretation of what believers take to be divinely revealed.

In recent years these confusions have been multiplied by the rise in the number and variety of interpretational approaches used to understand revelation. Whereas in the past there appeared to be a rather limited number of these, nowadays the list seems endless. Culturalist, sociological, literary, psychoanalytical, historical, political, philosophical, and feminist interpretations, to name just a few, abound. But are all these legitimate? Do they make sense when applied to religious texts? These and other questions cry out for answers that seldom are even attempted in the pertinent literature. Most often it is assumed that the interpretational approach used is simply a matter of individual or community preference. But does this make sense, and does it help to bring about understanding and agreement?

There is room and need, then, for a discussion of these issues from a nonpartisan perspective, which explores the tacit assumptions that underlie them. In particular, we need an evenhanded examination of the roots of disagreements concerning the interpretation of revelation and the obstacles on the way to their resolution. Much has been written on divine revelation and its interpretation, but most of it has been written from particular religious perspectives. Indeed, even books that claim neutrality often betray a definite apologetic agenda, with the result that little progress has been made toward the resolution of religious conflicts and disagreements among religious communities.

But there is another, perhaps even deeper reason why an investigation into the interpretation of revelation is important. If we assume that God exists and that he has revealed himself to humanity, surely then the understanding of that revelation is without a doubt fundamental for humans. What else could be more fundamental, or even as fundamental, as what God has to tell us about himself, the world, and his relationship to us? What else could serve better as the basis for our views, actions, and plans? And how could we ever claim any kind of completeness to our knowledge without incorporating God's message into it? No wonder that some Christian theologians hold that all knowledge is meaningless without theological knowledge because all knowledge is ultimately reducible to theology.[2]

Indeed, even if there were no God, understanding the significance of what a large part of humanity considers as divine revelation would still be a very important business. We need to know how this revelation came to be regarded as such, how the notion of God developed, and the reasons that led human beings to come up with these ideas. Understanding revelation, even if both revelation and God are nothing but anthropological creations, would tell us important things about ourselves, our history, and our future. The death of God, so frequently proclaimed in many quarters, does not diminish the need to understand revelation and its interpretation.

In this book, I do not address the issue of whether divine revelation comes from a divinity (or divinities) or is merely a result of human ingenuity. Nor do I discuss criteria of genuine divine revelation. The answers to these questions, *malgré* Kant, ultimately depend on theological views.[3] Faith could furnish their foundation, but this is not a theological treatise. My aim is to understand the nature of revelation and the most general conditions of its interpretation from a philosophical standpoint. This means that some of the theses I defend are hypothetical, as they ultimately depend on answers to theological questions that a book of this nature cannot give, but not all the theses I propose are of this sort. Indeed, the main ones apply, regardless of the answers one gives to questions concerning the theological underpinnings of revelation. Moreover, the views I propose have important implications for theology and religious hermeneutics. They concern the proper way to interpret revelation, the possibility of definitive interpretations, and the relativity of those interpretations, all fundamental issues in both.

The general perspective from which this book is written is Western; I frequently speak of "God" rather than "gods," and the examples I use are taken primarily from the Judeo-Christian tradition. But most of what I say applies to all that is regarded as divine revelation, regardless of its source. The question of whether all religions have a concept of divine revelation, or even of just revelation, is controversial and need not detain us here.[4] As long as a religious tradition accepts the notion of a divinity (or divinities) who has bestowed a revelation on humanity, much of what I say is pertinent. The cases in which it is not should be evident as we go along. Moreover, I do not assume that the Judeo-Christian tradition is the model for others. Although one frequently finds this attitude present in hermeneutical discussions, it seems presumptuous and unwarranted if left unexamined, a result of Western insularity and a misguided sense of superiority in all things. Naturally, as a Westerner, I am also liable to fall prey to this attitude, but I try to counteract its effects whenever possible.

Four developments in particular have prompted the book: the rise in popularity of literary and sociological interpretations of divine revelation; the increasing disrepute in which theological interpretations are held; the almost general rejection of the possibility of definitive interpretations; and the widespread acceptance of relativism. All four are closely interconnected and pose serious challenges for religious communities, insofar as (1) the interpretational practices of these communities are frequently not in step with the theories behind these developments and (2) the views with respect to those of rank-and-file members of the communities in question often conflict with those of their leaders. We need, then, to examine the theoretical foundation of these developments and determine their implications and the extent to which they adhere to sound hermeneutical principles.

The main thesis I defend is that divine revelation may be interpreted in various legitimate ways but that the primary and essential component of a satisfactory interpretation of divine revelation is theological. This applies to all kinds of interpretations, including such different ones as the literary, sociological, and authorial. This by itself is a controversial and disputed view today. There are a few exegetes of Christian scriptures, for example, who explicitly advocate and practice theological interpretations of revelation, but no one has yet to articulate a sustained philosophical argument to support these efforts. My thesis, moreover, is even more daring in that I claim that theological interpretations are relational: A theological interpretation is not in fact, as many mistakenly hold, the understanding of what a divinity wishes believers to understand, but rather of what a theological tradition considers to be a divine message. This naturally raises questions about the possibility of definitive interpretations and the relativity of interpretations, so I also propose parameters within which the notion of definitive interpretation makes sense and explain the ways in which an interpretation of divine revelation is relativistic and the ways in which it is not.

I stay away from the much traveled roads of religious language and epistemology of both revelation and religious belief and omit discussion of criteria for recognizing or evaluating religious truth. In particular, I avoid discussion of the relation between revelation and religious belief, the means of assessing the meaning and truth of revelation, and the nature of divine speech. These topics have been extensively treated in many books, including Nicholas Wolterstorff's profound *Divine Discourse* (1995), Richard Swinburne's now-classic, *Revelation* (1992), and George Mavrodes's well-known *Revelation and Religious Belief* (1988). The present book has profited from these but nonetheless charts a different course. My concern is rather with the kinds of interpretations that are appropriate to revelation and their relation to the lack of agreement regarding the import of revelation among religious communities. Hence, I do not discuss issues involved in the meaning and significance of religious language and the conditions that need to be satisfied by religious knowledge and belief. One can easily understand why contemporary philosophy of religion has been so concerned with these linguistic and epistemic matters. After all, apart from the philosophy of mind, modern and contemporary philosophers seem preoccupied primarily with language and epistemology. But there are good reasons to explore other, less exhausted areas and approaches as well.

The discussion is divided into eight chapters. The first two are primarily propaedeutic and clarificatory in nature, although they do make some important substantive claims. They provide the conceptual framework on the basis of which later analyses are undertaken. They are necessary because terms like 'revelation' and 'interpretation' are frequently used without precision in the literature, giving rise to confusion, ambiguity, and avoidable disagreements. Chapter 1 deals with the controversial and difficult notion of revelation; it raises the questions of what revelation is and how many are its kinds. Chapter 2 undertakes a similar task, but with respect to interpretation. The four chapters that follow these two are devoted to different kinds of interpretations of divine revelation: chapter 3 addresses interpretations that are meaning, rather than relation, based; chapter 4 takes up literary interpretations; chapter 5, sociological interpretations; and chapter 6, theological ones. The two chapters that follow explore more general issues: chapter 7 is concerned with the possibility of definitive interpretations of divine revelation, and chapter 8 with relativity in interpretation. The book ends with a conclusion that presents a general overview of the position articulated in the preceding chapters.

A few points about method: The discussion in this book is primarily theoretical. Contrary to tradition, I provide brief and pointed examples for the sake of illustration rather than engage in long and complicated exegetical analyses, for three reasons. First, although the latter would have been useful in some cases, in others they would have directed the attention of readers to matters only tangential to the argument and, therefore, created confusion rather than clarity. Second, they would have lengthened the text considerably and would have transformed the book into a different one. And third, they would have involved interpretation, and this is inconsistent with the general position I defend: I argue that interpretations should occur only within particular theological perspectives, and this book aims to be neutral in theological matters. I have also stayed away from questions concerned with the historical development of the issues I raise and the many answers that have been given to them in the history of religious hermeneutics. Again, this would have produced a different book. Finally, in spite of its present unpopularity in theological and religious contexts, I have adopted a systematic and largely analytic approach for the sake of completeness and clarity. Although I have no quarrel with discussions of religious issues that are unsystematic or use ambiguity for the sake of insight, edification, or enlightenment, I find myself dissatisfied with them insofar as they often fail to produce clear understanding. Because my aim is clear understanding, I adopt what some might think is a rather austere method, but one that in the end I hope will produce the effect I seek.

Readers should keep in mind that the general theoretical background of this study is to be found in two previously published books, although some parts of the theory have been modified substantially: *A Theory of Textuality: The Logic and Epistemology* (1995) and *Texts: Ontological Status, Identity, Author, Audience* (1996). More directly connected to the particular point of view presented concerning the interpretation of revelation are six articles:

"Borges' 'Pierre Menard': Philosophy or Literature?" (2000), "Sociological Accounts in the History of Philosophy" (2000); "The Interpretation of Revealed Texts: Can We Know What God Means?" (1999); "Relativism and the Interpretation of Texts" (1999); "Interpretation and the Law: Averroes's Contribution to the Hermeneutics of Sacred Texts" (1997); and "The Philosopher and the Understanding of the Law" (1996). All these are listed in the bibliography, and I am grateful to the pertinent presses and editors of the journals for allowing me to rely on them.

Many friends, colleagues, and students have helped me with their criticisms and suggestions in the preparation of this book. I am particularly grateful to Michael Gorman, William Irwin, and John Kronen. Their detailed and perceptive comments and criticisms were invaluable. The first gave me the benefit of his analytic and theological training; the second challenged my views on interpretation based on his own, fully articulated position; and the third helped me understand the classic texts of early modern theological speculation in Lutheran Europe. Bruce Reichenbach, John Sullivan, and Sandy Menssen also offered detailed and useful comments. John Bruin and Peter Hare read very early drafts of the manuscript and made valuable suggestions. Fabio Escobar, John Rock, Marcus Marenda, Jeffrey Dueck, William Fedirko, and Anthony Moulesong helped in various ways. And Michael Rota, Nicholas Wolterstorff, Majid Amini, Leslie Stevenson, and Bernie Cantens, among others, raised challenging questions when I presented a section of the book at the meetings of the Society of Christian Philosophers that took place at St. John Fisher College in the Winter of 2001. Jonathan J. Sanford compiled the indexes and proofread the manuscript. Finally, I must mention Gayatri Patnaik, from Palgrave, for without her interest and encouragement this book would not have seen the light. My sincere thanks to all of them.

Chapter 1 ⊷

Revelation

What is divine revelation and what is its function? This is perhaps one of the most controversial and disputed issues in religion and theology today. Indeed, the confusion is explicitly and frequently acknowledged.[1] The positions theologians and religious communities take with respect to it are wide apart. Some conceive revelation as a set of scriptures or texts; others think of it as a divine act; and still others regard it as certain pieces of information a divinity has made available to humans. These are just three of the most common ways of thinking about revelation, but there are others, as we shall see presently. So how should we conceive revelation?

The answer to this question is fundamental to the issue that concerns this book, for without a clear notion of revelation we cannot expect to develop a credible and effective theory about how to interpret it. Indeed, what we think about revelation will substantially affect how we should proceed in interpreting it. If revelation is a divine act, our task as interpreters will be different than if it is a set of texts or pieces of information. A text is a linguistic entity, but acts and information are not. An act is something one does; information is something one has; and a text is something one reads or hears. This means that the first step we need to take toward a sensible view of how to interpret revelation is to be clear about what revelation is. Otherwise we might create more confusion than is already present in discussions of this topic. To paraphrase a philosopher's well-known saying, a little confusion at the outset can result in great confusion at the end.

Let us begin, then, by saying something about revelation in general, and then turn to divine revelation in particular.

Revelation in General

But how should we proceed to determine what revelation, considered in general, is? One way is to look at the ways in which we speak about revelation.

Ordinary language holds our basic intuitions about the world, and thus its analysis should help us develop a general map of the ways we think, consciously or unconsciously, about revelation. Let us, then, consider a few sentences of ordinary language to see if we can derive from them some understanding of how the term 'revelation' is commonly used:

1. An artist *reveals* her nature through her work.
2. He *revealed* a special gift for trickery.
3. His clothing *reveals* his taste to anyone who pays attention.
4. She *revealed* the truth to the jury through her sworn statement at the trial.
5. Nature *reveals* its uniformity in the law of gravitation.
6. Her words *revealed* her belief in his guilt.
7. The moment I arrived, the dynamics of the situation were *revealed* to me.
8. A see-through veil *revealed* her sad expression.
9. The mob's behavior *reveals* their intentions.
10. The light, shining through the trees, *revealed* the path to the wanderers.
11. The effect *reveals* the cause.
12. The sculptor *revealed* the statue to the audience by pulling away its cover.
13. The Oracle of Delphi *revealed* her destiny to the pilgrim, but she failed to grasp it.
14. The confessor *revealed* the murderer's secret to his torturers.
15. Contrary to his intention, his gesture *revealed* his true feelings toward her.
16. Pamela *revealed* herself by coming into the room.

These sentences suggest that 'to reveal' means to communicate, make known, disclose, uncover, make manifest, or tell. This does not entail that revelation is equivalent to each and every one of these considered independently, or to all of these taken together. It means only that it is the same as one or more of these in some cases, or that it may imply one or more of them in others.

To tell may involve revealing, but revealing can take place without telling (e.g., 1, 2, 3); one may reveal by showing (e.g., 3, 9, and 12), for example, rather than telling. To uncover is not the same as to reveal. I may uncover the facts of the murder but never reveal them. Communication, again, may be involved in revelation, but it does not appear to be equivalent to it. The former has to do with making some piece of information common, so it seems to require that all parties involved in it be affected, even if differently, but this is not always the case with the latter (e.g., 13).[2] What counts in a revelation is not that some information has been actually made common to two or more parties, but that one party aims to affect another in a certain way. Similar points could be made about making known, disclosing, and making manifest. Revelation is closely related to these, and in certain contexts it may be equivalent to them, but it is not the same thing.

Depending on the circumstances, revelation may involve seven different factors: the thing revealed, the receiver of revelation, the agent that reveals, the intention to reveal, the act of revealing, the act of receiving what is revealed, and the means whereby the revelation is made.

A revelation always requires that something be revealed. From the sentences given above, it is clear that there are all kinds of things that can qualify as the *thing revealed:* a nature (in 1), a gift (in 2), a taste (in 3), truth (in 4), the uniformity of Nature (in 5), beliefs (in 6), a sad expression (in 8), intentions (in 9), and so on. These various things may be grouped in different ways. For example, they could be divided into properties and non-properties, concepts and non-concepts, and so on. One appealing possibility is to divide them into things and their properties on the one hand and views or beliefs on the other. According to this division, the thing revealed is sometimes something like an Aristotelian substance (e.g., this horse, this man), or the property of such a substance (e.g., the horse's weight or the man's intelligence).[3] In 2 above, for example, what is revealed is a special gift for trickery, and this surely is a property. And something similar occurs when a person reveals herself, as happens in the event described in 16. On the other hand, what is revealed sometimes appears to be a certain view, belief, piece of information, or doctrine, such as we have in 6 and 14.

Sometimes it is assumed that the difference between these two kinds of revealed things lies in that the second is propositional whereas the first is not. By propositional is meant that what is revealed can be expressed by a sentence that is either true or false. Thus, it is taken for granted that a property (e.g., his gift for trickery) or person (e.g., Pamela) revealed is not propositional, because whatever properties or persons are, they are not the kinds of things that can be expressed by a sentence that is true or false. On the other hand, a view or belief involves one or more propositions in the sense that it can be expressed by sentences that are either true or false. Thus, her belief in his guilt (in 6) is propositional because it can be expressed in sentences such as 'She believes he is guilty' and 'He is guilty.'[4]

I do not see this as a significant difference, however, for even the revelation of a property or person involves facts that can be expressed propositionally. The revelation of his gift for trickery (in 2) is nothing other than that "he has a gift for trickery." The revelation of the uniformity of Nature (in 5) is that "Nature is uniform." And the revelation of herself (in 16) is nothing but that "she is present, is such and such, or did such and such."

These are not different from the revelation of a view or belief in which the view or belief is expressed propositionally. The revelation of her belief in his guilt (in 6) is that "she believes in his guilt." The distinction between things and their properties on one hand and views and beliefs on the other cannot be cashed out in terms of their propositional character. The attempt to do so rests on a confusion between what is revealed and the means of revelation. What is revealed is always expressible in a proposition, although there are two exceptions to this: (1) when the aim of revelation is not to produce understanding but some other effect on the receiver, such as an emotion; and (2) when revelation is deemed to be beyond intellectual grasp, as happens with mystical experiences. However, the means of revelation, as we shall see immediately, is frequently not propositional.

The distinction between views and beliefs on one hand and things and their properties on the other rests rather on their relations to knowers. The first are entertained, believed, held, and so on, by knowers; the second are perceived or known by knowers and verify or falsify what knowers think. The first amount to ways in which we think about the world; the second to ways in which the world is. The second we might call facts; the first, views about facts. An example of a fact is that the Earth moves around the Sun. Examples of views about facts are that "the Earth moves around the Sun" and that "the Sun moves around the Earth." The first view is true because it corresponds to the fact it describes; the second is false because there is no fact to which it corresponds.

This means that one may reveal a fact or what someone (including oneself) thinks is a fact (i.e., a view). In the first case, one reveals what is the case; in the second, what someone thinks is the case (whether it is so or not). Of course, holding a view, or having a belief, is itself a fact, although the view or belief itself is not. That he believes she murdered her husband is as much a fact as that she murdered her husband. But the view, "she murdered her husband," is different from the fact that she murdered her husband insofar as facts cannot have truth value, whereas views do. However, both facts and views are propositional in structure.

Some authors hold that not all that is revealed need be propositional because, in some cases, what is revealed is not a thing, a property of a thing, a view, or a belief. Mystics often speak of revelations that are beyond linguistic expression and propositional understanding and, therefore, cannot be considered to be propositional in any sense. But this is an entirely different approach, which falls outside the kind of analysis provided in this book.

Naturally, a revelation may involve a plurality of things revealed. When a man reveals a special gift for trickery (in 2), he reveals only one fact, but when a woman reveals the truth at a trial (in 4), all sorts of facts may be involved.

It is possible to distinguish at least between two *receivers of revelation:* actual and potential. The first is someone who *does* receive the revelation, whereas the second is anyone who *could* receive it but has not received it. In 7, when the dynamics of the situation were revealed to me, I was the actual receiver of revelation; and in 12, the audience is the actual receiver of the revealed sculpture. On the other hand, in 3, the revelation of his taste is given to a potential audience, those who pay attention; and in 5, Nature reveals its uniformity to those who are observant, a group that may contain potential receivers.

Actual and potential receivers of revelation may be intended or unintended. In 4, her revelation in the trial is directed to an intended audience, namely the jury, whereas in 15 he did not have her as the intended receiver of the nature of his feelings.

A revelation always requires a receiver, even if he or she never actually receives it and therefore remains potential. Although some authors hold that if something has been revealed, there must be an actual receiver of the revelation,[5] this does not appear to be necessary. It is quite possible that an agent of revelation has revealed something in a document but that no one ever gets to see the document. Revelation requires only a potential receiver. An actual receiver is only a requirement of successful, or effective, revelation. The need for a potential receiver is quite evident in most sample sentences given above, but particularly in 10, 13, and 14. In all others, it is tacitly assumed. Note, however, that it is not always necessary that a revelation have an intended receiver to the extent that intention on the part of an agent is not always required for revelation, as we shall see below.

The receiver of revelation is generally a human being, although there is no reason why other beings (e.g., angels, extraterrestrials) could not receive revelations as well. In principle, even a divinity could be the receiver of a revelation as long as the divinity is not conceived to be omniscient. If the divinity is omniscient, then it is impossible for it to be the receiver of a revelation because it knows everything, and nothing could be revealed to it that it does not already know. However, this does not preclude someone who does not know that the divinity is omniscient from intending, or trying, to reveal something to it. I return to this condition of revelation later.

It goes without saying that the receiver of revelation has to have the capacity to grasp what is revealed. In cases in which the thing revealed is a fact or a view, this capacity must involve propositional understanding, and in cases in which the revelation is made through some means like a particular language, the receiver must also be capable of understanding the means or language in question. Moreover, if what is revealed is some kind of mystical, non-propositional insight, the receiver must likewise have the capacity to grasp it in the fashion appropriate to it.

I have been speaking as if the receiver of revelation were always one, but it does not need to be so; groups can do as well. We speak of a group of persons, such as a set of jurors, and other pluralities functioning as receivers of revelation. Henceforth, whenever I refer to the receiver of revelation I mean to include groups, although I generally avoid using the plural for stylistic reasons.

A first intuition might lead one to think that a revelation always requires an *agent of revelation* who does the revealing, and that the agent must be capable of understanding propositionally. From the sentences given earlier, however, the existence of an agent does not always appear to be required. For example, in 7, it is clear that there is no agent of revelation: No one revealed to me the dynamics of the situation—somehow, these became apparent by themselves.[6] Moreover, *prima facie* the agent of revelation does not appear in general to need to be capable of understanding propositionally, or even to have any kind of mental awareness at all. This seems to be confirmed by several sentences above. In 3, 5, and 6, we have non-intelligent entities doing the revealing: in 3, it is clothing; in 5, it is Nature; and in 6, words. The case of clothing, however, is misleading insofar as "his clothing" reveals something only because it is a sign of something that pertains to "him" and in which he had a hand. And something similar could be said about words. If the clothing had not been chosen by a human being, then it would not reveal anything. And if words had not been chosen and used by a human being, they would not reveal anything. The case of "Nature," on the other hand, cannot be dismissed so easily, for who is the mind behind it? For some philosophers it is God, but this is not accepted by everyone. It appears possible, then, that there are cases in which the agent of revelation may not be mentally aware at all. And, of course, a non-intelligent agent of revelation cannot be required to be capable of propositional understanding.

Keep in mind that just as the receiver of revelation can be a plurality, so can the agent of revelation. There is no reason why the agent of revelation need be one, rather than several, although from now on I generally refer to the agent of revelation in the singular.

Another factor that plays a role in revelation is the *intention to reveal* on the part of the agent. This may be regarded as a certain mental disposition: To intend to do something is to be mentally disposed to do it, that is, to be in a certain kind of relation to what is to be done. Intentions require subjects in which they are present and on which they depend; they do not exist by themselves. In revelation, the subject is the agent. This means that if there are cases of revelation in which there is no agent, or the agent is not capable of intentions, there cannot be an intention to reveal (e.g., 7, 8, and 10). But, even when there is an agent of revelation capable of having intentions, there may not always be an intention to reveal. Revealing a special gift for trickery (in 2) may be completely unintended. Indeed, in some cases (as in 15), revelation goes contrary to the intention of the revealing agent. Again, the intention on the part of the agent of revelation may be one or many, simple or complex, depending on the case.

The *act of revealing* is an act in which an agent engages when he or she reveals something. That this is an act is quite clear from the use of the verb 'to reveal' in sentences 1–16. Consider 4, in which a wife reveals her guilt at a trial when she confesses: "I killed my husband." This is an act whereby this woman reveals this fact to the jury. This act must be distinguished from other acts in which the agent may also engage. Our woman, for example, engages in the act of uttering the sentence whereby she reveals her guilt. But the act of uttering is not the same as the act of revealing. Consider as evidence of their distinction that the act of uttering the sentence is tied to particular sounds that are not essential to the act of revealing. The woman could have uttered a Spanish sentence instead of an English one and still revealed the same thing by saying: "Maté a mi marido." Or she could have uttered no sound, but rather written something on a piece of paper, made some signs in the language of the deaf, or used whatever other means were available to her to reveal her guilt. She could even have made someone else do the talking for her. All these acts are only accidentally connected to the act of revealing.

Because what is revealed need not always be expressible propositionally and in language, the act of revealing cannot always be considered a speech act on the part of the agent of revelation. Indeed, one might conceive of this act in various ways. Three of these have been recently suggested.[7] The act could be one of manifesting something, as when I uncover a statue wrapped in cloth. It could be conceived as communicating something, as when I inform someone that I am going to be late for an appointment. Or it could be taken as causing someone to do something, as when I get Peanut, one of my cats, to step down from the table.

Another important point to keep in mind is that if agents are not always necessary for revelation, then acts of revelation are likewise not necessary. And, indeed, sentences 5, 8, and 10 illustrate the point. In none of these do we have acts of agents. Nature, clothing, and light do not engage in acts of revealing, even though they seem to reveal something or to contribute to a revelation taking place. Finally, although so far I have been referring to the act of revealing as a single act, there is no reason why it need be one; it could be a group of acts, or a complex act composed of many others.

The act of revealing is not the only act involved in revelation. In order for a revelation to be successful, there must also be an *act of receiving* what is revealed. An actual act of receiving revelation is not a necessary condition of revelation. If there can be revelation without an actual receiver, it cannot be credibly argued that an actual act of receiving it is required. However, such an act is expected and necessary for a revelation to be successful or effective, and it is necessary potentially insofar as a potential receiver is necessary.[8] In the case described in 4, the audience must understand what the woman at the trial says in order for the revelation to be successful, and the potential act of understanding is necessary in order for the revelation to be a revelation at all. The act of receiving a revelation need not always be an act of propositional understanding, insofar as the thing revealed is not always propositional and the receivers of revelations need not always be capable of understanding propositionally. There are cases of mystics who speak of grasping things that are beyond propositional understanding. The act of receiving a revelation, then, does not have to be an act of understanding in which a proposition expressed, or expressible in language, is entertained by the mind of the receiver. It could be an act of non-propositional enlightenment. Moreover, this act, like the act of revealing, could be more than one, or be a complex act composed of many others.

Finally, there is also the *means of revelation*. This factor is not present in all revelation, for some revelations are immediate.[9] When the fact revealed is immediately presented, there is no means of revelation separate from the fact itself (e.g., 2, 7, and 11). The unveiling of a statue is a kind of revelation, but there is no means of revelation apart from the statue involved. Of course, if the unveiling of the statue were observed by way of a videotape, then we would have both the thing revealed, namely the statue, and the means of revelation, namely the videotape (e.g., 1, 3, and 9). The revelation of views would appear *prima facie* to require a means insofar as there must be some language through which they are expressed and communicated. But this may not in fact be so. One could imagine cases of telepathy or direct brain hookups in which whatever is present in one mind is automatically and immediately made present in another without any intervening means.

The means of revelation can be of at least two sorts. In some cases, it consists of entities that are not sentences of a language. Clothing can be the means of revealing taste (in 3), and a see-through veil can reveal the expression of a face (in 8).[10] In other cases, the means consists of entities that are sentences of a language, as when a person reveals the truth in a trial (in 4). In cases in which the means of revelation consists of sentences, often these sentences express propositions (as in 4). In other cases, the sentences do not, as in the biblical commandment "Thou shalt not kill." In both, however, the fact revealed is propositional, for even the second can be expressed as "God commands us not to kill."

As we have seen, and depending on circumstances, not all factors involved in revelation are necessary conditions of revelation considered in general. We speak about revelation without one or more of the following:

agents, intentions on the part of the agents, acts of revelation, actual receivers of revelation, actual acts of receiving revelation, and means of revelation. The only necessary conditions of all revelation are the thing revealed, an actual or potential receiver, and an actual or potential act of receiving, although further conditions also pertain to particular kinds of revelation.

Revelations may be classified in various ways, depending on which of the factors mentioned is considered. Most important for our purposes, however, is the classification in terms of the agent, for it is the nature of the agent that distinguishes divine from non-divine revelations. A divine agent renders a revelation divine.

Divine Revelation in Particular

Apart from always having a divine agent, divine revelation has other characteristics of which we need to take note. These are best discussed in the context of the seven factors involved in revelation.

Most frequently, theologians speak of the thing revealed as being either propositional or non-propositional. Those who speak of it as propositional generally refer to it as either (1) facts[11] or (2) information,[12] although they also use the term 'proposition.'[13] Information is variously understood to consist of views or doctrines. Examples of facts divinely revealed are that "God created the heavens and the Earth," that "Christ is the Son of God," and that "Muhammad is Allah's prophet." Theologians also say that sacred scriptures reveal the doctrines according to which God created the heavens and the Earth, Christ is the Son of God, and Muhammad is Allah's prophet. I shall speak of "views" for the sake of convenience and economy.

Those who speak of what is divinely revealed as something non-propositional usually speak of it as either (1) a thing or a property of a thing[14] or (2) something that is beyond propositional understanding and linguistic expression.[15]

In principle, then, one may speak of a divinity revealing facts or views. This distinction is useful in cases in which divinities can err or are capable of deceiving. In such situations, divinities reveal their views, or the views they wish believers to believe, regardless of whether the divinities know the truth value of such views or not. In the case of divinities like the Judeo-Christian God, who is not only incapable of error, but also of deceiving, what he reveals must be either a fact or a true view.[16] For the sake of convenience, and considering that most readers of this book will assume divinities to be incapable of error or deceiving, I speak of facts, rather than facts and views. Keep in mind, however, that in cases in which the agent of revelation is not divine, or is divine but capable of error or deceiving, what I say needs to be adjusted.

Practitioners of religious hermeneutics who identify the thing revealed with facts do not agree on the nature of the facts in question. Within faiths in which the divinity is conceived in terms such that everything else is taken to be identical with, or part of, it (as in pantheism), or as its creation and imperfect image (as in Christianity), it makes some sense to claim that all that is revealed in some way concerns the divinity. If this is so, then all divine revelation is a form of divine self-revelation.[17] But this does not make sense in other cases. If the divinity is somehow limited, the fact revealed by the divinity could be some aspect of reality outside the divinity. Moreover, if the divinity is not regarded as creator of the world, then a revelation about the world does not necessarily convey information about the divinity. Finally, if the divinity is regarded as ineffable, that is, as beyond all understanding, as some theologians conceive the Judeo-Christian God to be, then again it makes no sense to say that divine revelation is self-revelation. In short, not all divine revelation need be divine self-revelation.

Often, however, theologians adamantly oppose the view that what is revealed is propositional at all, and therefore that it is a fact or a view. Some do this by arguing that what is revealed is either a thing or a property of a thing. Some Christian theologians say, for example, that it is the very person of Christ, or some property of that person, such as his divinity, that is revealed in Scriptures. Thus, Baillie writes: " . . . what is revealed to us is not a body of information concerning various things of which we might otherwise be ignorant. . . . in the last resort it is not information about God that is revealed, but very [*sic*] God Himself incarnate in Jesus Christ our Lord."[18]

However, even if we were to accept, as these theologians claim, that the primary role of revelation is to disclose or "manifest" the divinity rather than to convey any kind of propositional information,[19] three points can be made in favor of propositional revelation.[20] First, it is difficult to see how a divinity can disclose itself indirectly, through scriptures or other means, without conveying some propositional information about itself, for what would the disclosure consist of? True, Christian believers say that Christ revealed his divinity by, for example, turning water into wine, and in this case the means of revelation is not language. So one may be tempted to argue that what is revealed is not propositional. But this is a mistake, for the fact revealed, such as that Christ is God, is indeed propositional even if the means of revealing it, namely the act of turning water into wine, is not. Second, if part of the divinity's disclosure concerns its acts and relation to believers, how can this be communicated non-propositionally? Again, we are talking about some fact about the divinity acting in such and such a way, or about the divine being in relation to this or that, and all these facts are propositional. Third, often what we mean by 'knowing a person' through revelation, be that human or divine, is rather complex.[21] In part we mean to make a propositional claim, but in part we may be referring to some emotional state. Knowing a person is knowing that, say, the person is divine (i.e., knowing a fact). But knowing a person may also involve having certain feelings toward the person, and this is not anything propositional. Of course, one cannot have feelings toward something one does not know at all, and this indicates the fundamental importance of the propositional claim.

Still other theologians speak as if they reject the revelation not just of facts or views, but also of things and their properties. The argument here seems to be based on the assumption that what is revealed is beyond everything we know, or can know, through our regular epistemic powers. The divinity is beyond all the categories of thought, and therefore the revelation we receive concerning it cannot be reduced to any category that we use in understanding.

Here, of course, we are in a realm of enlightenment that transcends ordinary thought and speech and, therefore, is closed to conceptual analyses such as the ones provided in this book. There is no point, then, in attempting a task doomed to failure. Nonetheless, this does not eliminate the need for the more modest project of this investigation, namely the understanding of the conditions of revelation, when this revelation is taken to involve propositional understanding. Divine revelation differs from non-divine revelation not only in that it requires divine agents, but also in that its agents need to be aware of what they reveal. But does this entail that every agent of divine revelation needs to be capable of understanding and to be aware of the propositional and linguistic expression of what is revealed?

Three responses may be given to this question. First, because not all divine revelations are propositional and linguistic, this requirement cannot apply generally. There may be revelations of the sort that defy propositional understanding and linguistic expression, which means that it would be inappropriate to require every agent of divine revelation to have an awareness of certain propositions and sentences in every case. The requirement can apply only to the agents of those divine revelations that are propositional and linguistic.

Second, because divinities are frequently thought to reveal through human agents, who are sometimes regarded as unaware of what they reveal, it cannot be a requirement of all agents of divine revelation that they have a propositional and linguistic awareness of what they reveal. In certain cases, these agents function as if in a trance or under sleep, and recall nothing of what they have said after they wake up, and this undermines the claim that the agent of revelation needs awareness of what is revealed.[22] Still, even if some agents are not aware of what they reveal, or at least of not all they reveal, there must always be, for every divine revelation, some agent who is.

Third, in principle it is possible that a divinity could have a mode of understanding that is not propositional or linguistic, and that the revelation it bestows on humankind is not propositional or linguistic. One can very well conceive that a divinity whose understanding is intuitive—such as we have when we sense, for example—could reveal something to her followers through some kind of non-propositional and non-linguistic experience. If this be so, the agent of revelation need not be a being capable of having understanding in propositional form and of expressing it in language. Of course, this is probably a requirement of a divinity such as the Judeo-Christian God, who is omniscient and omnipotent. In such a case, the divinity should be able both to understand propositionally and linguistically and to reveal something that is to be understood propositionally and linguistically, even if it can also understand in other ways and reveal things that are beyond propositional and linguistic understanding. But divinities who lack these attributes are not placed under similar constraints.

Divine revelations, unlike revelations considered in general, seem always to involve intention. This must certainly be so in the case of the God of Abraham, who is omnipotent and omniscient. It appears impossible for him not to intend to do what he does when he knows what he does and has the power both to do it and not to do it. In the case of deities who are neither omniscient nor omnipotent, on the other hand, it is in principle possible to posit unintentional revelation, although it does not make much sense to do so. Divine revelation seems to require a special effort on the part of the divinity, and it is unclear how this effort can take place without a corresponding intention.

Divine revelation, like all revelation, requires an actual or potential receiver of revelation.[23] It does not make much sense to speak of a divinity who intends to reveal something when there is no one either actual or potential who can receive it.[24] But divine revelation also imposes some particular conditions on the receiver of revelation that do not apply to all revelation. Indeed, it requires certain receptive capacities on the part of receivers, although this does not mean that the capacities in question and the mode of reception involved need be linguistic and propositional. The receiver of divine revelation need not be able, nor be required, to understand a proposition expressible in some sentence every time that he or she successfully grasps a divine revelation. There may be situations in which divine revelations take place in such a way that no language is used, and the receivers of revelation do not, or even cannot, express what they have grasped linguistically. One could have some kind of experience akin to sensation, in which neither the experience nor what one gathers from it can be put into propositional form. Indeed, mystics frequently and explicitly tell us this.[25] To deny this possibility without strong evidence to the contrary would be dogmatic.

Apart from these conditions on the part of the receiver of revelation, divine revelation appears to be directed toward believers, members of the religious community for whom the revelation is intended. So, we may ask, must the receiver of revelation be a believer? At first, this does not appear to be so, for the receiver of revelation is not always in fact a believer. After all, if the means of a revelation is a text in some language, say, this should be understandable to all those who know the language, regardless of whether they are believers, potential believers, or neither.[26]

This answer, however, fails to take note of three factors. First among these is the intention of the divinity. This seems to be directed primarily to an audience of believers or potential believers. I say potential because sometimes revelations are made to non-believers for the purpose of making them believe. Witness the case of St. Paul, who received a revelation that changed his life from one of unbelief to one of belief. Moreover, even when the immediate receiver of the message is not a believer or potential believer, the message is intended for the benefit of believers and is also a message for them. In this case, however, the message is indirect and may differ from the message intended for the non-believer. Consider the case with the message God sent to the Egyptian pharaoh through Moses: "Let my people go." The immediate recipient was the pharaoh, but the Hebrews at the time were also indirect beneficiaries of a message. They learned, say, that God wanted to liberate them. Moreover, all those who believe in the Bible as a divine book are indirect recipients of a revelation as well, insofar as they may learn something about God's relation to the Hebrews and to themselves (his people).

Second, revelations are often coded, so that only those who know how to decipher them can understand them. The language of revelation is frequently and purposefully obscure to those not privy to its proper interpretation.[27] Generally, revelations are intended for those who have the code to decipher them.

Third, even if not coded, revelations need to be recognized as such in order to be effective, and only believers do so. For these three reasons, then, it appears that believers are the proper receivers of revelation.

In terms of the means, divine revelations can be, like revelations in general, immediate or mediate.[28] A good example of an immediate divine revelation in the Christian tradition is Jesus Christ. For those followers of Christ who were alive during his presence on Earth, he was an immediate revelation. And certainly when he presented himself to his disciples after his death, this very presence was a revelation. In these situations, there is no intermediary between the thing revealed and the receiver because Christ was immediately present.[29] On the other hand, for those who did not live at the time Christ was here on Earth, he is revealed through the narratives of those who saw him (unless some direct supernatural or mystical experience is involved). In this case, Christ is revealed mediately, through the means of those narratives.

We saw earlier that the only three necessary conditions of revelation considered in general are the facts revealed, an actual or potential receiver, and an actual or potential act of receiving. In the case of divine revelation, however, we now see that the situation is different. Here, revelation is necessarily accompanied by at least three other factors: the divine agent, the intention to reveal on the part of the divinity, and the divine act of revealing. Whether revelation is accompanied by still other factors depends on particular circumstances.

So much, then, for the factors that play roles in revelation, some of which are necessary for all revelation and some only for divine revelation. Now we must turn to divine revelation itself, for although we have established the conditions under which it occurs, we still have not established what it is. This is a topic about which there is considerable disagreement.

In religious contexts in particular, the term 'revelation' is frequently used to refer to four of the seven factors mentioned: the act of revealing, the fact revealed, the act of receiving what is revealed, and the means used for revelation. For rather obvious reasons, it is seldom, if ever, used to refer to the agent,[30] the agent's intention, or the receiver of revelation.

We frequently find authors who refer to the act of revealing as a revelation.[31] Some say, for example, that God's revelation to humanity is continuous, which suggests that they are speaking about the act of divine revelation. It would not make much sense to say that the fact revealed is continuous, and the explicit reference to God precludes understanding this as a reference to the act of the receiver. Similar points could be made about the other two possibilities.

'Revelation' is also frequently used to refer to the fact revealed.[32] For example, when Christians say that Christ is the revelation of God to humanity, they appear to be speaking about the very thing that is revealed. Christ is not an act, and although he could also be thought to be a means of revelation, often Christ is taken to be the very thing God has revealed.[33] Indeed, Christians frequently speak as if knowing Christ were a sufficient condition for salvation, which is, after all, the ultimate aim of revelation in the Christian Faith.

'Revelation' is also sometimes used to refer to the act of receiving in which believers engage.[34] When believers say, for example, that they have revelations, sometimes this is taken as the very acts of understanding they have of the facts God has revealed; it is the reception by believers that is important in this case.

Finally, many speak of the means of revelation, for example the Judeo-Christian scriptures, as God's revelation.[35] In this sense, the means God uses to reveal is regarded as revelation.

These various uses of 'revelation' naturally tend to create confusion, and therefore we must keep them separate. In general, and assuming that divine revelation requires a divine agent, an intention and an act of revealing on the part of the divine agent, and an actual or potential believer who can engage in an act of understanding the revelation, we can summarize the four senses of revelation mentioned as follows:

1. A divine revelation is an act of a divine agent who intends to cause an act of understanding of a fact in a believer.
2. A divine revelation is a fact of which a divine agent intends to cause an act of understanding in a believer.
3. A divine revelation is an act of understanding of a fact intended to be caused by a divine agent in a believer.
4. A divine revelation is an entity used and intended by a divine agent to cause an act of understanding of a fact in a believer.

These formulas are still incomplete in some important respects, however, for if we were to take them as presented, we would have to conclude that any communication by a divinity to a believer is a divine revelation. Other conditions need to be added to narrow appropriately the field. One of these is that revelations require ignorance in the believer of what is revealed.[36] Indeed, the English verb 'to reveal' comes from the Latin *revelare,* to uncover. To tell someone what she already knows is not to reveal anything to her. Revealing always carries the connotation of disclosing something that was hidden, of unveiling what was veiled.[37] This does not mean, of course, that the receiver of revelation must be ignorant of everything contained in the revelation. A revelation appears to concern a central fact of which the receiver is ignorant before the revelation takes place, but this fact is usually accompanied by other facts of which the believer is aware before the revelation.[38] The facts revealed are usually complex and require on the part of believers that they already know other facts. This is why often revelation is taken as clarifying rather than informing, that is, as making clear what was obscure before.[39] Consider, for example, the revelation that God gave Moses in the Decalogue. The central point of this message was new to the Hebrews at the time it was revealed, but in order to understand it, they had to have some understanding of what a commandment is, of God, and so on.

Moreover, a fact revealed need not be available only through revelation.[40] Revelation often involves facts that can be known, or that some maintain can be known, through other means as well. For example, some Christian authors hold that God's existence can be learned both through divine revelation and through reason.[41] It is also possible that some of these facts are actually known by some believers before they became believers or even after they became believers but before they found them in revelation.

If the facts revealed are already known by believers, or are available to be known in principle through natural means, the question arises as to why have a revelation at all.[42] Many answers have been given to this question.[43] For one, such revelation is useful for apologetic purposes, showing that at least some beliefs are supported by means other than revelation. Moreover, not all members of a community of believers might know these facts or be capable, based on their natural abilities, of knowing them. Also, even though some of these facts may already be known, when they become part of a larger group of facts, their significance changes. In the new context, they make it possible for believers to understand things they did not understand before, namely, how facts they may have known before are related to other facts and how they form an integral whole. Divine revelation, then, does not require that every member of the community to which the revelation is given be ignorant of every fact revealed, a point generally overlooked by those who write on this topic.

Another condition of divine revelation not yet mentioned is that revelations seem to concern only what is important and momentous, that is, facts that are significant.[44] This often applies to revelation in general. No one would consider a statement about the weather a revelation, but the identification of a criminal is certainly a revelation. But it always applies to divine revelation. Anything a divinity deems worthy of revelation must be important and momentous. This feature, combined with the ignorance presupposed in the receiver, gives divine revelation its extraordinary and fateful character. Here is something fundamental believers did not know, and whose knowledge will alter their lives in perhaps major ways. Of course, not everything divinely revealed has the same degree of importance. For Christians, the revelation of Christ's divinity is certainly more important than the revelation of the Seventh Commandment. But all divine revelation is related, so that one piece of revelation leads to another. This is why, although having in principle various degrees of importance, all divine revelations are significant.

Let us, then, add the two factors mentioned to the prior formulas in order to make them more adequate for purposes of the present discussion.

1'. A divine revelation is an act of a divine agent who intends to cause an act of understanding of a significant fact in a believer who might otherwise be ignorant of it.

2'. A divine revelation is a significant fact of which a divine agent intends to cause an act of understanding in a believer who might otherwise be ignorant of it.

3'. A divine revelation is an act of understanding of a significant fact intended to be caused by a divine agent in a believer who might otherwise be ignorant of it.

4'. A divine revelation is an entity used and intended by a divine agent to cause an act of understanding of a significant fact in a believer who might otherwise be ignorant of it.

Of these formulations, 2' is metaphysically, epistemologically, and axiologically prior to the others. It is metaphysically prior because no revelation in any of the other three senses can take place without it. It is epistemologically prior because to know the significant fact is the aim of the whole process of understanding involved. And it is axiologically prior because to know this fact is what matters, is what is of value for the receiver of revelation, and is what the agent of revelation seeks to effect in the receiver. In Aristotelian language, this is that for the sake of which everything else is done.

Nonetheless, for our investigation, 4' is the one that matters, not only because it is the means used by the agent to cause an understanding on the part of the receiver of revelation, but also for two other, more important reasons: First, here we are concerned in particular with the hermeneutical task of interpreting what believers hold that a divinity has revealed, or has sought to reveal, to them; second, it is in the context of the means of revelation that most disagreements occur with regard to interpretation. The discussion of the fact revealed is not pertinent insofar as it does not require, although it may be subjected to, interpretation, and the same applies to the divine act of revealing. The act of understanding on the part of the believer is not pertinent insofar as it concerns rather epistemic questions not central to this investigation. Our concern is with the hermeneutics of revelation, and this has to do primarily with how the means used by a divinity to reveal needs to be interpreted.

The means of revelation can take many forms. It can be a burning bush, a voice, designs on a wall, natural phenomena, the position of the stars, the entrails of birds, events, and so on. Practically anything can be used to convey a message and certainly a divine message. But, regardless of their original nature, when these entities are selected, arranged, and used to cause understanding, they become texts, as I shall explain immediately. For this reason, we need to turn to texts at this point.

Texts

In order to explicate the nature of divine revelation conceived as texts, I must first clarify what I take texts in general to be. I adopt the following conception:

> A text is a group of entities, used as signs, selected, arranged, and intended by
> an author to cause certain specific acts of understanding in an audience in a
> certain context.[45]

From this definition, we can draw four important inferences for our discussion: (1) the entities that constitute a text are not the same as the signs of which the text is composed; (2) signs are not the same as texts; (3) texts are not the same as language; and (4) texts are not the same as discourse.

The entities of which texts are constituted can be anything whatever. They can be lines and figures drawn on a page; they can be gestures made by a person; they can be actions; they can be glass beads; or they can be stones. Consider such examples as a text printed on a page; a text put together out of pebbles on a beach; a text composed of sticks; a text drawn on the sand in the desert; a text made up of smoke or vapor spread over the sky by an airplane; a text constructed of blocks of ice; a text consisting of bumps on a page for the blind; a text spoken aloud; and so on. A text can be made up even of mental images. There is no *prima facie* reason why I cannot make up a text with visual, aural, or tactile images I contemplate in my mind. Indeed, I can very well imagine the sounds uttered when one says, "Excuse me," even when no one actually says it.[46] The only requirement that applies to the entities that constitute a text is that they be perceptual, when this is taken as either that they are capable of being perceived or that they are capable of being phenomenologically experienced as percepts, even if they are not capable of being perceived. Lines, figures, gestures, actions, events, and the like are examples of the first; mental images corresponding to these are an example of the second.

Apart from the perceptual character of the entities that constitute texts, there are other requirements of textuality as specified in the definition. These perceptual entities must be used as signs, that is, they must be taken in relation to meaning; and they must be selected and arranged in a certain way by an author who intends to cause an understanding of some specific meaning to an audience through them in a particular context.[47]

The entities that constitute texts are not signs when they are considered apart from the use they have to cause understanding. It is only when they are used to do this that they become signs.[48] For example, an ink mark in the shape of a circle is not by itself a sign. But when used to cause an understanding of, say, the letter 'o,' then it is a sign. And the same can be said about pebbles, sticks, lines drawn on the sand, smoke, blocks of ice, or sounds.

I refer to the relation between the entities that make up a text or a sign and the text or sign as "constituting," and I refer to the relation between signs and the text of which they are part as "composing." These ways of referring to these relations help to distinguish them. The letter 'E' is constituted by four lines arranged in a certain way, but the text 'God is great' is composed of the words 'God,' 'is,' and 'great,' and the period '.', arranged in a certain way. I use 'constitute' for the first because signs and texts are actually made up of these, as a human body is made up of water and certain minerals. I use 'compose' for the second because signs are parts of texts gathered together in the way dwellers compose a city.

The main difference between signs and texts is that the understanding of the meaning of texts is at least in part the result of the understanding of the meanings of the signs of which the texts are composed, but the understanding of the meanings of signs is not even in part the result of the understanding of the meanings of the signs of which they are composed.[49] This assumes, of course, that the signs are themselves composed of signs, as in *cat,* for often they are not composed of signs at all, as happens with the letter 'o.' The understanding of the meaning of 'God is infinite' is at least in part the result of the understanding of the meanings of 'God,' 'is,' and 'infinite,' but the understanding of the meaning of 'God' is not, even in part, the result of the understanding of the meanings of 'G,' 'o,' and 'd.'[50]

Clearly, both the claims I have made and the examples I have used suggest that I take a text to be something like what the readers of these words have in front of them. But in principle there is no reason why such things as "history" or even "the world" cannot function as texts of a sort. Indeed, some Christian theologians conceive revelation as history precisely because history is, in their view, like a text: God uses history to say something about himself.[51] And in the Middle Ages, theologians frequently spoke of two books: the book of Scriptures and the book of Nature.[52] The understanding of history and Nature strictly as texts is possible, although difficult. It is not easy to show how in fact they can meet the conditions made explicit in the definition of a text given earlier. But the issue is moot for us anyway insofar as our concern is not with these kinds of texts, if indeed they are texts, but with scriptural texts like the Bible and the Koran.

From the definition given earlier, we can also gather that texts are not languages. A language, like English or Spanish, is composed of a set of rules (a syntax) and a set of signs (a vocabulary). Texts are composed of signs arranged according to the rules of the language to which they belong. A text is language in use and not the same as the language to which it belongs;[53] nor is a language the same as the set of all actual or possible texts that can be constructed with it. There is a substantial difference between Spanish and *Don Quixote,* or even Spanish and all the texts that have been composed, will be composed, or could be composed in Spanish.

What has been said about the entities that constitute texts, signs, and language entails that texts should not be confused with any one of these. Texts are not the same as the entities that constitute the signs of which the texts are composed. A text is not just a group of sounds, of marks on a page, or of mental images; it is a group of sounds, marks, or images considered in relation to certain acts of understanding that it is supposed to produce. Nor are texts the same as the signs of which they are composed, for these signs must be arranged in certain ways and taken in certain contexts in order to convey meaning. And finally, texts are not languages, for languages merely establish the conditions that make texts possible. This is important insofar as those views of texts that conceive them as just the entities that constitute the signs of which they are composed, or, alternatively, as just those signs or as language, are predisposed to a hermeneutical view that rejects the possibility of definitive interpretations as a matter of principle. It is easier to argue for an infinite number of interpretations in the context of a word, a sign, or language than it is in the context of a particular text. The "endless semiosis" of which some authors speak[54] is more probable in the case of a term, say 'good,' considered by itself than in what I said to my wife this morning when I got up: "Good morning, dear." The position I adopt, however, leaves open this possibility. This is significant for the discussion undertaken in chapter 6.

Again, texts and discourse should not be confused. A text is a group of entities used as signs, but discourse consists of certain acts in which one who discourses engages. One good way to understand discourse is in terms of the notion of illocutionary act. To be engaged in discourse is to be engaged in the production of illocutionary acts. Indeed, discourse amounts to a series of illocutionary acts. When I say to a student in my class, "Begin reading from the top of page 7," I have carried out several speech acts. First, I have uttered certain sounds, a locution. The act of uttering these sounds is the locutionary act (or acts). Second, I have succeeded—if in fact the student proceeds to read—in getting my student to begin reading. This is the perlocutionary act; it is what my locution has caused. And third, I have commanded the student to read. This act of commanding is one of the illocutionary acts I have performed through the locution. The illocutionary act (or acts) is the discourse, whereas the locution considered as used to cause an understanding of some meaning is the text. Texts are not the same thing as discourse, even though they presuppose discourse. There cannot be texts unless there is, or there has been, discourse. Illocutionary acts are necessary conditions of texts.

Although most texts are used to do more than cause understanding in an audience, all texts are intended to convey some meaning, and thus to cause some understanding. When I say "I apologize," the apology is accomplished precisely because the interlocutor knows the meaning of 'I apologize.' If the interlocutor did not know this, the apology would not be understood and would not be effective. And when I say 'I apologize,' I intend the interlocutor to understand what I say, that is, the meaning of 'I apologize.'

Another important implication of the definition given is that texts are not to be confused with their meanings or the understandings of those meanings. Understanding is one of the things texts are supposed to cause. Understanding is something that happens in the author, the audience, or both, and therefore it is ontologically distinct from the text that causes it. The text is a group of entities considered in relation to the meaning these entities are supposed to convey. To understand the meaning of a text should not be conceived narrowly as involving always a proposition, for the meaning of a text is not always a proposition or a set of propositions. Understandings take place in the minds of the members of the audience, and of course also in the mind of the author. Some philosophers think they are mental acts, whereas others think they are qualities, relations, or physical events in the brain, to name just a few views that have been proposed. But the determination of the ultimate nature of understandings is not part of our task, which we can accomplish without settling the issue. For our purposes, any generally accepted view of understandings will do, and I propose to adopt the one that takes understandings to be acts in the mind. Moreover, I want to keep the notion of understanding broad, so that we may speak of understandings that are not propositional. The reasons for this will become evident later on.

Likewise, meanings are neither understandings nor texts. In a very general sense, the meaning of a text is whatever we understand when we are said to understand the text. The meaning of 'Christ raised Lazarus from the dead' is, say, that Christ raised Lazarus from the dead. I do not say meanings are concepts, or propositions, or facts, or anything else in particular, in order to avoid unnecessary wrangling about an issue that has received considerable attention in contemporary philosophy.[55] We might say that meanings, as it were, are the objects of understanding—provided an object is taken merely as what we think about rather than necessarily as an individual thing, a particular kind of thing, or a property of a thing—and their understanding is accomplished through texts. A text makes possible for me to grasp what someone wants me to understand. There are no meanings of texts without texts and understandings, but the meanings of texts should not be confused with them.[56]

Even this conception of the meaning of texts, however, is not general enough to accommodate all the work that we need it to do in this book. In some cases, we need to be able to include in meaning certain properties about texts, like rhyme, that are perceived rather than propositionally grasped. By this I do not intend to make a claim as to the ultimate nature of these properties or of meaning. I merely wish to leave the notion of the meaning of a text as broad as possible at this stage. I shall return to it in chapter 4.

In short, we have been speaking of at least four ontologically distinct items: (1) a text, (2) its meaning, (3) the understanding of the text by an audience, and (4) the understanding of the text by an author. Keep in mind that the conception of texts provided here is quite broad. It includes such different things as a sentence, a paragraph, and a whole book. Length, complexity, or even the ontological character of the entities that constitute a text do not qualify or disqualify something as a text. Likewise, texts can be uttered, written, acted, or thought; they can be simple or complex; they can be difficult or easy to understand; and they can be vague or clear. There is no reason why any of these considerations should make a difference when it comes to the classification of something as a text. Texts come in many varieties.

Finally, I need to say something about the identity and metaphysical status of texts. The first has to do with the conditions that a text must satisfy in order to be the text it is; the second has to do with an analysis of a text in terms of the most general categories available.

The question of identity is complex, for it may involve either an individual or a universal text. Philosophers generally refer to an individual text as a *token* and to a universal text as a *type*. Consider the following two sentences:

1. God is great.
2. God is great.

Here we have two tokens of one type text. In the case of a token text, identity involves the set of necessary and sufficient conditions satisfied by the token; in the case of a type text, identity involves the set of necessary and sufficient conditions satisfied by the type. Obviously, some of the conditions of the token and the type are common; for example, the tokens and the type of 1 and 2 have the same meaning. But some of the conditions are not the same. Perhaps more obvious among these is that tokens 1 and 2 are non-instantiable instances, whereas the type of 1 and 2 is instantiable, instantiated in fact in 1 and 2. A more controversial condition is that 1 and 2 are located in space and are interchangeable, but their type is neither spatial nor interchangeable with either 1 or 2.

In the case of identity, whether of a token or a type text, the conditions are particular in the following senses. In the case of a type text, they are the kinds of conditions that are made explicit in a particular definition. If, instead of texts, we were speaking about geometrical figures, and triangles in particular, the conditions of identity could amount to those present in the definition of a triangle, say, a geometrical figure with three angles. In the case of a token text, the matter is controversial, for there is no agreement on the conditions of individuality, but in any case the conditions are particular; for example, some favor spatiotemporal location, whereas others favor bundles of features, and so on.[57] One could argue that it is the spatiotemporal location of 2 above that makes that sentence a token, or one may alternatively argue that it is rather the unique bundle of features it has, such as the color of the lines, the shape of the lines, and so on.[58]

When we come to metaphysical status, the conditions are not just general rather than particular, but most general.[59] Suppose, for the sake of illustration, that we were working within an Aristotelian categorial framework. In this context, the conditions of triangularity are given by the category, or categories, identified by Aristotle within which triangles fit, such as quantity, relation, and so on. And the same can be said about individuals. In this context, we are not speaking of a particular spatiotemporal location, shape, color, and so on, but of location in general, shape in general, quality in general, and so on. We seek to determine about texts the same thing we determine about humans when we say they are substances; about white and black when we say they are qualities; about motherhood when we say it is a relation; about three when we say it is a quantity; and so on.

Naturally, the issues of both identity and metaphysical status are complex and require the kind of attention that cannot be provided in passing. Because I have engaged in a detailed discussion of these issues elsewhere, I hope a summary of that discussion is sufficient here.[60]

It is important to keep in mind that there are several theories about the metaphysical status and identity of texts, for the view adopted has significant consequences for the understanding of revelation and interpretation. According to one, texts are the same as the entities of which they are constituted and have the same characteristics they have.[61] Differences in these entities, then, imply differences in identity. Consider the following two texts: 'God is great' and 'GOD IS GREAT.' According to this view, these texts are not tokens of the same type and, therefore, are not the same text, insofar as the entities that constitute the first do not have the same characteristics as those that constitute the second. Certainly 'D' has a different shape than 'd' when considered not as a letter, but as a certain mark on the page. Indeed, 'D' is as different from 'd' as it is from 'b,' and one might even want to argue that 'D' has more in common with 'b' than with 'd,' insofar as the bulge in 'D' and 'b' are on the same side of the vertical line.[62]

Another view holds that texts are meanings, and therefore that the entities of which texts are made up have nothing to do with their identity or metaphysical status. The status of texts is the same as the status of their meaning, whatever that may be.[63] This view is quite contrary to the first. Not only would it say that 'God is great' and 'GOD IS GREAT' are the same text to the degree that they have the same meaning; it would have to hold that 'God is great' and 'Dios es grande' (its translation into Spanish) are also the same text because the meaning is the same.

A third position holds that texts are speech acts, and here there are several possibilities if we follow Austin's classification.[64] A text, according to this view, is an act in which the author of the text engages, such as an act of writing, an act of informing, or even an act of performing.[65] Consider an author who says: 'God is great.' Here we can distinguish several speech acts. First, there is the locutionary act of uttering the sounds; second, there is the act of praising God, and this is the illocutionary act; and, finally, there is also the act of making those who hear this praise bow their heads in acquiescence, and this is the perlocutionary act. The text, according to this position, is one of these acts.

According to a fourth position, texts amount to the entities that constitute them when they are considered as meaningful, that is, as having meaning, although no particular meaning. Consequently, the identity of a text is not tied to any meaning in particular. Meanings can change and the text remains the same, although changes in the entities that constitute the text result in changes in its identity.[66] For example, in the case of 'God is great,' certain changes in the physical makeup of the entities would change the text. If instead of 'God,' we wrote, or said, 'Dog,' that would alter the text, but changes in meaning would not. 'God is great' would be the same, regardless of whether it meant a single, omniscient, omnipotent, and good being or an evil divinity with limited knowledge and power.

All these views have unacceptable consequences. The view that texts are the same as the entities that constitute them is unacceptable because these entities in themselves do not function as texts. They become texts only when they are considered in relation to the meanings that someone wishes to convey. A burning bush is nothing but a burning bush; it becomes a text only when its components are understood in relation to certain meanings.

The view that texts are meanings is unacceptable because, among other things, it does not take into account that one can understand and express the same thing in different languages. The notion of translation makes no sense unless one includes in the identity conditions of a text some of the characteristics of the linguistic entities that constitute it.

The speech-act view of texts is right insofar as it establishes a strong connection between texts and their authors through the acts in which the authors engage when they speak or write. But it neglects two important factors: the entities that result from the acts of the authors and the meanings. The entities are important because texts appear to have an existence that goes beyond that of the acts in which the authors engage when they produce them. And the meanings are important because meanings are what authors and audiences of texts understand through them.

The conception of texts as groups of entities with an indeterminate meaning does not sufficiently fix the identity of texts. Indeed, if this were the case, the text of Genesis and that of Leviticus could be regarded as the same if someone understood them to mean the same thing, which makes no sense at all.

Finally, the view I favor, in line with the definition provided earlier, holds that a text is the same as the entities that constitute it when considered in relation to a specific meaning. Therefore, changes in that meaning or in the entities that constitute the text result in changes in the identity of the text.[67]

Apart from the distinction between type and token texts, there are other classifications of texts that are pertinent for our discussion. One may, for example, distinguish among historical, contemporary, intermediary, intended, and ideal texts. The *historical text* is the text that the historical author produced, although again one could speak of a token or a type. In the case of a written text, the token would be the autograph, that is, the actual piece of writing the author produced; the type would be the universal of which the autograph is a token along with other copies of it.

The *contemporary text* is the text that we have at a particular point in history. In some cases, this could be the autograph if this text has survived, but in many cases the contemporary text is merely a copy of the autograph or of some other copy of the autograph. The contemporary text is, again, a token of the same type of which the autograph is a token, although often there are differences, and sometimes important ones, between the tokens we have of a text and its autograph.

The *intermediary text* is any text that mediates between the autograph and the contemporary text but is no longer available. It was a contemporary text for some audience from the past, but it is no longer one. If it were, of course, then it would be a contemporary text.

Some practitioners of hermeneutics like to speak as well of the *intended text*.[68] This is the text the author intended to produce but did not actually produce. Those who use the notion of intended text frequently are not clear about what it means. It makes sense only if one thinks of it as a mental text that does not get produced extramentally in the way it was anticipated, or as a set of ideas that are not properly expressed by the text produced. In the first case, we in fact have two texts, the mental and the one produced. So intended texts are simply texts that exist in the minds of their authors, which they wish, or wished, to produce but have not yet produced, or did not produce, outside the mind. In this sense, it is not merely intended, because it does in fact exist, insofar as it does exist in the mind of the author, even if not outside it. In the second case, taken as a set of ideas in the mind of the author, we do not have a text at all, for ideas by themselves, whatever they may be, are not texts.

Finally, the *ideal text* may be conceived in three ways. First, as an inaccurate version of a historical text produced and considered by an interpreter as an accurate copy of a historical text; second, as a text produced by an interpreter who considers that it expresses perfectly the view that the historical text expresses only imperfectly; and third, as a text produced by an interpreter and considered as the text that perfectly expresses the view the historical author should have expressed.

These distinctions will be of use in our discussion of revealed texts. We shall return to them later.

Divine Revelation as Divinely Revealed Texts

Equipped with this conception of texts, we can better grasp the conception of divine revelation used in this book. For present purposes, I regard a *divine revelation as a text through which members of a religion believe a divinity they worship intends to cause them to understand significant facts about which they might otherwise be ignorant.* The Bible is a revelation in this sense because Christians believe it is the means through which God seeks to make them understand significant facts he wishes them to know and of which otherwise they might be ignorant. Likewise, the Koran is a divine revelation because Muslims believe Allah intends them to understand significant facts through it.

Not all religious texts are to be considered revelations or parts of revelations. Prayers, catechisms, and theological treatises, for example, are religious texts, but they are not regarded as conveying a message from a divinity. Catechisms and theological treatises aim to cause understandings of matters fundamental to the religion, including doctrines about the divinity, but these texts are not believed to originate in the divinity. They are taken as products of the attempts by a community of believers as a whole, or by some of its members, to articulate, systematize, and understand what they consider pertinent religious knowledge. Prayers have another function: Traditionally their aim has been taken to be to communicate something to the divinity rather than vice versa, although there is considerable dispute among believers concerning the actual aim and result of prayers. Of course, there are prayers, like the one Jesus taught his followers, that are part of revelation. In these cases, prayers have a revelatory function that they normally do not have.

The conception of revealed texts I have proposed leaves open the question of which texts are truly revealed and which are not, as well as questions concerning the bases on which one can decide on this matter. These are important questions that must be considered in any attempt to develop a comprehensive hermeneutical theory of revelation, but they are marginal to the issue under discussion here. My concern is rather with the interpretation of texts that are thought and treated as if they were revealed, and this requires a broader notion of revelation than one would accept under different constraints. This understanding is in keeping with the general philosophical approach I am using, according to which the issue of the truth of particular religious beliefs is left open. Finally, the proposed conception of revelation rules out texts that are believed by a religious community to have divine origin but whose function is not to cause an understanding in the community, but rather, for example, to make the members of the community have certain feelings or experiences. Whether ultimately these texts should be included in the category of revealed text or not requires separate discussion. For present purposes I exclude them.

The conception of revelation I have proposed makes its function clear: to cause understanding in certain persons chosen by the divinity. Here, again, one might wish to raise the question of what exactly is the revelation in question. We saw that texts are complex entities and that there are several conceptions of what a text is. A text can be taken as (1) the entities that constitute it, (2) meaning, (3) speech acts, (4) the entities that constitute a text considered in relation to meaning, and (5) the same as (4) but with a specific meaning. This entails that the view one adopts of a text will determine the view one should adopt concerning revelation.

The view of revealed texts as the entities that constitute the texts, say the lines and shapes that constitute 'God is great,' makes very little sense. For, what would it be that the divinity means believers to understand in this case? The lines and shapes? This position makes sense only if believers are intended to understand a meaning other than the very lines and shapes that constitute the text. This requires the text to be not just the entities that constitute it, but those entities considered in relation to a meaning, and this is a different position altogether.

The view that identifies a revealed text with its meaning appears to make more sense at the outset. It does to the extent that we do not have to worry about the identity of the entities that constitute the text, but rather about the meaning the divinity wishes to be understood. However, this position inherits general problems from the view that texts are the same as their meanings and also generates specific problems related to the notion of revelation. When most religions speak of revelation as texts, they do not in fact speak of the meaning the divinity wishes to convey, but of some scriptures or verbal messages the divinity is supposed to have made available to them. The reason is that they are referring to the means whereby the revelation is given to humans and not to the facts revealed. Indeed, if we adopt the view of a revealed text as a meaning, the distinction between the facts revealed and the means of revelation collapse, and as a result the whole question of interpretation becomes moot.

Understanding revealed texts as speech acts of some kind poses problems of its own. In the first place, one has to decide whose speech acts are pertinent: those of the divinity, or those of the human author through whom the divine message is supposed to be conveyed? One problem with the first alternative is that it is not uncontroversial to attribute speech acts to a divinity, particularly in cases in which the divinity is conceived, as it is in most Western religions, as immaterial, unchanging, and transcendent.[69] Those who argue against God's speech point out that speech can only be attributed metaphorically to a being who, unlike humans, has no body and is immutable and transcendent.[70] If, on the other hand, the speech acts in question are those of a human author, then the message seems to be human rather than divine, and therefore unacceptable to those who believe otherwise. But, even apart from these problems, this position radically divorces the entities that are generally taken to constitute texts from revelation, and even from the facts that are being revealed. For there is no reason why different acts and different entities cannot be used to convey the same facts. And yet, religions generally consider the original form of revelation, the very entities that constitute the text regarded as revealed, as somehow essential to the revelation.

The position that identifies a revealed text with the entities that constitute it considered in relation to meaning, but to no specific meaning in particular, is also unacceptable insofar as it leaves open the content of revelation, which is after all what matters.

The view that makes most sense considers a revealed text to be the entities that constitute it taken in relation to the meaning the text is intended to convey. This is the view of texts I favor and one that appears consistent with the attitude of most believers. Revelation, considered as these texts, then, consists of certain entities used as signs that are related to a meaning the divinity intends believers to understand through them. This way of conceiving revelation does not conflict with the primary sense of revelation as the fact revealed. One can still hold that the primary sense of revelation is the fact, as it were, and to this extent revelation is not a text, but rather what is to be understood through a text. But when revelation is taken as a means and this refers to a text, then revelation turns out to be the entities that constitute the text considered in relation to the fact the divinity wishes to be understood. In this way, we can preserve the primary sense of revelation and at the same time take into account the attitude of believers toward revealed texts. This attitude is that these texts are essential for the conveyance of the facts they reveal; the original textual artifact is indispensable.

A qualification is in order here, however. First, some religions hold that the original individual artifacts are important in themselves. We have a case of this sort with the Commandment tablets given to Moses. The ancient Hebrews regarded these tablets as sacred and built a temple around them. Other religions also accept the importance of original documents, although not because of any intrinsic value they may have. Their view is that original documents are important as controlling devices that ensure the authenticity of copies, rather than because they have any value or power in themselves. To understand this better, we must go back to the distinction between a type and a token text introduced earlier. Using the notions of type and token, we can say that for some religions the token text is essential not just epistemically, as a paradigmatic instance against which all other instances of the text should be compared, but rather as a sacred thing. For other religions this is not so. The important text is the type, and the original token is important only insofar as it is a faithful instance of the type text through which the divinity has revealed a fact to a community of believers.

For purposes of interpretation, the latter view is most appropriate, unless one holds that the original token has some power that other tokens of the text do not have. Most religions would hold the original token to be somehow sacred because of its association with the first moment of revelation, the divinity, and the human instrumental author, but they would not regard it as having any power to help us understand appropriately the facts the divinity wishes believers to understand. A facsimile, or even a transcript, of this text would do as well as the original to the extent that it is faithful to anything that could have semantic or hermeneutical significance.

Conceiving a revealed text in the way I have proposed is useful because it allows us to explain both the hermeneutical importance that religions attach to the original tokens of revealed texts and the hermeneutical importance of the original context in which revelation took place. Revelation always occurs at a time and in a place, and is therefore eminently historical. The cultural and historical circumstances within which it occurs are essential for its understanding.[71] This also explains why revealed texts come in the shape in which they do. These texts are produced within a culture and are given to the members of that culture in the forms and genres they understand. And this is not just a matter of language; other factors are also at play.

Consider the Old Testament. The genealogies it contains were a customary way in which societies kept records at the time. There is a story about the beginning of the world, again typical of the times. There are songs, and there are books of laws. All these fit nicely within the cultural context of the times, and made the revealed text understandable to the people for whom it was first produced. Cultures and traditions, then, make possible the understanding of the message the divinity is trying to convey.[72] If the message contained in the Old Testament had been revealed in a scientific treatise of the sort we are accustomed to today, or as a play similar to those of Shakespeare, the message would have been incomprehensible to the ancient Hebrews. And, of course, they did not have videos and phonographs, so the message could not have been presented through these means.

There is no particular genre, or form, that is essential to revelation when this is conceived as text. The form or genre in which a revealed text is presented depends very much on the historical and cultural circumstances in which the revelation takes place. This prompts an interesting question, namely: Why is the divinity's revelation given to the same people, sometimes even at the same time, in different genres? Why a genealogy and a set of songs in the Bible, for example?

Several possibilities suggest themselves immediately. One could say that (1) even within the same society, different individual persons require different means to convey the same message, because they have different capacities, education, dispositions, and so on; (2) the nature of the message requires different kinds of texts; (3) it is not so much the nature of the message, but rather the effect the divinity wishes to have on the audience that imposes such requirements; and (4) the message requires the cooperation of the members of the community, and this process in turn deepens its desired effect; and so on.[73] Obviously, this issue is anything but simple, and deserves more attention than I can give it here, so I must put it aside for another occasion.

Finally, we saw earlier that apart from the historical token text, there are four other texts one may consider: contemporary, intermediary, intended, and ideal. For most religions, the importance of the original token is fundamental, because it is the ultimate controlling device of the message from the divinity. If the contemporary text we have is in fact the autograph, then we have a most fortuitous situation. But this is seldom the case. In most instances, we have only a contemporary text that we know relies on intermediary texts all the way back to the autograph. This means that we do not know to what extent we actually have a text that is like the autograph. In this situation, the notions of both intended and ideal texts become useful. The former is useful because it brings out that the text we have is not the one intended by the divinity or the instrumental author. The notion of ideal text is useful because it helps in our attempts to get at that intended text, insofar as the text we have is the result of the labor of not just the divinity and the instrumental author, but also of copyists and others who helped shape it. In this sense, we are measuring the result of the labor of several authors by what we think the text should be.

Conclusion

In sum, for our present purposes, it is most appropriate to conceive divine revelation as a text regarded by a religious community as intended by a divinity to cause certain acts of understanding in an audience. This audience is composed of members of the religious community in question, and the revelation concerns certain significant facts of which the community might otherwise be ignorant. For this reason, not only the message, but also the means through which the message is conveyed is essential in revelation. Indeed, the token of the revealed text is most important as an accurate instance of the revealed type that can be used to control the accuracy of its copies. Armed with this conception of revelation, we can now turn to interpretation.

Chapter 2 ➤

Interpretation

To address the issue of how revelation is to be interpreted, we need a clear understanding not only of revelation, but also of interpretation. And here we encounter problems similar to those we faced with revelation, for interpretation is understood in different ways by different people, including philosophers and theologians. This is obvious from the many objects of interpretation to which we refer in ordinary language. We talk about interpreting events, elections, people, actions, motives, views, arguments, symbols, signs, the world, authorities, and so on. And surely, in many cases, the differences among these objects suggest that what we are doing, when we are interpreting them, are quite different things. To interpret a motive seems to be quite a different thing from interpreting an authority, and likewise with a view or symbol. Indeed, if we go back to the different views of revelation we saw earlier, it appears that they also involve different interpretations. Recall that revelation was taken to be at least four different kinds of things: acts of revealing, facts revealed, acts of receiving what is revealed, and the means used to reveal. The interpretation of a fact would appear to be something different than the interpretation of an act of revealing, an act of receiving a revelation, or the means used in revealing. Fortunately, in the last chapter we settled on the means of revelation as the proper source of our inquiry, and we identified this with texts regarded as revealed by a community of religious believers. This makes our task much easier.

Two Senses of 'Interpretation'

Insofar as our task has to do exclusively with revealed texts, there are two senses of 'interpretation' that are particularly pertinent for our discussion.[1] In one way, call it *interpretation$_1$*, it means understanding. Thus, for a particular person to have an interpretation$_1$ of a text is the same as for that person to have an understanding of it. In this sense, an interpretation$_1$ is a kind of mental act (or acts) that is produced in relation to a text. Thus, whenever I understand the first verse of the Gospel According to St. John, I have an interpretation$_1$ of it, and the interpretation$_1$ is the act (or acts) of understanding I have. The first verse of the Gospel According to St. John, on the other hand, is the object of the interpretation, that which is to be, or is, interpreted. As the object of understanding, this verse is not an act (or acts) of understanding, and therefore it is neither part of the interpretation$_1$ nor similar in nature to it. Nonetheless, the interpretation$_1$ is intentionally directed toward it and contains both a reference to it and an understanding of the relation between it and the acts of understanding caused by it.

We might, then, distinguish two things that play a role in an interpretation$_1$: an *interpretandum* and an *interpretans*. The first is the text under interpretation, that is, the object of interpretation. An example would be, as noted, the first verse of the Gospel According to St. John: Ἐν ἀρχῇ ἦν ὁ λόγος. The *interpretans,* on the other hand, is composed of the acts of understanding an interpreter has in relation to the *interpretandum*. It has two main parts. One consists of certain acts of understanding that, by themselves, do not appear related to the *interpretandum;* for example, the understanding "In the beginning was the Word." The other part consists of certain acts of understanding that relate the first set of acts to the *interpretandum.* Let us call the acts that establish this relation *referential.* Now, a referential act requires both a sign that refers to the *interpretandum* and a concept that makes clear the relation between the *interpretandum* and its understanding. If, say, 'X' is the sign that is used to refer to the text, "Ἐν ἀρχῇ ἦν ὁ λόγος' and "means" is the relating concept, then the referential act of understanding would be "'X' means." The interpretation$_1$, in turn, would be a set of mental acts composed of the referential act and the other acts of understanding mentioned, so that our example would amount to: "'X' means 'In the beginning was the Word.'" Of course, the *interpretandum* (e.g., "Ἐν ἀρχῇ ἦν ὁ λόγος') can take the place of the referential sign (e.g., 'X'), so that the interpretation, in our example, could also be something like: "Ἐν ἀρχῇ ἦν ὁ λόγος' means 'In the beginning was the Word.'" This should make clear that in an interpretation$_1$ the *interpretandum* is not ontologically of the same nature as the interpretation, and therefore cannot be part of it, although it is represented in it by a sign that is considered in the referential act of understanding.

In accordance with the definition of texts adopted in chapter 1, texts have authors, but if interpretations$_1$ are understandings, then they do not appear to have them. It seems misleading to speak of me as the author of my own understanding, for authorship seems to entail some construction and originality: I am not the author of something that has already been created by someone else. Of course, one might be able to speak of the author of a copy, insofar as someone is responsible for its production, but the author of the copy is not the author of the original. Even if I produce a perfect replica of Picasso's *Guernica,* I am the author of only the replica, not of *Guernica.* Applying this to the understanding (i.e., interpretation$_1$) of texts, we can see that I cannot be the author of an understanding of Genesis if someone else has already had this understanding. On the other hand, if my understanding of Genesis is different from earlier understandings of this text, there is no reason why I cannot be said to be the author of it. Interpretations$_1$, then, can have authors, although only if they satisfy certain conditions.

In another way, call it *interpretation$_2$,* an interpretation is a text rather than an understanding. But here, as in interpretations$_1$, we can distinguish between two different things that play a role in the interpretation: an *interpretandum,* or text under interpretation, and an *interpretans,* or text added by the interpreter.[2] In interpretations$_2$ also, as in interpretations$_1$, the *interpretans* is composed of two parts: a text that is supposed to cause an understanding and a reference to the *interpretandum* that makes clear that the understanding in question is related to the *interpretandum.* And as in the case of interpretations$_1$, the reference in the *interpretans* can be the *interpretandum* itself. As noted, the main difference between interpretations$_1$ and interpretations$_2$ is that the first are understandings, whereas the second are texts.

Consider a situation in Mexico in which a Mexican who knows no English tells an American tourist who knows no Spanish, "Pare." Obviously, the American has no idea of what has been said to her, but there is a third party close by who knows both English and Spanish and comes to the rescue. If the third party simply said, "Stop," the American tourist would not be able to connect this text with the original text, unless of course the context made the connection clear. The third party would have to say something like, "He means for you to stop," or "He means stop," or "'Pare' means stop," in order to convey his message. In all cases, even when the original text is not explicitly included in the second text, there is an elliptical reference to it, for without the reference the American tourist would not be able to connect the first text to the second. Now, all three sentences, 'He means for you to stop,' 'He means stop,' and '"Pare" means stop,' are examples of interpretations$_2$, but the most frequently applied to revealed texts is the third kind. This is the case, for example, with Augustine's *Literal Commentary on "Genesis,"* in which the *interpretandum* and the *interpretans* are integrated into a single text.

In this last sense, then, an interpretation$_2$ resembles a definition in structure. One of its two parts, the *interpretandum,* corresponds to the *definiendum,* and the other part, the *interpretans,* corresponds to the *definiens.* Just as in the definition "A human being is a rational animal" we have a *definiendum* (A human being) and a *definiens* (is a rational animal), so in Augustine's *Literal Commentary on "Genesis"* we have the text of Genesis and his discussion of it.

The fact that interpretations$_1$ are understandings and interpretations$_2$ are texts is significant. In the first, the *interpretandum* can never be part of the interpretation because the *interpretandum* and the *interpretans* are ontologically different, but in the second, the *interpretandum* and the *interpretans* can be integrated into a single text, as we have seen in the examples given. Indeed, even though interpretations$_1$ must contain a reference to the *interpretandum*, the latter remains as the object that is being understood, and therefore as something that is not ontologically part of the acts of understanding that constitute the interpretation$_1$. Using a metaphor, one might say that in interpretations$_1$ there is a break between the understanding and the text, or between the interpretation and the *interpretandum*, that is not present in interpretations$_2$, because in the latter the *interpretans* and the *interpretandum* are ontologically similar. Consider that an interpretation$_2$ of the Greek text cited above is a sentence such as Ἐν ἀρχῇ ἦν ὁλόγος means "In the beginning was the Word.'" This sentence shows clearly that the *interpretandum* (i.e., the Greek text) and the *interpretans* (i.e., the English text) are of the same kind. Indeed, the very term 'means,' used in the *interpretandum* to clarify the relation between *interpretandum* and *interpretans*, is also textual in nature. An interpretation$_1$ of the same text, on the other hand, would be quite a different thing insofar as it would be a mental act, or acts, of understanding with a reference to the Greek text.

This also makes clear another point about interpretations$_2$ that should be obvious: That an interpretation$_2$ often includes the *interpretandum* does not entail that the author of the interpretation$_2$ is the author of the *interpretandum*. The author of Ἐν ἀρχῇ ἦν ὁλόγος means "In the beginning was the Word'" is not the author of the sentence Ἐν ἀρχῇ ἦν ὁλόγος. Moreover, although interpretations$_2$ are texts, and as such have authors, their authors, just like the authors of other texts, need not be the authors of their components. Indeed, we are seldom the creators of the signs we select and arrange to compose the texts of which we are authors. I also assume that for an interpretation$_2$ to have an author, it must not have been produced before. If it has, then it has only a user, not an author, unless the person in question was unaware of it. Just as I am the user of 'Good morning,' a text of which I am not the author, in principle I can be the user of Augustine's *Literal Commentary on "Genesis,"* even if this appears unlikely.

It is important to keep in mind that *interpretanda* are often part of interpretations$_2$. This is particularly evident in literal commentaries, in which the *interpretandum* is often woven so tightly into the *interpretans* that the latter makes no sense, sometimes even grammatically, without the inclusion of the former. Modern editors of such commentaries have to resort to all sorts of artifices to distinguish the words that compose the *interpretandum* within the interpretation. They might, for example, capitalize all letters in the *interpretandum,* or use italics or boldface.[3] The way this is done is not of any consequence; what needs to be noted is the close integration of both texts.

In short, interpretations$_2$ are quite different from interpretations$_1$ in several ways, two of which are quite important for our purposes. First, in an interpretation$_2$, the *interpretandum* can be, and often is, part of the interpretation, whereas in interpretations$_1$ this cannot be so. Second, interpretations$_2$ are texts, whereas interpretations$_1$ are acts of understanding. Both of these differences have important consequences that will become apparent as we go along.

Often, the *interpretans* of an interpretation$_2$ is the textual expression of the *interpretans* of an interpretation$_1$. For this reason, most of the points I make here apply regardless of whether one adopts the first or the second conception of 'interpretation,' but there are certain advantages to the use of the second, and so I begin with it, although I return to the first sense later.

As a text, an interpretation$_2$ is a group of entities, used as signs, selected, arranged, and intended by an author to cause certain specific acts of understanding in an audience in a certain context. Just as authors of interpretations$_2$ should not be confused with the authors of the texts under interpretation because they add textual elements to these texts, and thereby change their identities, the audiences of interpretations$_2$ should not be confused with the audiences of *interpretanda*. Moreover, the contexts of interpretations$_2$ are not the same as the contexts in which the *interpretanda* were produced, but rather correspond to the contexts of the audiences of the interpretations$_2$.[4]

Consider the case of Augustine and his *Literal Commentary on "Genesis."* The *Commentary* is a text of which Augustine is the author, even if it includes the text that Augustine is trying to make us understand. Moreover, the historical audience and context of the *Commentary* are different from those of Genesis, even though the contemporary audience of both may be the same, namely, you and I, for example. Note that, as a text, Augustine's *Commentary* is itself, like Genesis, subject to interpretation, both interpretation$_1$ and interpretation$_2$. But this does not make any difference for the purposes of the issue we are considering here.

At least one aim of all interpretations, whether they are taken as understandings (i.e., interpretations$_1$) or as texts of the kind we have been discussing (i.e., interpretations$_2$), is to develop understanding either in interpreters themselves or in their audiences. Interpretations are generally produced by interpreters for their own benefit or the benefit of others. Interpreters want to understand, or to make audiences understand, something about the texts under interpretation. A teacher, for example, engages in this kind of procedure in class when she lectures on Aristotle's *Metaphysics*. The teacher wants, first, to develop an understanding of Aristotle's text in herself, and, second, to cause a similar understanding in her students.

Apart from understanding, interpretations may have all sorts of other aims. Some of these are generic to all texts. For example, interpretations may be used to arouse or vent emotions, prompt or prevent actions, make a profit, generate fame, and so on. This raises some interesting issues that, however, I must put aside here insofar as they are not germane to our topic. Apart from these generic aims of interpretations, there are other, more specific ones, to which I turn presently, because they have significant implications for the interpretation of revelation. I begin with different kinds of interpretations$_2$.

Kinds of Interpretation$_2$

For our purposes, it is important to distinguish among several kinds of interpretation$_2$ based on the functions they have. These functions are the uses to which interpretations are put, and are determined by the specific aims they are intended to achieve. Aside from the general function of causing acts of understanding in an audience with respect to an *interpretandum,* interpretations$_2$ may have many other functions. Four of these I gather under the heading *meaning interpretations* and the rest under the category *relational interpretations.*[5] The fact that interpretations$_2$ are classified on the basis of function implies that unless their functions conflict, different kinds of interpretations$_2$ are not mutually exclusive. Different kinds of interpretations$_2$ of the same text may coexist without difficulty because the same interpretation$_2$ may be intended to, and effectively, carry out several functions simultaneously or at different times.

Meaning Interpretations$_2$

Meaning interpretations$_2$ always aim to cause an understanding of the meaning of the text under interpretation, but the meaning in question may be taken in four different ways: as what the historical author understood or intended (authorial interpretation$_2$); as what a particular audience understood (audiencial interpretation$_2$); as independent of what the historical author understood or intended or a particular audience understood (independent-meaning interpretation$_2$); or as any one of these three senses but including its implications (implicative interpretation$_2$). These interpretations are intended to cause an understanding of a text and its meaning, rather than of a relation of a text, or its meaning, to factors brought to bear on it by an interpreter.

The function of an *authorial interpretation*$_2$ is to cause in an audience acts of understanding similar to those the historical author had or intended in relation to the *interpretandum*. I call it *authorial* because it aims to capture the meaning of a text as understood or intended by its author.[6] These interpretations$_2$ roughly take two forms. One form is: A understood Q by P, where A is the historical author, Q is composed of additions the interpreter makes to the historical text, and P is the historical text. In this sense, an interpretation$_2$ of a text tries to reveal the author's understanding of the text. An authorial interpretation$_2$ of the Gospel According to St. John I, 1, for example, would be something like this: "The author understood 'In the beginning was the Word' by Ἐν ἀρχῇ ἦν ὁ λόγος." Another form of authorial interpretation$_2$ is: A intended that Q be understood by P. In this sense, the interpretation$_2$ tries to reveal the meaning that the author intended to be understood through the text. An authorial interpretation$_2$ of the same text we have considered would be something like this: "The author intended that Ἐν ἀρχῇ ἦν ὁ λόγος be understood to mean that in the beginning was the Word."

Keep in mind that an authorial interpretation tries to capture the meaning either understood or intended by the historical author, that is, the person (or persons) who composed the historical text. Other authors, such as the composite, the interpretive, and the pseudo-historical, about whom I shall have something to say in the next chapter, are not pertinent. In the case of revealed texts, where there are two authors, a divinity and a human being, the latter of whom functions as the instrument of the divinity, the matter becomes complicated. I return to this in chapter 3.

The function of an *audiencial interpretation*$_2$ is very similar to that of the authorial kind, except that the interpretation is intended to cause acts of understanding in an audience similar to those a particular audience, rather than the historical author, had in relation to the *interpretandum*. Moreover, unlike the case of authorial interpretation$_2$, these take only one form, insofar as they concern the understanding of audiences only, not their intentions. These interpretations$_2$ take the form: A understood Q by P, where A stands for a particular audience. An interpretation$_2$ of this sort of the Gospel According to St. John tries to capture the understanding a particular audience, such as the historical, had of it rather than the author's own understanding of what he or she wrote or his or her intention as to how it is supposed to be understood. This audience can in principle be one person, but more often than not it is composed of many persons. In audiencial interpretations$_2$, we are often dealing with a social understanding rather than a single person's understanding. In some ways, this is more difficult to accomplish, but in other ways, it is easier, because social understandings leave more markers than do individual ones.

Most audiencial interpretations$_2$ concern historical audiences, that is, the audiences contemporaneous with the historical texts and part of the cultures to which the authors belong. (More on this in chapter 3.) The reason is that, generally, interpreters tend to be interested in them more than in other audiences. In principle, however, there is no reason why other audiences cannot be included. If so, we would have as many different audiencial interpretations$_2$ as audiences selected. And since any person or group of persons may in principle be the audience of a text, the number of possible audiencial interpretations$_2$ is potentially infinite. By 'possible audience' I mean logically possible, not factually possible. It is certainly possible to give an interpretation$_2$ of what Alexander the Great would have thought had he had access to Borges' "Pierre Menard," even though it is factually impossible for Alexander to be the audience of this text. The various audiences in question may be classified in several ways, some of which are discussed in chapter 3.

The function of an *independent-meaning interpretation$_2$* is to cause in an audience acts of understanding of the meaning of the *interpretandum,* irrespective of whether that meaning was understood by the historical author or any particular audience of the text or of the understandings they may have had of it. This kind of interpretation$_2$ presupposes that the meaning of a text is not necessarily determined by what the historical author or any particular audience understood by it.[7] Independent-meaning interpretations$_2$ roughly take the form: P means Q, where P is the historical text and Q is composed of the additions the interpreter makes to P in order to cause an understanding of the text. In this case, an interpretation$_2$ of the Gospel According to St. John would try to cause an understanding of the meaning of the text in an audience independently of what the author, or any particular audience of the text, actually understood by it. An independent-meaning interpretation$_2$ of St. John's Gospel I, 1, would be something like this: "'Ἐν ἀρχῇ ἦν ὁ λόγος means 'In the beginning was the Word.'" Clearly, this kind of interpretation$_2$ does not have a historical aim. Moreover, it assumes that it is possible that neither the author nor any particular audience fully understood, or understood at all, the meaning of the text. This sounds scandalous, but it is widely accepted nowadays that historical authors, or even particular audiences, are not always the final arbiters of the meanings of texts and that the meanings of texts are not always exhausted by any single audience's understanding of them.[8] Texts are supposed to have a life of their own.[9] And, indeed, I believe this view is correct with respect to the author, insofar as we often say things we do not mean and we often mean things we do not say. Any writer, or even any speaker, should have experiences that vouch for this. And something similar applies to particular audiences, at least in the case of some texts.

The function of an *implicative interpretation$_2$* is to cause in an audience acts of understanding of the meaning of an *interpretandum* taken together with its implications. This kind of interpretation$_2$, then, proposes a richer understanding of the meaning of a text than others might. Indeed, it presupposes two things: First, the historical author, or any particular audience, may not be aware of the implications of the meaning of the *interpretandum*—this distinguishes this kind of interpretation$_2$ from the authorial and audiencial in particular; second, what we called earlier the "independent meaning" of the *interpretandum* neither is the same as nor includes the implications of that meaning—this distinguishes this kind of interpretation$_2$ from independent-meaning interpretations$_2$.[10] Implicative interpretations roughly take the form: P implies Q, where P is the meaning of the historical text apart from its implications and Q is the meaning of the additions made to P by an interpreter. In this case, the interpreter tries to make an audience aware, for example, of the implications of the Gospel According to St. John, regardless of whether the author himself, or any particular audience, was or was not aware of them. For example, one might argue that the meaning of Ἐν ἀρχῇ ἦν ὁ λόγος implies that Christ is the locus of Platonic Ideas, as Augustine thought he was, even though the author of the Gospel does not say so.[11] Of course, the meaning of a historical text, even when considered apart from its implications, can be taken in various ways, and this gives rise to as many interpretations$_2$ of it.

All four kinds of meaning interpretations$_2$ mentioned are intended to cause in an audience understandings of the meaning of texts apart from any relations the texts, or their meanings, may have to other things. Yet, each of these four kinds of interpretation$_2$ conceives differently the understanding it aims to produce.

Relational Interpretations$_2$

The function of *relational interpretations$_2$* is to cause an understanding of a text in relation to factors brought into the interpretive process by the interpreter. I call it *relational* because this kind of interpretation$_2$ is primarily focused on the relation of a text, or its meaning, to something else.[12]

Of course, every interpretation$_2$, as every text, has a context that will, as it does in all texts, play a role in the identity, meaning, and understanding of the interpretation$_2$. When I say, "Ἐν ἀρχῇ ἦν ὁ λόγος means "In the beginning was the Word,"" there is a context to my remark—a place, a time, an audience, and an author. But only part of this context is relevant for the interpretation of the text. The relevant context is composed of anything that affects the meaning and understanding of the text. Consider, for example, the text 'Fire!' If this is said by a rank officer in the trenches, it means one thing; when it is said by a guard in a crowded store in which there is the smell of smoke, it means another; and when it is said by a punk in a theater when there is no evidence of fire, it means something else still. Clearly, the speaker and the circumstances alluded to are part of the relevant context of the text. But such other factors as the time of the day, the weather, and the chemical composition of the fibers that make up of the clothing of the speaker are not part of the relevant context because they do not affect in any way the meaning or the understanding of the text.

Moreover, in every interpretation$_2$, including meaning ones, interpreters consider and bring into play various factors in order to accomplish the interpretive function. For example, in order to provide an effective meaning interpretation$_2$ of St. Paul's First Epistle to the Corinthians, the interpreter has to learn Greek and take into consideration not just Greek customs and Greek culture but also Hellenistic and Jewish cultures. In addition, the interpreter must take into account the language, customs, and culture of her own audience in order to cause the appropriate acts of understanding in it.[13] These factors are often taken to constitute the basis for an objection against the distinction between meaning and relational interpretations$_2$. But this is misguided. Bringing in these factors is compatible with the meaning functions and does not undermine the distinction between meaning and relational interpretations$_2$. These factors play merely an epistemic role in the interpretive process and are not supposed to change the function of the interpretation$_2$, even if in fact they affect the resulting interpretation$_2$ and, consequently, the understanding that the audience will derive from it. Surely, an adequate or inadequate knowledge of Greek will affect the interpretation$_2$ that an interpreter produces of St. Paul's First Epistle to the Corinthians, but it does not alter the function of the interpretation$_2$, be that authorial, audiencial, independent-meaning, or implicative.

Perhaps the point can be made clear by referring to the distinction between the means and the end: The means used affects the end achieved, but this does not entail that it affects the end pursued. The end of an interpretation$_2$ can still be an understanding of the meaning of a text and at the same time use and consider all sorts of other things in order to achieve it. The use of particular means, or of any means at all, does not change the nature of a meaning interpretation$_2$.

Relational interpretations$_2$ differ from meaning ones in that their function is to produce an understanding of a text in terms of, or in relation to, factors other than those considered in a meaning interpretation$_2$. In the latter, this understanding is considered *independently* of other factors, even if those factors are used to establish the goals of the meaning interpretation$_2$. It is one thing to try to cause an audience to understand that 'X is Y' and another to try to cause the audience to understand the relation between 'X is Y' and 'Z is V.' For both, I need to refer to and use all sorts of things, such as how 'X,' 'Y,' 'Z,' and 'V' are used in the language to which they belong.

But this is not the same thing as aiming to establish a relation between 'X is Y' and 'Z is V.' Consider a concrete example: It is one thing to get an audience to understand the meaning of the Anselmian formula *Credo ut intelligam* (whether that meaning is taken to be authorial, audiencial, independent, or implicative) and another to get the audience to understand that the Anselmian text owes a debt to Augustine. For the second, the interpreter has to bring Augustine in, and the understanding effected is of a relation between the Anselmian formula and Augustine, rather than just of the meaning of the formula. A different, although also informative, example is an interpretation$_2$ a Freudian analyst gives of a text that describes the action of a son who kills his father. Again, it is one thing to get an audience to understand the meaning of the text as, say, understood by the author, and another to understand that the action described was prompted by an unconscious Oedipus complex of which neither the perpetrator of the action nor the writer who described it were aware. Clearly, the second kind of interpretation$_2$ brings into the interpretive process a theoretical framework missing in the first. The first understanding concerns whatever the author understood—that an action took place. The second concerns the relation of that action to certain unconscious motives that are revealed only if one assumes a certain theoretical stance and considers the action in terms of it.

The function of a relational interpretation$_2$ is different from that of a meaning interpretation$_2$ in that the use of the factors the interpreter brings into the interpretation$_2$ is not merely epistemic but has an ontological dimension. These factors control and affect the end pursued; they are not just instruments that get us to the end. Going back to a point made earlier, in a relational interpretation$_2$ the nature of the end depends on the means, whereas in a meaning interpretation$_2$ the achievement of the end may depend on the means although the nature of the aim does not. This can be illustrated by the two examples given earlier. First, the understanding of the Augustinian basis of Anselm's formula may help us in turn to cause an understanding (epistemological role) of the meaning of the Anselmian formula in an audience, but it is not the aim pursued in a meaning interpretation$_2$ of it, nor should it affect it (ontological role). Likewise, the understanding of the unconscious Oedipal motives of the parricide may be instrumental in causing an understanding (epistemic role) of the textual description of this action in an audience, but it is neither what is sought in a meaning interpretation$_2$, nor should it affect (ontological role) the understanding of what the author of the descriptive text understood.

An analogy might help. Consider a microscope and certain bacteria one can see only by means of the microscope. The microscope is indispensable to see the bacteria, and in many ways determines what we see and how we see the bacteria. But the assumption behind the use of the microscope is that the nature of the bacteria is not affected by this use. Now think of the meaning of a text as the bacteria and of the various hermeneutical tools used by interpreters to get it as a microscope. The understanding of a text that meaning interpretations$_2$ aim to produce, just like the bacteria, is not supposed to be affected by the means used to get at it, just like the microscope, even if in fact it is. But the understanding of a text that relational interpretations$_2$ aim to produce, unlike the bacteria, is supposed to be affected by the means used to get at it.

Of course, it is altogether possible, and indeed it is frequently the case, that interpreters aim in theory to provide meaning interpretations$_2$ whereas in fact they engage in procedures that, instead, involve relational ones. Thus we could make a distinction between what one might call a nominal intention and a real one. The nominal intention is the one the interpreter has in mind; the real one is the one he or she actually pursues. This entails that interpretations$_2$ may not always be what interpreters think they are, a fact that needs to be considered for the characterization and evaluation of interpretations$_2$ and that has a bearing, as we shall see in subsequent chapters of this book, on the kind of interpretation that is appropriate for revealed texts.

The possibility that interpretations$_2$ may not be what interpreters think they are raises the question as to how one can decide the matter. Is the interpreter's nominal aim to be ignored and the real one accepted, or is the nominal aim to be taken at face value and the real one discarded? I do not see how one can easily answer this question, for both alternatives seem undesirable when considered in the abstract. Perhaps the best way to solve this problem is not to choose for all cases, but to consider the question on a case by case basis. If it should turn out that there is a particular case in which a choice is not possible, then perhaps the best thing is to provide two characterizations with their respective evaluations.

In short, then, that all interpretations$_2$ rely on factors interpreters have to bring into the interpretive process for epistemic reasons does not undermine the distinction between meaning and relational interpretations$_2$. Still, there are other grounds on the basis of which this distinction may be questioned. I shall take up two of these briefly.

Consider the difficulty, or as some claim, practical impossibility, of achieving meaning interpretations$_2$, particularly authorial ones. I shall pay greater attention to this and other related difficulties in chapter 3, but for now let it suffice to say that an objection formulated on this basis is not effective for three reasons. First, even if it were in fact practically impossible to achieve meaning interpretations$_2$, this does not entail that the notions of meaning and relational interpretations$_2$ are logically indistinguishable. And as long as it is logically possible to distinguish them—and I believe I have made this clear—it is appropriate to do so in order to maintain clarity in the discussion. Second, as will become clear later, one important claim in my overall thesis in this book is that theological interpretations of revelation are relational, a point I make against those who argue that they are authorial. So, even if it turned out that all interpretations₂ were relational, this would not undermine my claim. Third, to present one view I oppose, namely that interpretations of revelation are authorial, I need to distinguish these from relational interpretations, even if only provisionally.

There is one more way in which the distinction between meaning and re-lational interpretations₂ might be undermined that I wish to take up here. Some might argue that, in addition to the general means we need to use in the interpretations₂ of texts, we always bring to the interpretation of texts certain personal views in terms of which we cause their understanding in others. And it is not clear how these personal views function differently from, say, the Freudian and feminist conceptual frameworks that I have ar-gued, when used in interpreting, yield relational interpretations₂.

The answer to this objection is that, of course, personal views, if used not merely epistemically, but to mold understanding, do yield relational in-terpretations₂. And, indeed, we often acknowledge this when we talk about some interpretations₂. We say, for example, that they are personal, or idio-syncratic, or peculiar, and so on. In doing this, we recognize that they are not what we expect, which is, say, an understanding of what Anselm un-derstood by *Credo ut intelligam.* We do not expect to understand what someone thinks such a text means when filtered through his or her personal viewpoint. Of course, as in the previous objection, one can always claim that this understanding is practically impossible, but this does not mean it is logically impossible. Nor does it mean, certainly, that a claim to that ef-fect should be accepted without critical inspection, particularly when we mostly assume, in ordinary life, not only that we aim to understand what others tell us but also that we do understand it. Meaning interpretations, including authorial and intended, then, can and should be distinguished from personal understanding.

There are many kinds of relational interpretations₂. Psychological, psycho-analytic, philosophical, historical, Marxist, feminist, and Christian interpreta-tions₂ are all relational. Consider, for instance, a Christian interpretation₂ of Aristotle's *Metaphysics.* The function of this kind of interpretation₂ is to cause in an audience an understanding of the *Metaphysics* in terms of Christian prin-ciples and doctrines, rather than an understanding of what Aristotle thought or intended to be understood, what some audience of the text understood by the text, and so on. Thus, one might argue that Aristotle's "Unmoved Mover" is the Christian God and that the movers of the spheres are in fact angels. As is well known, this is indeed what Thomas Aquinas did. So, in this sense, one could argue that Aquinas's *Commentary on Aristotle's "Metaphysics"* is not, say, an authorial interpretation$_2$ insofar as the understanding of Aristotle's *Metaphysics* Aquinas's audience would get from the *Commentary* is not of the meaning of the text as understood, or intended to be understood, by Aristotle, but rather the understanding of Aristotle's *Metaphysics* in terms of the Christian Faith. For surely no one could seriously argue that Aristotle did think that his Unmoved Mover is the Christian God or his movers of the spheres are Christian angels. One could argue, perhaps, that what Aristotle meant by the Unmoved Mover is in some respects what Christians mean by God, but not that he understood or intended it to be understood so. In short, Aquinas's interpretation$_2$ may not be a meaning interpretation$_2$ at all, for it does not appear to be an independent-meaning or an implicative interpretation$_2$ either. Aquinas's *Commentary on Aristotle's "Metaphysics"* appears to be rather a Christian interpretation$_2$, and therefore relational.

This does not imply, however, that Aquinas may not have also had other functions in mind, either for the whole text of his *Commentary* or for parts of it, or even that he realized exactly what he was doing. For example, he may have also been trying to produce in his audience an understanding of what Aristotle understood in the *Metaphysics,* or of the meaning of the text and the implications of that meaning. To this extent his interpretation$_2$ may not be purely relational. Keep in mind also that just as there may be several interpretations$_2$ of a text, contingent on various goals the interpreter wishes to reach, there is no reason why the same interpretation$_2$ may not have more than one function and achieve several ends.

This brings me to another important point. Generally, the functions of the interpretations$_2$ of particular texts are seldom of a single kind. Most often they are mixed, in part because interpreters are not fully aware of different kinds of interpretive tasks; in part because, even though they may be aware of them, they find these tasks not easily separable, or not separable at all, in practice; or in part because, being aware of them and their separability, they choose to keep them together. Moreover, one must remember that many texts under interpretation are very long, and this facilitates a multiplicity of specific interpretive goals for different parts of the texts. This does not preclude, however, that some interpretations$_2$ may have an overall, primary, or overarching function that supersedes the others. For example, one could argue that the overall, primary function of Aquinas's *Commentary on Aristotle's "Metaphysics"* was to produce in his contemporary audience an understanding of Aristotle's text in terms of Christian beliefs, even if in order to do this Aquinas felt the need to cause in the audience an understanding of what Aristotle himself understood by the text as a whole or in part.

Finally, it is also important to note that different relational interpretations bring different factors into the interpretive process, which in turn may be related to the text or its meaning in various ways. A historical interpreter concerned with influences may try to relate the text under interpretation to some other text in order to produce some understanding of their relation. So here the factor brought in is a text. A Freudian interpreter, on the other hand, may not bring a text into the interpretive process, but rather a psychological theory. A Christian who aims to produce a Christian understanding of Aristotle's *Metaphysics* in a Christian audience, may bring in a set of Christian doctrines. And so on. In short, what is brought in, and how it is used, varies with the kind of relational interpretation$_2$ in question. Common to all these, however, is both the relational aspect involved and the fact that the understanding sought is ontologically different from that sought in meaning interpretations.

This does not mean, of course, that relational interpretations may not rely, or even require in some cases, meaning interpretations$_2$. Indeed, if I am to cause an understanding of the relation between the meaning of Anselm's *Credo ut intelligam* and the meaning of some text of Augustine, surely I need to cause an understanding of the meanings of the two texts before I can cause an understanding of their relation. On the other hand, this is not necessary for some other interpretations$_2$. For example, when I try to cause an understanding of the relation of a text to a certain date (say, that it was written on that date), I may not need to take into account the meaning of the text. It might be sufficient to establish its date based on a reference to it found in some other text or on the relation of the text to some event, and so on.

Achronic, Synchronic, Diachronic, and Panchronic Interpretations$_2$

Apart from the functional taxonomy of interpretations$_2$ into meaning and relational, they can also be classified as achronic, synchronic, diachronic, and panchronic. This classification is particularly important in the case of revelation. Synchronic, diachronic, and panchronic interpretations$_2$ are intended to cause the understanding of texts at one time in particular (synchronic), at two or more particular times (diachronic), or at all times (panchronic). Achronic interpretation$_2$, on the other hand, would have to cause an understanding of a text in audiences outside of time, which is impossible, for all interpretations$_2$ are texts whose aim is to cause acts of understanding in particular audiences, and these audiences are temporally located.

Interpretations$_2$ are always synchronic, diachronic, or panchronic. When I am functioning as a translator in a particular situation—for example, trying to help a non-speaker of English in an airport—my interpretation$_2$ (i.e., translation in this case) is not meant to be achronic. My aim is to cause an understanding of a particular text at this time. But there are many interpretations₂ that aim to be diachronic or panchronic. For example, when I make a translation of a Spanish novel into English, my aim is not just to make present English readers understand the text, but also English readers at some future time (diachronic). Indeed, it is possible that my intention is to produce a translation that will be useful for all readers of English at all times (panchronic), even though it is doubtful that I could ever succeed.[14]

In the case of revelation in particular, it appears that some interpretations₂ are intended to be synchronic, whereas others are intended to be diachronic or panchronic. Some interpretations₂ of texts regarded as revealed are intended for particular persons at particular times in order to help those persons deal with particular questions and problems. Consider the case of Augustine's interpretation of Romans 13:13 in the famous garden scene described in the *Confessions*. Other interpretations₂, however, aim to be diachronic. Detailed commentaries on sacred scriptures seem to be intended not just for the contemporaneous audience of the interpreter, but also for some other, subsequent audiences. This would be the case of Augustine's *Literal Commentary on "Genesis."* Moreover, there are some interpretations₂ that aim to be panchronic, that is, they aim to cause an understanding of a text in audiences at all times. This seems to be the case, for example, of papal encyclicals whose aim is to clarify a point of doctrine based on some scriptural exegesis. Most panchronic interpretations₂ are given by a person or body considered to be authoritative by the faithful.

Interpretations₂ and the Interpreter's Dilemma

Some interpretations₂ pose an interesting problem, which elsewhere I have called the *Interpreter's Dilemma,*[15] for they include both an *interpretandum* and an *interpretans.* This kind of interpretation₂, then, is a text different from the historical text. Now, the interpreter produces the interpretation₂ because the historical text by itself does not cause understanding, or the proper understanding, in the interpreter's audience. But, by adding something to the historical text, the interpreter changes its identity conditions, and this suggests two, equally unacceptable, possibilities in relation to the audience's understanding: (1) The audience understands a text, but this text is not the historical text, or (2) the audience understands a meaning that is not the meaning of the historical text. In both cases, it appears that the audience does not understand the meaning of the historical text and, therefore, the interpretation has failed.

This dilemma is the result of two mistaken assumptions. First, an interpretation₂ that includes both the *interpretandum* and the *interpretans* changes the identity conditions of the historical text and misleads the audience into thinking that the meaning it understands is that of the historical text, whereas in fact it is the meaning of the interpretation$_2$. Second, the addition of the *interpretans* to the *interpretandum* necessarily precludes the understanding of the meaning of the *interpretandum*. The first assumption is unwarranted as long as the interpretation$_2$ is given in such a way that the boundaries between *interpretandum* and *interpretans* are preserved and there are clear indications that the additions of the *interpretans* to the *interpretandum* aim to cause an understanding of the latter. Indeed, both conditions are frequently satisfied by interpretations. Even a simple case such as "*Buenos días* means 'Good morning'" clearly satisfies the conditions.

The second assumption is unwarranted insofar as different causes can produce the same effect. I can get a headache from overexposure to the Sun, from drinking too much champagne, from lack of sleep, and so on. Likewise, the understanding of a particular meaning may be produced through a text in Spanish, English, or German. So there is no reason why a different text (i.e., the interpretation composed of the *interpretandum* and the *interpretans*) cannot produce in an audience the same kind of understanding that the historical text (i.e., the *interpretandum*) produced in its author or its historical audience. The Interpreter's Dilemma, then, can be easily escaped.

I have framed the Interpreter's Dilemma in terms of meaning interpretations$_2$ because it is easier to see how it applies to them. However, there is no reason why the dilemma cannot be framed, *mutatis mutandis,* in terms of relational interpretations$_2$. Because a similar solution can be found for these cases, there is no reason to take up the matter here.

Identity Conditions of Interpretations$_2$

Because interpretations$_2$ are texts, what was said concerning the identity of texts in chapter 1 applies to them as well. We can speak of token and type interpretations$_2$, as well as historical, contemporary, intermediary, intended, and ideal interpretations$_2$. A historical interpretation$_2$ is a text produced by a historical interpreter, that is, an interpreter contemporaneous with the historical author. A contemporary interpretation$_2$ is a text some other interpreter produces at any time other than the time when the historical text was produced. An intermediary interpretation$_2$ is any interpretive text that is neither a historical interpretation$_2$ nor a contemporary interpretation$_2$, but occurs sometimes between the two. An intended interpretation$_2$ is either (1) a mental text that a historical interpreter intended to produce but did not produce extramentally or (2) certain ideas that a historical interpreter had but never expressed in a text. And an ideal interpretation$_2$ is either (1) an inaccurate version of a historical interpretation$_2$ considered by a subsequent interpreter as an accurate copy of the historical interpretation$_2$ in question,

(2) a text produced by a subsequent interpreter who considers that it expresses perfectly the view that a historical interpretation$_2$ expresses only imperfectly, or (3) a text produced by a subsequent interpreter who considers it as the text that perfectly expresses the view a historical interpreter should have expressed. Moreover, these interpretations$_2$ can in turn become *interpretanda* for still other interpretations, both interpretations$_1$ and interpretations$_2$. But there is no need for us to dwell on these matters, because whatever we have said and will say about texts in general applies also to interpretations$_2$.

Kinds of Interpretation$_1$

The classification of interpretations$_1$ follows, *mutatis mutandis*, the taxonomy of interpretations$_2$. Interpretations$_1$ are understandings rather than texts, but like interpretations$_2$, they can be divided into meaning and relational. Meaning interpretations$_1$ are understandings of the meanings of texts or the implications of those meanings, or they are understandings that seek to be similar to those that historical authors had or intended or that particular audiences had. Relational interpretations$_1$ are understandings of texts in terms of factors brought into play by an interpreter. An understanding of the Song of Songs, for example, in terms of Freudian principles, is a relational interpretation$_1$ of the Song of Songs.

Something similar can be said concerning achronic, synchronic, diachronic, and panchronic interpretations$_1$. An achronic interpretation$_1$ of a text is an understanding of the text apart from considerations of time. On the contrary, synchronic, diachronic, and panchronic interpretations$_1$ of a text take time into account.

This claim needs further clarification, however, for the chronicity of understanding may be taken intensionally or extensionally, that is, it may refer to the content of what is understood (intension) or to the act of understanding (extension). Extensionally, all understandings are temporal because they are mental acts of individual persons and they happen at particular times. Because of this, they are always synchronic, although they can also be diachronic or panchronic. But, intensionally, not all understandings are like this, because what one understands can be understood as applying in four different ways: regardless of time, at a particular time, at two or more times, or at all times. Consider my current understanding of $2 + 2 = 4$. Extensionally, my understanding is synchronic insofar as I understand $2 + 2 = 4$ at this, or some other, particular time. Acts of understanding are always temporal but they can take place at one time and one time only (synchronic), at more than one but less than all times (diachronic), or at all times (panchronic). Consider the following examples. When I understand "$2 + 2 = 4$" or

"Josephine married Napoleon," I can understand these now and only now (synchronic), now and at some other time(s) but not at all times (diachronic), or always (panchronic). The last possibility is a matter of principle, not fact, for no one understands anything in particular at all times (only an eternal being could do it), even within the span of a human life.

Intensionally, however, matters are different, for the chronicity in this case applies to the content, rather than the act, of understanding. Thus one can understand something apart from time (achronic), at a particular time (synchronic), at more than one but less than all times (diachronic), and at all times (panchronic). An example of the first is the understanding of "2 + 2 = 4"; of the second, "Jorge Gracia was born in 1942"; of the third, "Clinton campaigned for the presidency in 1996 and 1992"; and of the fourth, "Human nature is always unpredictable."

The chronicity of interpretations$_1$, then, is quite a different phenomenon from the chronicity of interpretations$_2$. In the latter case, I used the notion in order to emphasize the time(s) at which the understanding of an interpretation$_2$ is supposed to take place. Indeed, it would not make sense to use it in any other way, insofar as interpretations$_2$ are texts, and texts only exist as temporal tokens. In the case of interpretations$_1$, I used the notion in order to emphasize the times at which an act of understanding in reference to a text actually occurs (extension) and the temporal or non-temporal nature of what is understood (intension).

Because interpretations$_1$ are not texts, we cannot properly divide them into token and type interpretations$_1$. This does not mean, however, that we cannot speak of them as individual and universal. As acts of understanding, they can be individual when the act in question is an instance of a universal act of understanding. My understanding, now, that 2 + 2 = 4 is an individual act of understanding, and so is yours. But both are instances of understanding that 2 + 2 = 4, which is therefore a universal act of understanding. Acts of understanding are universal when they are capable of instantiation; they are individual when they are instances incapable of being instantiated.

One may also speak of interpretations$_1$ that are ideal, contemporary, and so on, as we did with interpretations$_2$, although they are not texts. But clearly, in these cases what is meant is different from what is meant when these terms are applied to texts. Indeed, in some religions, these distinctions are essential insofar as the divine author is conceived as completely transcending any conception that humans can possibly have of him or her. But even in other religions, the distinctions are also pertinent to the extent that the conception believers have of the divinity may vary and may contain errors that in turn affect the way the revelation is interpreted. For our purposes, the further exploration of these distinctions would not add anything important to the discussion.

Conclusion

In sum, interpretations of texts come in two classes, understandings and texts. The first, which I call *interpretations₁*, are mental acts; the second, which I call *interpretations₂*, are texts composed of the text under interpretation (*interpretandum*), or a reference to it, and something added to it (*interpretans*), which, taken together, are intended to cause acts of understanding in the audience for which the interpretation is provided.

Interpretations are further divided into meaning and relational. The function of the first is the understanding of the meaning of a text when this is taken in one of four ways: (1) what the historical author understood or intended to be understood, (2) what a particular audience understands, (3) considered independently of authorial intention or authorial and audiencial understanding, and (4) any of these including its implications. The function of relational interpretations, by contrast, is the understanding of a text in relation to factors brought into play by an interpreter, such as historical events or Freudian theories.

The history of hermeneutics can be seen as a battle over which of these two kinds of interpretations is primary or even legitimate. On the one hand, some hold that all interpretations are relational, and indeed some go so far as to maintain that only certain interpretations of the relational variety are valid. For example, many contemporary authors practicing hermeneutics are biased in favor of sociological interpretations, as we shall see in chapter 5. According to them, all legitimate interpretations of texts have to do with understanding texts in terms of, or in relation to, the social factors surrounding the production of the texts. The mistake these philosophers make is to confuse the epistemic means required for every interpretation with their function. They fail to realize that the epistemic role of certain factors, brought into play in the interpretive process by interpreters in order to cause understanding, does not necessarily alter the function of an interpretation.

On the other hand, there are those who take a contrary position, arguing that no relational interpretation is legitimate. An interpretation, by its very nature, should aim at the meaning of a text. These make the mistake of ignoring the legitimacy of various purposes that an interpreter may wish to pursue in the interpretation of a text. Why is it wrong to understand a text or its meaning in terms of certain factors that are deemed important by an interpreter?

All that has been said concerning interpretations in general applies also to the interpretation of revealed texts. We turn, then, to the meaning interpretation of these in the next chapter.

Chapter 3 ⊷

Meaning Interpretations

The notions of revelation and interpretation developed in the two previous chapters prepare the ground for the discussion of the proper way to interpret revelation. Revelation is nothing other than a set of texts regarded as revealed by a community of religious believers. Interpretations, on the other hand, come in several kinds, depending on the functions they have. In relational interpretations$_2$, the function of the interpretation is to cause an understanding of a text in an audience in terms of, or in relation to, factors brought into the process by an interpreter. On the other hand, meaning interpretations$_2$ aim to produce understandings of the meanings of texts unrelated to other factors. The case of relational and meaning interpretations$_1$ is similar. In some of these, the function is one of understanding in terms of factors brought into play by an interpreter, whereas in others it is the understanding of textual meaning.

From the view of revelation presented in chapter 1, it would appear to follow that the proper interpretation of revealed texts is of the meaning variety. If a revelation is a text whose aim is to produce an understanding of certain significant facts a divinity wishes a community of believers to understand, then it would seem only natural that the interpreters of this text seek to have, or to produce, an understanding of the meaning of the text. Indeed, it would appear completely inappropriate to interpret the text in terms of factors that the interpreter brings into play and that therefore may be irrelevant to textual meaning. This appears to rule out relational interpretations, but the matter is not this simple. In this chapter, I examine the claim that the interpretations of revealed texts must always be meaning interpretations, and because there are several different kinds of these, I divide the discussion into several sections.

Authorial Interpretations

The Claim

The view that an interpretation aims to be (interpretation$_1$), or to cause (interpretation$_2$), an understanding of what the author of a text understood by, or intended to convey through, the text has a long history. Elements of that history go back to Plato and can be documented throughout the Middle Ages.[1] Its most recent history, however, begins in the nineteenth century, with Schleiermacher.[2] It is not important for us here to dwell on the exegesis of Schleiermacher's writings on this matter or the exact nature of his position, as our aim is not historical, but rather to discuss the merits of the authorial interpretation. Let me, then, in abbreviated form, present the version that its most notorious and recent exponent gives of it.

According to E. D. Hirsch, Jr., the aim of the interpretation of a text is to re-create the meaning the author of the text intended. Although the intention of the author "is not the only possible norm for interpretation," it is "the only practical norm for a cognitive discipline of interpretation."[3]

The issue between Hirsch and his critics may be formulated in terms of the following question: Can the interpretation of a text be based on something other than authorial intention when the aim of the interpretation is to understand a text? Hirsch's answer is negative.[4] His view, painted in very large strokes, is that the purpose of an interpretation is to reveal what an author intended to convey through a text. Moreover, it is also clear that he thinks it is possible to achieve this goal, even if we cannot be certain that we have achieved it. This means that definitive interpretations are possible, even if we may not know that we have them.

Hirsch finds the justification for this position in an ethical maxim he considers fundamental:

> Unless there is a powerful overriding value in disregarding an author's intention (i.e., original meaning), we who interpret as a vocation should not disregard it.[5]

There are some exceptions to this rule, but there are precious few. One is the fudging necessary on authorial meaning for the sake of young, impressionable children. But other than such cases, authorial meaning is backed up by a strong ethical presumption. To do differently, and use an author's words for our own aims, disregarding his or her intentions, is to violate, in the realm of language, the counterpart of Kant's moral imperative. According to this principle, human beings should be treated as ends in themselves rather than merely as means to the ends of other human beings. We can transfer the Kantian imperative to the realm of language because speech is an extension and expression of men in the social domain, and also because when we fail to conjoin a man's intentions to his words we lose the soul of speech, which is to convey meaning and to understand what is intended to be conveyed. . . . [6]

Interpreters, then, are under a moral obligation to understand a text in accordance with the author's intention. This is why, Hirsch adds, "in ethical terms, original meaning is the 'best meaning.'"[7] Hirsch's point is clear: We are morally bound to interpret a text in this way, for anything else is to break one of the most, if not the most, fundamental moral rule: To treat others as ends and as we ourselves wish to be treated.[8]

Hirsch is aware of some of the possible objections that can be brought against his view. Of these, one is particularly pertinent here because, in answering it, Hirsch clarifies his position further. The objection is that there is a distinction between speech and writing, and the hermeneutical rules that apply to one do not apply to the other.[9] Whereas speech should be understood in terms of the speaker's intentions, writing need not be.

Hirsch answers that he is not impressed by this objection because no literary theory has yet succeeded in formulating an acceptable distinction between ordinary written speech and literary written speech. For this reason, the ethics of language are applicable to all language, whether oral or written, in literature or in philosophy. And he eloquently puts it thus:

> I am not impressed with the view that this ethical imperative of speech, to which we all submit in ordinary discourse, is not applicable to written speech or, in particular, to literary texts. No literary theorist from Coleridge to the present has succeeded in formulating a viable distinction between the nature of ordinary written speech and the nature of literary written speech. . . . To treat an author's words merely as grist for one's own mill is ethically analogous to using another man merely for one's own purposes. I do not say such ruthlessness of interpretation is never justifiable in principle, but I cannot imagine a situation where it would be justifiable in the professional practice of interpretation. The peculiarly modern anarchy of every man for himself in matters of interpretation may sound like the ultimate victory of the Protestant spirit. Actually, such anarchy is the direct consequence of transgressing the fundamental ethical norms of speech and its interpretation.[10]

Hirsch is not content to leave his response to the objection at that. He goes on the offensive, arguing that interpreters who do not accept his view are inconsistent, if not plain dishonest, for they apply a different standard to themselves than the one they apply to others:

> The question I always want to ask critics who dismiss authorial intention as their norm is one that could be transposed into the categorical imperative or

simply into the golden rule. I want to ask them this: "When you write a piece of criticism, do you want me to disregard *your* intention and original meaning? Why do you say to me 'That is not what I meant at all; that is not it at all'? Why do you ask me to honor the ethics of language for your writings when you do not honor them for the writings of others?" . . . Few critics fail to show moral indignation when their meaning is distorted in reviews and other interpretations of their interpretations. But their sensitivity is often one-way, and in this they show an inconsistency amounting to a double standard—one for their authors, another for themselves. They are like the tenant farmer whose belief in redistributing everybody's property extended to land, money, horses, chickens, and cows, but, when asked about pigs, said: "Aw hell, you know I gotta couple of pigs."[11]

The point of this passage is clear, but not everything about Hirsch's position is. Indeed, there is an ambiguity in the formulation of Hirsch's view that is common among those who discuss the authorial interpretation of texts. Sometimes Hirsch speaks as if what is involved in the interpretation of texts is the understanding the author had of the text. Indeed, as we saw earlier, he speaks of the author's meaning as being "the best meaning," and sometimes even as being "the meaning" of the text. But sometimes he uses the notion of "authorial intention" instead. The latter suggests that the function of the interpreter is to cause an understanding not of what the author understood by a text, but of what the author intended to convey through the text. What an author understands by a text need not be the same as what the author intends an audience to understand through it. Of course, the author may understand what the audience understands by the text, but the author may also understand much more, and even something quite different. This, as we shall see, has important consequences for the authorial view.

Our present concern, however, is not with the authorial interpretation of texts in general, but rather with the authorial interpretation of revealed texts in particular. Is authorial interpretation appropriate for revealed texts, and if so, is it the only appropriate kind of interpretation?[12] In order to answer this question, we must take into account the identity of the authors of revealed texts.

The Authors of Revelation

It is generally acknowledged by exegetes and other interpreters of texts who believe in their divine origin that these texts, unlike most others, have at least two authors. One is the human author who actually composed the original token of the text. This is the historical person who wrote or spoke the text. Most often, this author is called the *instrumental author* because it is believed that he or she acts as an instrument of the real author of the text, who uses him or her for the purpose of producing the text.[13] The *real author* of the text, however, is the divinity, for it is the divinity who initiates and controls the process of production.[14] There are, of course, disagreements as to how this process takes place, and also about the degree of accuracy with which the instrumental author produces the text the divinity wishes to be produced.[15] Some go so far as to speak of the divinity as "dictating" to the instrumental author.[16] But these matters are of no immediate concern for our topic.[17]

Not generally acknowledged by those concerned with the interpretation of revealed texts is that the notion of an instrumental author does not do justice to the complexity of the situation concerning the identity of the human author of a revealed text.[18] Consider, first, that the human author may not be a single person, but a group of persons. In this case, it would be misleading to speak of *a* human author, and it would be more accurate to speak of *a composite author.* The case of Genesis illustrates the point well. It is now widely accepted that Genesis contains at least two accounts of the creation of the world, and that these two accounts make sense only when one posits at least two authors of the text. Indeed, there may have been three or more authors: the author of the first account, the author of the second, the author who put the two accounts together into one book, and so on.[19]

The existence of more than one author does not apply only to texts, such as Genesis, that are known to be compilations of other texts. Except for autographs directly traceable to their historical authors, most texts are the result of additions and modifications by the scribes who copied the texts, editors who modified the style, and so on. This is particularly evident in the case of ancient and medieval texts, where the original manuscripts of the autographs have long since been lost and what we have are copies several times removed from the originals. In the process of copying, words and even sentences and paragraphs are inadvertently, and sometimes purposefully, left out. Scribes often do not understand what they are reading, so it is easy for them to skip parts of the texts in the tedious process of reproduction. Those who understand what they are copying often disagree with parts of it or simply try to fix problems they perceive in it, and this leads them to introduce changes. Readers also play a role in this process, for some of them add comments on the margins, which are sometimes later incorporated by other scribes into the texts because the scribes think they were accidentally left out of the texts and were added subsequently as corrections. In all these cases, the texts are the result of these modifications and therefore cannot be said to have only one author, insofar as anyone who changed the text in some significant way is in part an author of the text as we have it.

We seldom have the original token of a revealed text produced by the historical author. Generally, we have only copies of it, sometimes separated by centuries and mediated by many other copies. Moreover, because most texts regarded as revealed are ancient, the copies we have of them were produced by hand, by different scribes, with different degrees of skills and notions about how faithful they were supposed to be to the text from which they copied. This means that the revealed texts available to us may in fact have more than one human author, insofar as many persons may have contributed to the shape of the text, including the modern editor.[20] A revealed text, then, may have not just one, or more, historical instrumental authors; it may also have other authors who altered it in important ways. It is important to keep this in mind when considering both the interpreter and the understanding of revelation.

There are, moreover, other cases of collective authorship, such as, for example, when two or more persons cooperate in the creation of a text. This is similar to what happens in artists' workshops, where a master directs a process in which many apprentices take part. A text may turn out to be the result of the conscious cooperation of several persons. In order to facilitate matters, whenever we have a text that is the product of more than one author, I speak of the author as the *composite author.*

In the case of revealed texts, all these possibilities are realized. In particular, when revealed texts pass through a process of oral transmission, it is difficult to distinguish an original traceable to the instrumental author, or authors, and the text available to interpreters. The task of establishing this distinction is paramount in religions that accept the divine character of only the autograph. Religions that accept notions of unfolding revelation through a divinely guided process put less emphasis on the importance of the autograph and its distinction from copies.[21]

This is not all that needs to be said about the notion of instrumental author, however, for this very notion may be taken in two senses. In one sense, it may refer to the person who produced the text at a particular time and place, and only at the time and place. The author of St. Paul's Epistle to the Corinthians is St. Paul at the time when he wrote the Epistle. But there is also another possible sense of instrumental author, for he or she may be taken as the person who at some point in his or her life produced the text in question. In this case, we would not be speaking of St. Paul as the person at the time of writing the Epistle, but rather of St. Paul as the person who wrote the Epistle and lived many years before and after that. This is important, because persons who author texts often change their views over the course of their lives and would not produce the same texts at different times. For example, it would be inconceivable that Wittgenstein would write the *Tractatus logico-philosophicus* toward the end of his life and the *Philosophical Investigations* toward the beginning. Moreover, some authors go back to their texts and modify them, thus altering the identity of the original. In the case

of revelation, the distinction between the author and the person who authored the text is not as crucial as in the case of other texts, because the instrumental author of a revealed text is not as important as the author of a
non-revealed text. The important author in revelation is the divinity, not the
human instrument the divinity uses to convey the message.

Another consideration that must be kept in mind when speaking about
the human author of a revealed text is that the person we identify as the author might not be the actual author of the text, or, alternatively, that what
we know about the author is only partly accurate. In short, the picture we
have of the author of a text may not be correct, and it might be completely
mistaken. Indeed, it is questionable whether we can have a complete picture
of the author of any text, since our knowledge of persons is rather superficial and limited. For this reason, we need to distinguish between the actual
human author of a revealed text and the construct we have made of that author. I call the first *historical author* and the second *pseudo-historical author.*
I use the expression *pseudo-historical* because this author is not an actual person, but rather the made-up picture, more or less accurate, that interpreters
have composed about the historical author. In some cases, historical authors
themselves create the pseudo-historical author, a fictional figure to whom
authorship is assigned.[22]

At first, it may appear that this is not a very significant distinction in the
case of revelation. After all, one could argue that the interpreter of revelation
is interested in the divine author's message, rather than what the instrumental
author may have thought. For a non-revealed text, the distinction is important
because the text is supposed to be the product of this author, and what we
know about the author is pertinent for the understanding of the text. But for
revelation, what we know about the human author appears less pertinent.

Further reflection, however, indicates that what we know about the instrumental author may be quite important for revelation, and perhaps as important as for non-revealed texts. The reason is that a revealed text is
presented in the context of the instrumental author—his or her culture, language, and world-view. In most religions, the interpreter's understanding of a
revealed text is mediated through the text, because the divinity does not produce a direct understanding of it. So, the instrumental author and his or her
views, culture, and historical location become of paramount importance, for
they help the interpreter understand the text. And because culture, language,
and world-views change, it is important for the interpreter of revelation to
know about the precise historical and cultural location of the instrumental
author of a revealed text in order not to confuse the divine message.

Finally, there is also another human author that must be mentioned: the
interpretive author. A text is a group of entities used as signs for the purpose
of producing understanding in an audience. This means that the conditions

of identity of a text include the conditions of identity of its meaning. If someone understands that meaning differently than it is, then the text that is being understood is also different. Therefore, when interpreters understand texts differently than what is warranted by their meaning, they are in fact understanding some other texts, of which in a way they may be regarded as authors. This means that interpretations, whether we take these to be interpretations$_1$ or interpretations$_2$, often change the identity conditions of the text under interpretation. In such cases, we no longer have an interpretation of the original revealed text, but rather of some other text that is in part a construct of the interpreter. This change of identity is often subtle and in many ways more insidious.

So much for the human or instrumental author. Now let us turn to the divine author and ask: Is there something about the identity of the divine author that we have not said about the human author? Perhaps this: that there is at least a difference between the divine author, who is supposed to have actually guided the process of revelation, and the construct or conception interpreters have of this author. In some religions this distinction is essential, for the divine author is always conceived as completely transcending any possible conception that humans can have of him or her. But, even in religions that do not share this view, the distinction is important insofar as the conception believers have of the divinity may vary and can contain errors that in turn could affect the way revelation is interpreted.

The situation of the divine author parallels that of the human author, where there is a historical author and a pseudo-historical one. Of course, since the divine author is not often conceived as a historical entity, we could not refer to him or her as historical. We might simply talk, then, about the *divine author* and the *pseudo-divine author*. Except for the composite author, in cases in which the divine author of the text is more than one, the other kinds of human authors discussed do not have parallels in the divinity. Now let us see how all this affects the viability of authorial interpretation in the case of revealed texts.

Difficulties with the Authorial Interpretation of Revealed Texts

The multiplicity of authors we have identified creates problems for the theory of authorial interpretation when applied to revealed texts. We saw that initially one may speak of at least two authors of revealed texts: the divine and the human. But, insofar as there are two authors, there can also be two different understandings of the same text and two different intentions as to what the text is supposed to convey to the audience. Consider first the case of understanding. In principle, the understandings of the two authors could be different and even in conflict. In either case, we can ask: Which is the understanding that an audience is supposed to have? That of the instrumental author, or that of the divine author? And the same applies to the intention. The distinctions introduced earlier between intended understanding and just understanding and between the instrumental and the divine authors allow for several possibilities. Indeed, the situation becomes quite complicated. The imperative to understand a text in accordance with the author's understanding or intended meaning cannot be easily pegged down, and in principle can be a source of difficulty. If the instrumental author's understanding is different from that of the divinity, or their intended meanings are different, the choice of one automatically betrays the other.

This problem becomes more complicated if we take into account the other authors mentioned: the pseudo-divine, the pseudo-historical, the composite, and the interpretive. And even if we were to ignore all these, arguing that only the divine and the historical human authors matter, we would still need to resolve the question raised before.

But let us, for a moment, assume that in spite of what the instrumental author may think (it is generally acknowledged that most human authors of divinely revealed texts never thought of themselves as writing for a divinity), he or she is not the real author of the text and the real author is the divinity. In other words, let us assume that a revealed text has only one author, the divinity, and that the presumed human author functions merely as a pen would for a human author. Obviously, then, what counts is the understanding or intended meaning of the divine author.[23] Nevertheless, this does not solve all the problems raised by the authorial position. If at stake are acts of understanding in an audience similar to those the divinity has in relation to the text, then the interpretation of revealed texts is impossible to the degree that the divinity is conceived as transcendent, infinite, and omniscient, as is the Judeo-Christian God. Indeed, even if we were to grant that such a divinity understands what humans understand when we understand a revealed text, the divinity would understand much more than a human being would.

Consider a simple biblical text: 'Abraham begat Isaac.' This is a text one would be tempted to say that both a transcendent, infinite, and omniscient being and any human being with a minimum intellectual capacity would understand in the same way. Yet, most theologians appear to disagree. The understanding God has of this text is supposed to be much deeper than any understanding humans could have of it. The reason is that the understanding of humans is conditioned by the way humans understand. And this extends to the understanding they have both of individuals and of their natures. It is often acknowledged by theologians that God's understanding of individuals and their natures is, in proportion to God's being, infinitely greater than whatever understanding of these humans could possibly have.

Indeed, some theologians argue that the understanding of individuals is mediated through an understanding of their natures. To understand Mary requires an understanding of human nature. But God's understanding of natures is far deeper than our understanding of them. God knows natures directly insofar as they are the models he used in creation. Humans, on the contrary, know natures indirectly, through a process of abstraction from sense experience they have of individuals. God knows humanness in itself; humans' knowledge of humanness is derived from their sense experience of Mary and Pedro.

This claim may be illustrated also in the following way: Let us assume a descriptivist theory of proper names, in which a name stands for a certain description.[24] In the case of a human knower, the description for which a proper name like 'Abraham' stands will be necessarily limited by the information about Abraham that the human knower in question has and can have. For example, it may be something like the following: the father of Isaac; a Hebrew patriarch; the man King Nimrod sought to throw into a fiery furnace; and so on. But in the case of an omniscient knower, like the Judeo-Christian God, the description in question would involve everything there is to know about Abraham, including things that no human being knows or could ever know; and this includes Abraham himself. This knowledge would include God's knowledge of Abraham's nature, of his humanity—and this, as theologians frequently note, is superior to anything humans can possibly have. For God's knowledge of human nature, as the creator of that nature, is much deeper than the indirect and derivative knowledge of that nature humans have. Indeed, if we accept the view that all human knowledge is based on experience, and we also hold that humans are more than physical entities, then it is clear that whatever knowledge of humans we have is mediated and limited by such experience. But presumably God is not limited in the same way.

From this it follows that the ethical force of the argument given by Hirsch concerning the interpretation of texts in terms of authorial understanding fails in the case of revealed texts insofar as one cannot hold someone responsible for something one cannot do. If it is impossible for humans to have an understanding similar to the understanding God has of a text, it makes no ethical sense to require that they do. We cannot be held responsible for actions we cannot do or things we do not know. Ethical responsibility requires possibility and knowledge. The purpose of the interpretation of revealed texts cannot be, then, the understanding of what the divine author understands, provided this author is conceived as the Judeo-Christian God is. Indeed, even if the divinity is not conceived in such exalted terms, but is nonetheless thought to be superior in knowledge to humans, the same conclusion applies.

This conclusion, however, does not exhaust all alternatives. Still open is the possibility of understanding what the divinity wishes or intends us to understand, rather than what the divinity understands. In short, we are supposed to understand through a revealed text what the divinity knows we can understand and intends us to understand, which may be only a limited portion of the divinity's understanding.

One could still argue that the divinity's understanding of what he or she wishes or intends us to understand is always different from what we understand and that this is an obstacle to this position. Say that the divinity wishes us to understand by 'Abraham begat Isaac' simply that Abraham was a human being and it was his seed that fertilized the egg of Isaac's mother and produced Isaac. Even then, one could argue that the divinity's understanding would also be different from ours because the understanding the divinity has and the one we have of 'human being,' 'seed,' and 'egg' are entirely different. Moreover, the context within which the divinity understands this is different, deeper, and broader than the context within which a human being would understand it. God cannot know but as he knows, and we cannot know but as we know.

This argument is not without flaws, however. First, it confuses part and whole. Even when I understand a whole, I can also understand the part, independently of the whole. I can understand the nature of oxygen apart from understanding the nature of water.[25] So, in principle, I could communicate with someone who understands the nature of oxygen and does not understand the nature of water, even if I also understand the nature of water. Likewise, that God understands more does not necessarily mean that God cannot understand what we understand just as we understand it.

Second, the argument misses the point that one can always understand less within more. That is, I can understand how an eight-year-old child might understand something even if I understand much more by it because I have more information and experience. Indeed, teachers explain complex things to students who know less than they, and they are able to do it because they narrow down their understanding for purposes of communication. Often they are able to understand what the student understands, and also the limits of that understanding, precisely because their own understanding is broader and deeper.

Finally, to say that the divinity could not understand what we understand as we do has the unwelcome consequence, for those who hold the divinity to be omnipotent, that the power of the divinity is restricted. This argument, of course, does not apply except within very particular religious traditions, but it does make clear that God's power makes it possible for him to understand just what we understand.

So much, then, for the argument that God understands something different than we understand. Now, if the meaning of a revealed text is not conceived as the meaning the divinity understands, but rather as the meaning the divinity wishes or intends believers to understand, then it is in principle possible for humans to understand revealed texts insofar as the understandings in question are within the capacity of humans to have. In this case, authorial interpretations do not have to do with the re-creation by an audience of the divine understanding of a text, but with the re-creation of what the divinity intends to be understood through the text. And there is nothing wrong in principle with holding that there can be an interpretation along these lines of the text 'Abraham begat Isaac.' Indeed, as unlikely as it may seem, it is logically possible that this very text, as an English translation of the Hebrew, is an interpretation$_2$, and a definitive one at that, of the Hebrew text for English-speaking audiences (we will have more to say about definitive interpretations in chapter 7).

This view of the interpretation of revealed texts makes considerable sense. If it is right, then the meaning of revealed texts is not necessarily fixed for all times and places, but changes with changes of audiences and circumstances. The same text can be used to convey what the divinity wants conveyed in different ways and in different circumstances to different peoples. This view takes into account the changing nature of cultures and the usefulness of revealed texts in different contexts and situations. But we shall return to this later, under independent-meaning interpretation.

Apart from this alternative, and because revelation also has an instrumental author, one could argue that the understanding of revealed texts involves the understanding of what the instrumental author understood, or intended to be understood, rather than of what the divinity understood. But immediately some difficulties arise. The first is that this seems to interfere with the very notion of revealed text. If the understanding of revealed texts is to be determined by the instrumental authors of the texts, then in what sense can we say that these texts are divinely revealed? Does not this mean that the object of understanding has nothing to do with the divinity?

The answer to this is not difficult if what counts in the interpretation of revelation is what the divine author wishes us to understand, rather than what the divine author understands. For then one can easily respond that what the divine author wishes us to understand coincides with what the instrumental author understood, or wishes to be understood. God revealed himself through St. Paul's words to the Corinthians precisely because he wants us to understand what St. Paul thought he was saying, or wanted to say, to the Corinthians, nothing more and nothing less. Removing the hermeneutical locus from divine understanding to divine will or intention seems to solve this objection. However, we should keep in mind that the instrumental author of a text often functions not just as the author who has a certain understanding of what he or she wishes to convey to an audience, but also as an audience of the text at times other than the time of composition. He or she may come back to the text after its composition and then have an understanding of it that may even in fact be different. In this way, the author is no longer functioning as the author of the text, but rather as an audience of it. Because of this, we deal with the author in this capacity in the next section.

A second difficulty has to do with the perennial and transcultural value of revelation. If revelation is to be effective throughout time and history, and in different cultural contexts, then one cannot identify its understanding with the time and culturally bound understanding of the instrumental author. If the message of the Epistle to the Corinthians is intended not just for St. Paul and the Corinthians but for all humans regardless of the time at which they live, then it makes no sense to say that we are supposed to understand St. Paul's understanding of the message and nothing more. What St. Paul understood, or wanted understood, when he was writing to the Corinthians cannot be all we are supposed to understand, because his understanding was limited in important ways by the historical circumstances and culture in which he lived.

Perhaps a different example might help us here. Consider the case of the text of Genesis 1 and 2, in which God is said to have created the world in six days. Surely it would be difficult to argue cogently that the author of this text understood 'days' to mean long periods of time comprising millions of years each. And yet, this is precisely how most contemporary theologians understand this text. Clearly, they do not understand the pertinent text of Genesis in the way its instrumental author understood it. The task of the interpreter, then, cannot be to understand a revealed text in just the way its instrumental author understood it, or intended it to be understood. Apart from this, a third difficulty may be considered that undermines the ethical imperative for interpreters proposed by the authorial view. If an instrumental author's understanding of a text is confused and imprecise, for example, even though the text may be understood quite clearly and with precision by someone else, are we also supposed to understand the text with the same degree of imprecision and confusion present in the author? Most intentionalists answer affirmatively. But, regardless of the answer they give, this issue should not arise in the context of divine revelation. In the case of a revealed text, there is no question about the divine author being confused or unclear about what he or she wishes the instrumental author to say, provided the divinity is conceived as omnipotent and omniscient. This means that even if the instrumental author is confused, what he or she says should not be so, unless the divinity wishes the text to be confusing. This difficulty, then, cannot apply to revealed texts in the form we have presented it.

Consider further what happens when instrumental authors make mistakes in what they say. What do we make of slips of the tongue and such phenomena? Consider the case in which someone says "Stop it!" when she means to say "Step on it!" And consider further that as a result the driver to whom the order was given kills someone. Surely in this case it is as important to understand what the speaker said as what she meant, for this is the only possible way to exonerate her. This entails that, in principle, the meaning of a text ("Step on it!") is not the same as the author's meaning ("Stop!"), and an interpretation cannot ignore one in favor of the other. Of course, one could argue along the same lines followed before, that no divinely revealed text can have any mistakes. Certainly it cannot have any mistakes of divine origin if the divinity in question is omnipotent and omniscient. And it would be difficult to argue that the origin of the mistakes is the instrumental author insofar as the divinity is held to be in control of the instrumental author and the process of production of the text.

The standard response to this difficulty is that it is not the instrumental author, but copyists of the text who introduce mistakes. But suppose the divinity is omnipotent and omniscient and yet decides not to control the process of textual production to ensure accuracy. Can this divinity be benevolent, then? How can we hold that a benevolent, omnipotent, and omniscient divinity does not take the necessary steps to ensure that his or her message to those who believe in him or her is conveyed accurately? Revealed texts, then, must be inerrant. But much scholarship on texts regarded as revealed suggests that they have mistakes, factual mistakes, originating in their authors, for which later scribes cannot be blamed. This raises questions concerning how faithful divinely revealed texts are to what the divinity wishes them to be, and therefore questions about the power of the divinity or about his or her knowledge, the control the divinity exercises over these texts, the instrumental authors, the process of production of the texts, and the nature of revelation involved. All of this creates serious difficulties for the authorial view.

This makes way for a fourth and even more basic objection. Just as one can distinguish between what a divine author understands and what he or she intends for us to understand through a text, one can distinguish between what a human author understands and what he or she intends for others to understand, and this raises the possibility of authorial manipulation. That is, is it not possible that the author, for example, wants to hide what he or she knows and make us understand only a portion of what we could understand, for reasons that are entirely unethical, and if not unethical, at least misguided? It is not possible to raise this difficulty in a context, such as Christianity or Judaism, in which the divine author of a revealed text is taken to be benevolent, but there are religions in which this is not so, and therefore this objection would apply. Of course, the difficulty can be raised with respect to the instrumental author as long as the divinity is not considered omnipotent and omniscient or is not in complete control of the process of textual production.

Under these conditions, are we really morally bound to understand any text, including one regarded as revealed, as the author wishes us to understand it? Surely not. If the intention of an author is unethical or contrary to our well-being, if an author intends to do us harm by having us understand what he said or wrote in a way that is different from the way he actually understands it, surely we are not bound to understand the text as the author wants us to do. For this would entail that we would be morally bound to be unethical or to do harm to ourselves, and this is certainly not justifiable on ethical grounds. Morally, we should not be forced to be unethical or to do harm to ourselves. Moreover, if it is a question of harm, and the harm in question is not to ourselves, then the case becomes even more compelling.

Apart from the difficulties of the authorial view arising from the specific divine or human authorships of revealed texts, there are two general objections to this position. One has to do with the epistemic inaccessibility and mysterious ontological character of intentions in general and divine intentions in particular. In the case of human intentions the case has been repeatedly made by both analytic and Continental philosophers. Authors like Quine, for example, have complained about the inaccessibility of mental entities such as meanings, let alone intentions. For empiricists like him, these entities are beyond our epistemic grasp; we have access to only empirically perceptible phenomena, like linguistic behavior. But linguistic behavior can be interpreted in various ways. This is the point of the Quinean view of the impossibility of translation.[26] And Continental philosophers have pointed out the same using what has come to be called the Hermeneutic Circle.[27] In both cases the point amounts to the same, which perhaps we can express through the following conundrum: We can know authorial intentions only through the meaning of texts, but we can know the meaning of texts only through authorial intentions. If one holds that the meaning of a text is determined by the author's intentions, then knowledge of those intentions becomes indispensable for understanding the meaning of the text. But how are we to know those intentions? For intentionalists, the only source is the text itself, and therefore they necessarily fall into an unbreakable hermeneutical circle. Just consider the text we saw earlier: "Abraham begat Isaac." The intentionalist will say that the meaning of this text is what the author of the text intended for it to mean. But the only way we have access to that intention and meaning is through the text. So we are left in a hermeneutical limbo, a fact that has not escaped interpreters of revelation.[28]

In the case in which God is supposed to be the author of a text, the situation becomes even more difficult for the intentionalist for at least two reasons:

First, the meaning of the language used in the revealed text does not depend on ordinary use and meaning. Divine language is, or at least can be, different from ordinary language. Indeed, it is standard for believers to argue that it is so. Second, the language of revelation often relies on conceptions particular to only some members of the community of language speakers, who have especial reasons to be privy to them. Therefore, even if one were able to reject the Hermeneutic Circle in the case of human authors and texts based on common cultural, natural, and communal features, something else has to take its place in the interpretation of revelation.

Here is a situation in which the author of a text is a supernatural being and therefore not a member of the community at large in whose language the text is composed. This means that the rules of the language in terms of which the community ordinarily interprets texts come into question. Do they apply when the author is not, in virtue of his or her divinity, an ordinary member of that community? Do some of them apply and others not? Are there special rules that apply only in this case? The situation is further complicated because the divinity is supposed to be addressing only some members of the community, that is, the group of people who believe certain doctrines not accepted by other members of the community. This raises further fundamental questions, for among the pertinent beliefs there may be some that concern the way revealed texts are to be interpreted. Or should the same rules that apply to other texts in the same language be also applied to the texts regarded as revealed by the community after all? If there is disagreement between believers and non-believers concerning these issues, we need to go outside the texts to decide. In short, in order to understand a revealed text, we cannot refer back to the text or the intention of the divinity; we must refer to something else that gives us the key as to how to understand the text.

The other general objection to the authorial position has to do with the fact that the author of revealed texts—whether human or divine—has been treated in a more simple fashion than warranted. I have spoken of this author as if he or she were the being, whether human or divine, who is ultimately responsible for a text. But much contemporary criticism has brought out the fact that the notion of author is far from being uncontroversial.

Earlier, I distinguished various ways of understanding an author. For example, I distinguished among the historical, pseudo-historical, composite, and interpretive authors. If we take these into account, it is clear that the picture we have painted so far needs altering. Consider, for example, that interpreters have access to only pseudo-historical authors. Under these circumstances, what do we do about the ethical requirement proposed by the authorial theory, according to which the aim of an interpretation is to re-create in an audience the understanding or intentional meaning of an author? Does it really make sense to talk this way at all, when the interpreter is working with a mere construct of the author? For, indeed, under the conditions described, it could turn out that the ethical imperative applies to an author who is not the author of the text. In the Middle Ages, everyone thought that the author of the *Fons vitae* was a Christian, named Avicebron. So, according to the authorial view, the ethical imperative in the Middle Ages was to interpret this work in accordance with Avicebron's understanding or intentions. But the Christian Avicebron was not the actual author of the *Fons vitae;* the historical author was a Jew, Ibn Gabirol. This problem applies, *mutatis mutandis,* to a divine author insofar as this author in most religions remains hidden at least in part.

From all this, it should be evident that the difficulties with the authorial interpretation of revelation are very serious. Indeed, none of the versions of this view we have examined, except for the one in which the interpretation sought is the understanding of what the divine author wishes or intends believers to understand, is even acceptable in principle. But even this exception encounters a very difficult challenge: When subjected to inspection, it remains a mere formal desideratum without content. To say that in understanding a revealed text we need to grasp what the divine author intends for us to grasp through it is not saying anything about how this grasp is to be achieved. In implementing this desideratum, then, we are left without guidance. What are we exactly to understand? Who can tell us? What criteria will determine the validity of an understanding? It will not do to refer us back to the divinity, for different interpreters claim different understandings of what the divinity wishes us to understand and even of the identity and nature of the divinity itself. The text itself is of no use without reference to the divinity and rules according to which it should be interpreted. This position is justified with various arguments, but often by an appeal to the gaps in the text that have to be filled by audiences.[29] A particular audience would not help unless there are criteria external to both God's meaning and the text whereby it can be chosen. So where do we go for direction? How can we determine what God intends for us to know? How can we break the Hermeneutic Circle? In short, the authorial interpretation of revelation, taken merely as such, is fraught with difficulties, even when the understanding sought is not that of the divinity, but rather of what the divinity wishes or intends believers to understand. Something else is required, as we shall see later.

In conclusion, it does not make sense to apply the hermeneutical imperative, according to which texts are to be interpreted only in terms of what their authors understand, or intend to be understood, across the board to revealed texts. Interpretation in terms of authorial understanding, and even intention, is at best one aim of interpretation and, therefore, cannot be held to be canonical with respect to interpretation in general. At worst, it involves in-surmountable difficulties. Moreover, the ethical justification for this kind of interpretation is unacceptable. Interpretations come in a great variety and de-pend ultimately on many factors. One of the mistakes made by those who adopt the authorial view of interpretation is that they try to make paradig-matic one of the functions of interpretation. In doing so, they misunderstand its nature and miss the multiplicity of functions that interpretations can have. In this, much contemporary hermeneutical theory is right, insofar as the aim of the interpretation of texts is not always to figure out what the authors of the texts understood, or intended to be understood, through them, but it is wrong to the degree that the search for authorial meaning is legitimate in some cases. When applied to revealed texts, however, the difficulties of au-thorial interpretation are compounded to such a degree that it must be dis-carded. Only in one case, in terms of divine intention, does it make any sense at all. But even here, by itself, it leads nowhere, as we have seen.

Audiencial Interpretations

Another possible aim of meaning interpretations is the understanding of what a particular audience of a revealed text understands through it. If there is one thing that recent criticism has made clear, it is that meaning is not *in* a text itself.[30] Now, our question is whether an audiencial interpretation makes sense in the case of revelation. Because the audience can be taken in various ways, however, we must examine these cases separately, and there are at least five possibilities: the author, when he or she functions as audience; and the historical, intended, contemporary, and intermediary audiences.[31] Consider the text of Augustine's *On the Teacher*. The author functioning as audience would be Augustine himself when he tried to understand the text he had produced. The historical audience was contemporary with Augustine and, belonging to his culture, had, or could have had, access to *On the Teacher*. The intended audience is the group of persons for whom Augustine wrote the treatise. The contemporary audience lives today, when 'today' is taken to refer to any time at which a reader is trying to interpret Augustine's text. And the intermediary audience may exist, or may have existed, at any time between the contemporary and the historical, such as during the nine-teenth century. Naturally, when the texts in question are revealed, then the situation is not quite the same, as will become clear immediately. Moreover, it should be obvious that several of these audiences may overlap. For exam-ple, the historical may overlap with the contemporary and the contemporary with the intended, depending on the circumstances.

The *author* may be considered to be an audience in at least two ways. During the time and process of composition of texts, authors constantly go back and forth to parts of the texts they are composing in order to change what has already been composed or to add other parts to them. As such, they function as audiences to their own texts or to the part of the texts they have already composed. Also, after authors complete texts, they often go back to them: sometimes in order to remind themselves of what they have produced; at other times as critics of their own views, finding fault with them and producing other texts in which they take back, modify, or alter what they said in the original text; and still at other times as interpreters, producing interpretations, particularly interpretations$_2$, for the sake of audiences.

When authors function as audiences, their relations to the texts they compose and to the interpretations they develop of them may be quite different from those they had when they functioned as authors: A distance is introduced that was not present before. Moreover, any time that elapses, between the time of composition of the text and the time of interpretation, allows for changes in the understanding the authors had at the times of composition. The change of role from author to audience and the time that may elapse between roles also facilitates changes in interpretive aim. For authors, *qua* authors, the only interpretations that make sense are interpretations$_1$, in which the interpretations amount to the authorial understandings of the texts. But, once authors assume the role of audiences and some temporal distance is introduced, other kinds of interpretations may be possible, and the aims authors pursue may change. For example, they may function as critics, or they may want to relate their texts to other factors they now think need to be brought into the picture. This changes the interpretations from authorial (i.e., What did I understand by this?) to relational (i.e., Does what I said make sense? or How does what I said relate to X?).

Revealed texts introduce a further complication because they have at least two authors, the divine and the human. Presumably, it would be possible in principle for a divinity to act as audience of revelation, but this requires that the divinity in question be in time and lack omniscience. If the divinity is not in time and is omniscient, as happens with the God of Abraham, then this possibility makes little sense. On the other hand, in principle the question makes sense with respect to the human author, although further reflection uncovers difficulties that were considered in the previous section and that we need not repeat. In short, the audiencial interpretation of revealed texts does not make sense when it is the author who assumes the role of audience.

The *historical audience* is the audience contemporaneous with the author of the text and is also part of the culture to which this author belonged. In the case of revealed texts, the pertinent author is the instrumental author, not the divinity, insofar as the divinity may not be subject to time and culture. This is the audience contemporary with, say, St. Paul when he wrote his letters to the Corinthians. This is a very important audience, and one whose understanding of a text is significant insofar as one expects that this audience was best equipped to receive the revealed message from the instrumental author. It is an audience that usually has the same native tongue as the instrumental author, and shares with him or her much that facilitates communication between them. For these reasons, it may be argued that what this audience understood by a text is especially pertinent in the interpretation of revealed texts. If the divinity has produced a revealed text with the aid of a human author at a particular time and place, and this text is expressed in a particular language and in the context of a particular culture, then what better way is there to understand the text than in the way the audience that was contemporaneous with the author, and part of the same culture, understood it?

This argument, however, makes two important assumptions that undermine it. The first is that the audience the divinity intends as recipient of the divine message is the historical audience. But this may not be the case. Indeed, according to most religions, the audience intended by the divinity is not the historical audience, but rather the audience composed of believers throughout history.[32] This means that whatever the historical audience understood is only partly pertinent for the understanding of the text.

The second assumption is that the historical audience understands the text in the way it is supposed to be understood. But here again, the general view of believers is that this often does not happen. Perhaps a few members of the historical audience do understand the text correctly, but often many members of that audience do not. After all, how could one explain otherwise the fact that Christ and St. Paul were both put to death for what they said? The first was put to death because some of his contemporaries presumably did not understand what he said in the way he intended it, otherwise they would have reacted differently to it—so the argument goes. And the second was put to death for similar reasons.[33] In short, the way(s) a historical audience understands a revealed text does not seem to be the proper criterion of how the text is to be understood, even if it turns out to be helpful or even necessary. Hence, it should not play a determining role in the interpretation of revelation.

The *intended audience* is the audience for which the text is intended. This is, for example, the audience for whom St. Paul intended the letters he wrote to the Corinthians. The locus of the intention in non-revealed texts is, of course, the author. But in the case of revealed texts, where there are two authors, the locus of the intention can be the divinity, the instrumental author, or both. This complicates matters for certain issues, but it does not affect the one that concerns us here.

To say that a revealed text should be understood in accordance with the way in which the audience intended for the text understands it seems to make considerable sense *prima facie,* insofar as this audience is presumably the body of believers for whose sake the text was produced. Moreover, this way of approaching the situation solves some of the problems that surfaced in the case of the historical audience. For example, one could argue that the audience for which Christ's words and St. Paul's words were intended was not the same as the audiences that put them to death; the intended audience was composed of believers who not only understood them correctly, but also had to suffer nefarious consequences on account of their beliefs.

Nevertheless, this position is not without difficulty. The most obvious is that the intended audience cannot be taken as being composed of just the group of believers contemporaneous with the author. It cannot because, if this were the case, it would exclude believers from other times and places; only those believers alive at the time of the revelation would count. But this makes no sense, insofar as the intended audience must be composed of all believers, regardless of the times and places in which they live.

This raises a second problem of demarcation. If the understanding of believers constitutes the criterion of interpretation of revealed texts, and believers differ in what they understand by these texts, how are we to settle these differences? At least three possibilities suggest themselves: (1) Any understanding by a believer is as good as any other; (2) only the understanding of some believers count; or (3) only the understanding common to all believers counts.

The first view cannot be sustained on rational grounds for two reasons: First, the body of belief can be potentially contradictory; second, it presupposes that the divinity makes his or her meaning known directly (and perhaps mystically) to every member of the community of believers with which he or she wishes to communicate.[34] The first reason is intolerable and the second goes contrary to the experience of most believers.

To say that the understanding of only some believers counts and, therefore, not that of others also creates problems.[35] The most important of these concerns the criteria for choosing those believers whose views count. Where do these criteria come from, and how can we know they are the right ones? The text itself cannot provide the answers to these questions, and a private, mystical experience cannot do, for reasons we have already stated. So where do we turn?

The third alternative is that only the understanding common to all believers counts, but this notion of "consensus"[36] itself generates problems of demarcation that cannot be solved with reference to interpretive doctrine. This in turn makes clear that this kind of interpretation is not really a meaning interpretation, but rather a relational one, insofar as it seeks to establish a relation between a text and its meaning on the one hand and certain views about the interpretation of revealed texts on the other.

Finally, if it is the understanding common to *all* believers that counts, how can any believer or group of believers at any given time be certain of an interpretation, not having access to the understanding of those who have not yet lived? This assumes, moreover, that there is access to the understanding of all believers from the past, something that is logically possible but practically unlikely.

The *contemporary audience* is composed of the members of a community who wish to understand a revealed text today, when 'today' refers to any time at which members of a community try to understand the text. For example, this can be you and I, when we try to understand St. Paul's letters, or it can be the audience contemporaneous with St. Paul, and so on. When an audiencial interpretation is conceived in terms of this audience, it has the peculiarity that its aim is not the understanding of some other audience's understanding of a text. Indeed, the contemporaneous audience functions as an interpreter, who in this case becomes the sole arbiter of the interpretation.

The matter is not this simple, however, insofar as for some the interpretive audience consists of individual persons,[37] whereas for others it consists of groups, or, as a proponent of this position puts it, "interpretive communities."[38] In both cases the argument is similar. The conditions of identity of a text include the understanding provided by an audience. A text is nothing but the entities, such as marks on a page, of which it is constituted, so that there is no text if there is no understanding provided by an audience. The understanding is supplied by the interpretive audience, which through this understanding completes or, perhaps better, creates the text. When the audience is an individual person, it is that person's understanding that completes the text, and it is up to that person, and that person alone, to do the interpreting. Of course, the understanding is related to the entities that constitute the text and the signs that these make up, so this understanding is not as free as one might think. Nonetheless, only the text imposes constraints on the interpreter's understanding—not the author or any particular community of readers.

For others, this is not enough insofar as there is another source of interpretive constraints. Individual interpreters are not free to do with texts whatever the texts will bear; interpreters are always part of interpretive communities that have rules of interpretation—even though these are generally unwritten—which establish legitimate ways to proceed and limit the parameters within which an individual interpreter works.[39] The particular aims of, and procedures used in, interpretations, then, depend on the community.

In both cases, whether individual or group based, an audiencial interpretation of this sort aims to satisfy the requirements imposed by a text and an interpretive audience and nothing else, and this is precisely the source of its weakness when it comes to the interpretation of revealed texts. For revelation has to do with a message that a divinity wishes to convey to a community of believers through a text. But in an audiencial interpretation in which the interpretive audience is the arbiter of proper understanding, there is no way of ensuring that the divine message is understood correctly. This is so not only when the interpreter is an individual person, but even when it consists of a community. In both cases, there is nothing beyond the interpreter, except for the entities that constitute the text and the signs of which it is composed, that can control the accuracy of the understanding of the divine message.

Finally, the *intermediary audience* is neither the historical nor the contemporary audience, but rather stands between these two. For example, this audience is neither the Corinthians to whom St. Paul addressed his letters nor present-day Christians who wish to understand God's message in St. Paul's letters. Rather it is, say, a group of people in the nineteenth century, or in the eighteenth, who developed interpretations of St. Paul's letters. The intermediary audience may in fact be many audiences, depending on how far apart in time the historical audience is separated from the contemporary and how many groups of people are involved. Again, it makes no sense to argue for the understanding of revealed texts in terms of this audience, because this audience has no basis on which to establish its interpretive authority.

In short, the audiencial interpretation of revealed texts makes no sense. Audience understanding cannot be held as canonical in the interpretation of revelation.

Independent-Meaning Interpretations

If neither the author nor a particular audience can be regarded as the arbiter of the understanding of revealed texts, perhaps the meaning considered independently of these should be regarded as determinative of legitimate understanding.[40] This is what some exegetes of revealed texts have in mind when they speak of a *sensus plenior:* a fuller meaning that goes beyond what the human author of the text or any particular audience can get out of it.[41] *Prima facie,* this makes considerable sense. If the meaning of a text is what is supposed to be understood when the text is understood, then it is the meaning that determines the understanding and whether the understanding is good or bad, accurate or inaccurate. Still, the formula we are using to describe meaning is highly ambiguous, for whose meaning is involved? Whose understanding should count when it comes to meaning? Meaning is always dependent on someone who understands as well as on a text through which this understanding is produced.[42] The formula we have provided assumes that a meaning requires both someone who understands it and a text through which it is understood. We do have the text, but who is the arbiter of the understanding? It could be the author, for we can certainly speak of an author's meaning. In the case of revealed texts this has to be further divided into the meaning according to the divine author and the meaning according to the instrumental author. And it could also be the audience. Here again, we have several possibilities in accordance with the various conceptions of the audience discussed earlier. So, which of these determines the meaning?

I have already argued that none of these possibilities makes any sense in the case of revealed texts if they are considered apart from what the divinity wishes believers to understand through the text. It seems that a precondition of the interpretation of all revealed texts, *qua* divinely revealed, is that they be understood in accordance with the wishes of the divinity. But this still leaves open the matter as to how that is to be determined.

Moreover, it would make no sense to say that the meaning of a revealed text is something the divinity does not understand. For, what would the divinity have in mind by the revelation then? Who would control this meaning if it were not the divinity? If meaning is always an object of understanding, in order for there to be meaning there has to be some being who grasps it. This possibility makes no sense in particular in the case of a being, such as the Judeo-Christian God, who is omniscient. God's understanding of the meaning of a revealed text is necessarily the meaning of the text insofar as there cannot be any meaning of the text of which God could not be aware. Indeed, one could even go further than this and argue that the meaning of a revealed text is God's meaning because God is not just the creator of the revealed text's particular meaning, but of meaning itself. Regardless of the argument used, however, it is clear that there can be no meaning of a revealed text that God does not know. And this seriously undermines the notion of an independent-meaning interpretation of revealed texts.

Implicative Interpretations

Implicative interpretations have as their function an understanding of the meaning of a text when taken together with its implications, and that meaning is taken in one of the ways in which we have discussed. This entails that this kind of interpretation is parasitic on the ones we have just considered. But these are not viable, so there is no need for us to dwell further on implicative interpretations.

Conclusion

Of the four different kinds of meaning interpretations of revealed texts we have considered in this chapter, the only one that makes any sense is the authorial. Even in this case, however, it is not any kind of authorial interpretation that makes sense, but only one that seeks to be, or cause, an understanding of what a divinity wishes or intends to have understood by an audience composed of believers. Yet, upon further examination, even this view faces serious difficulties. The main problem with it is that it remains an empty formulation insofar as believers must search elsewhere for the content of what is to be understood and for the criteria that can be used to establish what the divinity wishes them to understand. Moreover, this view must rely on other views—such as a particular conception of the divinity who wishes believers to understand—in order to make sense, and this entails that it is ultimately dependent on those views. But what is the source of these other views?

The answer to this question must be found outside the divinity, its intention, and the text. This is the only way to break the Hermeneutic Circle that vitiates the authorial position. And this brings us to relational interpretations. If meaning interpretations, including authorial ones, are inadequate, then the only alternative open to those who seek to interpret revelation is to turn to relational interpretations, a move characteristic of most approaches to revelation today. But what kind of relational interpretation is appropriate? Three suggest themselves. Two are highly favored by non-believers and believers alike: literary (although this need not always be relational, as we shall see) and sociological. The third kind, theological, is not fashionable today but is concordant with traditional hermeneutical procedures in certain religious traditions. I examine the merits of the first in chapter 4, of the second in chapter 5, and of the third in chapter 6.

Chapter 4 ⊷

Literary Interpretations

The failure of meaning interpretations to establish themselves as the proper ways to interpret revelation opens the door to the consideration of relational ones.[1] Indeed, these have become commonplace. But relational interpretations come in a great variety: Freudian, feminist, sociological, historical, psychological, political, philosophical, Christian, Lutheran, Roman Catholic, Marxist, Thomist, lesbian, capitalist, personal, materialistic, culturalist, spiritual, theological, and so on. They all have in common that they bring to a text factors provided by the interpreter, who then proceeds to understand the text (interpretation$_1$) or to compose a text to cause an understanding in the audience for whom the interpretation is being produced (interpretation$_2$) in relation to these factors.

In some cases, these factors consist of principles to which the interpreter is committed, and in other cases they consist of certain facts or events that the interpreter wishes to emphasize or take into consideration. A Freudian interpretation of a text is a good example of the first. In it, the interpreter wishes to understand, or cause an understanding of, a text in terms of certain views Freud developed. For example, the interpreter might try to do so in terms of the Oedipus-complex theory. The interpreter might present the protagonist of the text of a novel as acting in ways that conform to this theory, and this produces an understanding that is different from one in which the Freudian theory is not taken into account.[2]

A historical interpretation is a good example of one in which the factors brought into the interpretive process by the interpreter involve certain facts or events. Consider the situation in which an interpreter seeks to understand, or to cause an understanding of, a text in terms of the sources on which the author of the text relied.[3] For example, an interpreter of Augustine's *On the Teacher* might want to understand the text in terms of the neo-Platonic writings that Augustine might have used in the composition of the text but to which he never referred. In this situation, the understanding sought involves a relation of the text to factors that the interpreter has brought into play, for these factors—such as the influence of the neo-Platonic writings on which Augustine might have relied, the historical connections between Augustine and these writings, and so on—are not part of, nor even explicitly referred to in, the text.[4]

This is all very different from the kinds of interpretation we have called meaning interpretations, whose aim is to understand the meaning of the text, whether that meaning is understood apart from or in terms of the understanding of the author and particular audiences. In the case of relational interpretations, the understanding is based precisely on factors the interpreter brings into the interpretive process.

Relational interpretations are the rage these days. Indeed, many believe that they are the only ones that make any sense. Some of those who favor them argue that to think other kinds of interpretation are even possible is naive insofar as all interpretations are carried out by interpreters who always bring something with them to the interpretive process. The rise of postmodernism and deconstruction has aided the emphasis on relational interpretations and added support to this point of view. The realization that power relations, for example, play a role in interpretation has further eroded the belief in the possibility of non-relational interpretations. Does it make any sense to ask about the meaning of a text when in fact that meaning is always determined by those who hold power over others? How can the dominated understand anything but what those who dominate them determine they should understand?

Not every kind of relational interpretation, however, is favored in every field. In some areas, certain kinds of interpretations have established themselves more firmly than others. For example, in literary studies, Freudian interpretations have acquired a disproportionally prominent role. Much literary criticism today is Freudian or psychoanalytic.[5] One need not go very far to encounter these kinds of interpretations in literary conferences, publications, and college courses. On the other hand, in historical studies, it is frequent to find interpretations that aim to reflect class divisions and, therefore, advocate readings developed from the point of view of marginalized segments of society.[6] And we find similar diverse relational approaches in other fields, although in some the impact of what we might call *relationalism* has not been strong. In philosophy, for example, the influence of relational interpretations has been limited so far, although there are some active proponents of their value.[7]

The area of revelation has felt the impact of relationalism strongly. Texts regarded as revealed, in Western religions in particular, have been subjected to all kinds of relational interpretations, from Marxist to psychoanalytic.[8] In the current postmodernist world, literary interpretations of a relational sort especially are taken seriously by both believers and non-believers—by believers because they see the texts they consider to be revealed as literary pieces whose literary quality is essential for their identity and therefore for the understanding of what they are supposed to do with them;[9] for non-believers because even if there is no divinity whose message is to be gathered from these texts, there is still the possibility of gaining something from them as literary pieces.[10] Yet, there is no agreement on what is a literary, as opposed to a non-literary, text and a literary, as opposed to a non-literary, interpretation, even though no determination of the value of the literary interpretation of revealed texts can take place without a clear understanding of these distinctions.[11] Within the limits of the present discussion, then, I present and defend certain views about literary texts and their interpretation that may, or may not, satisfy readers, but that nonetheless should help them better to understand the issues involved.

The Literary vs. the Non-Literary

In a letter to his wife, to whom he dedicated the Eighth Symphony, Mahler wrote:

> It is a peculiarity of the interpretation of works of art that *the rational element in them (that which is soluble by reason) is almost never their true reality,* but only a veil which hides their form. Insofar as a soul needs a body—which there is no disputing—an artist is bound to derive the means of creation from the natural world. But the chief thing is still the artistic conception. . . . [In *Faust*] everything points with growing mastery toward his final supreme moment—which, *though beyond expression, touches the very heart of feeling.*[12]

Mahler's point concerns what is peculiar to works of art: They defy rationality and expression. By this, I take him to mean in part that works of art are not reducible to ideas and, therefore, cannot be effectively translated. This is the standard modernist view of philosophy and art—and, by extension, of literature—which has been one of the points of attack by postmodernists. But is this view correct, particularly in the case of literature? And, more generally, what is literature?

Three Popular Views of Literature

Philosophers have not shied away from giving answers to the last question. Indeed, the number and variety of opinions in this matter are staggering and the positions frequently conflicting. It is not surprising to find claims to the effect that literature is distinguished by the fact that it is concerned with life, whereas others claim that it is not about life but about itself.[13] Again, some claim that literature is about reality, contradicting others who say that literature is always fictional.[14] Others distinguish it in terms of its presumed non-cognitive nature.[15] And, more recently, some have argued that literature, *qua* text, refers only to other texts, whereas others object that literature is not about texts at all but about non-textual reality.[16] Here, however, I omit discussion of most of the many views that have been offered in this matter, limiting myself to three answers that are widely held but inadequate. The first I call the *institutional view;* the second, the *interpretational view;* and the third, the *particularist view.* After I present them, I turn to the position I favor, and which I shall call the *textual view.*

The *institutional view* holds something like this: There is no feature or set of features common to literary works and texts that distinguishes them from other works and texts. Indeed, the same works or texts have at different times been considered literary or non-literary, so it would be futile to attempt to find this distinction in anything that characterizes works or texts themselves. Literary works and texts are cultural creations, and the culture that creates them determines how they are regarded. Moreover, since this kind of task is usually left to an institutionalized segment of society, it is the institution in question that determines, through its members, whether particular works and texts are literary or not.[17] Hence, whether, say, Borges' "Pierre Menard" is a literary work or text depends on the institution or institutions in society that determine such questions, and in order to know the answer to the question, we need go no further than to pose the question to well-established members of the pertinent institutions who are known for their agreement with institutional views. In fact, since the question has to do with literature, we might just as well ask any bona fide literary critic whether a particular text or work is literary or not.

I suspect, however, that if we were to follow the procedure just suggested, we would get as many different answers to the question as persons asked, depending on the work or text in question. Some would answer yes, some no, some both, and some neither, but in all cases there would be so many qualifications that it would be difficult to find full agreement between any two answers. But perhaps I am being unfair to the institutional view. Perhaps it is not bona fide literary critics who should be asked. And yet, if not them, then whom should we ask? Moreover, who determines who should be asked? Indeed, I suspect that if we were to pose these questions to the readers of this book, we would again receive as many different answers to them as we would receive concerning the earlier question.

I imagine that by now the thrust of my objection is clear: The institutional view leads to a vicious circle or an infinite regress. It does so because it does not identify the feature or set of features that make something literary. To say that literary critics determine what is literary is either to beg the question or to postpone it again and again, *in infinitum*. But neither of these paths leads to closure. The institutional view is very popular today and is favored by many of the most fashionable and well-established literary critics in connection with various issues that have to do with aesthetics, but it certainly does not help us answer the particular question we are seeking to answer here.

The second view I want to consider briefly here is the *interpretational view*. According to it, works and texts are literary because their meanings are never completely clear—there are always ambiguities in them. *Don Quixote*, for example, is literary because there can never be a definitive interpretation of it; there can never be interpretive closure with respect to it. Non-literary texts and works, by contrast, may have definite and unambiguous meanings that can be identified.

This is a well-entrenched view. I heard it expressed for the first time in high school many more years ago than I would like to acknowledge, and have heard it voiced repeatedly ever since. Naturally, this view has also found its way into professional discussions of this issue.[18] Moreover, it has some backing from experience, for it looks as if, indeed, most literary works and texts have the kind of openness to interpretation that this position confers on them.

The problem this position encounters is not so much with what it holds concerning literary works and texts, but with what it holds concerning non-literary ones, for it cannot easily be claimed with a straight face that non-literary works and texts always have definitive interpretations and lack ambiguity and openness. It is perhaps *prima facie* possible to argue that some scientific works and texts are this way, but can we really say the same concerning all scientific works, let alone philosophical ones, for example? Are not some texts of theoretical physics, for example, open to different interpretations? And do not interpreters of Aristotelian works and texts argue endlessly about what Aristotle meant by them? Consider the meetings of the American Philosophical Association. How many different interpretations of Aristotle's works and texts are presented every year in them? And what about Plato? And could we not say the same about some works and texts of Freud, Boole, and Durkheim? In short, ambiguity and openness of meaning do not seem to be the demarcating criteria between literary works and texts and non-literary ones.

The third view is the *particularist*. It finds the distinctive character of literary texts and works in their concrete and particular content. Philosophy and science, so the argument goes, deal with common experience, whereas literature deals with individual experience. This is why literature always tells a story or presents a picture from an individual point of view.

Again, this is an often repeated position, and one that appears to have some basis in experience.[19] Novels and short stories, for example, always deal with individual lives and events. And even poetry, so it is claimed, when not concerned with individual lives or events, is nonetheless concerned with personal experiences.

Now, it is quite true that much literature is like this, but it is false that all literature is so. Moreover, it is also false that all that is not literary excludes the concrete and particular. There are many examples that could be cited to substantiate these claims. Much Enlightenment literature, for example, ignores the concrete and particular. Think of Alexander Pope. True, he is not a very popular writer these days, and some would even say that his works are not very good, but one should not confuse preference or even quality with nature. It would be hard to deny Pope a place in English letters and to consider his works not literary.

On the other hand, even the most universalist and abstract philosophers frequently engage in storytelling to illustrate their claims or even to raise questions that otherwise would be very difficult to raise. Indeed, in certain areas of philosophy, such as the philosophy of law, cases are never too far from the discussion and often direct it.[20] In short, it makes no sense to say that what distinguishes literature is its concern with the concrete and particular.

Clearly there are serious problems with the three views we have briefly examined. Does this mean, then, that there is nothing that distinguishes the literary from the non-literary?

Literary and Non-Literary Texts and Works: The Textual View

In order to answer this question, it is useful to introduce a distinction between texts and works. This is, of course, a much disputed topic. Because I have no space to engage in a discussion of the relative merits of various current views in this matter, I proceed instead by presenting my own position.[21] This will not be sufficient to establish it fully, but I hope it will at least clarify how I use it to articulate the view concerning the nature of literary works and texts I present.

In chapter 1, I introduced the notion of a text as a group of entities used as signs, selected, arranged, and intended by an author in order to cause certain specific acts of understanding in an audience in a certain context. The entities can be ink marks on a piece of paper, sculpted pieces of ice, carvings on stone, designs on sand, sounds uttered by humans or produced by mechanical devices, actions, mental images, and so on. Considered by themselves, these entities are not texts. They become texts only when they are used by authors to cause the understanding of specific meanings to audiences in certain contexts. Ontologically, this implies that a text amounts to these entities considered in relation to the specific meaning whose understanding they are supposed to cause. The marks on the paper on which I am writing, for example, are not a text or part of a text unless someone mentally connects them to a specific meaning. The situation is very much like that of a stone used as a paperweight. The stone becomes the paperweight only when someone thinks of it as a paperweight or uses it as a paperweight.

A work, on the contrary, is the meaning of certain texts. Not all texts have meanings that qualify as works.[22] 'The cat is on the mat' is a text as judged by the definition given, but no one thinks of its meaning as a work. By contrast, *Don Quixote* is both a text and a work. On the difficult question of which texts have corresponding works and which do not, there is much disagreement in the literature. The matter does not seem to depend on length, style, authorship, or the degree of effort involved in the production of the text. Fortunately, there is no need to resolve the question at this juncture.[23] The pertinent point for us is that texts and works are not the same thing: A text is a group of entities considered in relation to a specific meaning, whereas works are the meanings of certain texts. I leave the notion of meaning open, for what I am going to say later does not depend on any particular conception of meaning. But it is important to emphasize that meaning, taken in this general sense, need not be propositional. The meaning of a text may go beyond the propositional content that may be understood through the text.

The text of Genesis, then, consists of the marks on the page I am looking at, the sounds I hear when someone reads Genesis to me, certain images I have when I think about the marks on the page or the sounds uttered by someone reading, and so on, *as long as* the marks, sounds, or images in question are considered signs intended to convey a specific meaning. In contrast, the work Genesis is the meaning that those marks, sounds, or images are intended to convey.

Now we are ready to present what I take to be the distinctive mark of the literary. *The conditions of identity of a literary work include the text of which it is the meaning.* This is to say that the particular signs of which the text is composed, together with the arrangements of the signs and the entities that constitute the signs, are essential to the literary work in question. This is the reason why no work of literature can ever be, strictly speaking, translated. It is in the nature of a literary work that the text that expresses it be essential to it. This is not the case with non-literary works. It should not really matter whether I read Euclid's *Elements* in Greek or English. What should matter is that I get the cognitive, propositional meaning. The work is not essentially related to Greek, whereas Shakespeare's *Hamlet* could only have been written in English and Cervantes' *Don Quixote* could only have been written in Spanish.

Note, however, that the impossibility of translation may have various origins, and therefore it is possible that a non-literary work may not be translatable. In this case, however—and this is my contention—the reason it would not be translatable is not that the conditions of identity include its text, but rather some other reason. For example, "$0 + 1 = 1$" may not be translatable into the language of a culture that has no concept of zero, but this has nothing to do with its literary quality. Of course, there are things we call translations of literary works, but they are not strictly speaking translations; they are rather more or less close approximations. Translations of literary works are works different from the originals that share some of the properties of the originals. And their authors are the translators, not the original authors. Thus, the author of the English translation of the *Coplas* of Jorge Manrique is Longfellow, not Manrique, even though Longfellow apparently tried very hard to duplicate the work of Manrique.

One more point: One could argue that it is not logically impossible for a literary work to be translated. Consider a rather short literary work and a translation into a cognate language. Why would this be impossible? The answer is that it is in principle possible, as long as what the reader is supposed to get from the original work and what he or she gets from the translation are the same. Scholars, of course, believe this possible and strive for it, although they never quite achieve it. The reason: No language is exactly like any other, nor can it be exactly like any other, because languages are historical entities tied to chains of historical events that make them unique.

So much, then, for the distinction between literary and non-literary works. Now we can turn to the distinction between a literary text and a non-literary one. But this proves not to be difficult: *A literary text is one that is essential to the work it expresses, whereas a non-literary text is not essential to the work it expresses.* Now we can see the reason for the name of this view: Textual elements are essential not only for the identity of the text, but also for the identity of the work.

But perhaps I have gone too fast. After all, I have just stated my view and have not given any arguments for it. I could be wrong in holding that literary texts and works have a distinctive character. And even if not wrong about this, I could be wrong about the basis of their distinctiveness. To provide the kind of substantiation that this objection implies would take us too far from the central topic of this book, but I do need to say something in response to it. As a compromise, I offer some evidence to support my position.

First, in practice we do make distinctions between at least some non-literary and some literary works and texts, and we treat them differently. For example, what we do with philosophical works and texts differs from what we do with works and texts we regard as literary. This is a kind of pragmatic argument. Aristotle's *Metaphysics* is studied in different academic departments, by different specialists, and in different ways than is Shakespeare's *Hamlet*. We do act as if these works and texts were quite different in function and aim, and we use them for different purposes. Moreover, when we study them, we apply different methodologies. In the case of the *Metaphysics*, historians of philosophy and philosophers are concerned with the understanding of the views it proposes, with the arguments with which it supports them, and with the truth value of the claims and the validity and soundness of the arguments it contains. We do pay attention to the language and the way Aristotle expresses himself, but this is secondary and merely instrumental to the main purpose of the study, which is to determine the cognitive meaning and value of what Aristotle said. On the contrary, what we do with *Hamlet* is quite different. Here there may still be some concern about claims, but there is no concern about arguments. No literary critic I know has ever tried to apply logic to discourses contained in the play. Moreover, the overriding preoccupation is with the overall significance of the work and text, and by significance I mean the impact of the work and text on ourselves, others, society, and culture.[24]

Still, it is obvious that although we do use non-literary and literary texts and works in different ways, we could be wrong about this. Someone could argue that we do so simply because we are following certain modernist traditions and customs well entrenched in our society, and that there is nothing in the works or texts themselves that justifies the different ways in which we treat them.

To this I respond with a second piece of evidence, namely, the case of poetry. Here is a kind of work or text that seems clearly to fit the distinction I have drawn between the non-literary and the literary. Poetry involves certain structures, punctuation, and rhythm that stand out in contrast to the form of expression generally used in non-literary texts and works. Moreover, in poetry, such factors are as essential for the identity of the work or text as the views expressed by it. Even if this piece of evidence, however, were to convince us that at least poetic works and texts can be distinguished from non-literary ones, in that poetic texts are essential to poetic works, whereas this is not so with non-literary ones, the problem we still face is that not all literary works and texts are strictly speaking poetic. So what do we make of prose literary works and texts? How are we to distinguish them from non-literary ones, and vice versa?

My contention is that still there is a sense in which the identity of prose literary works depends ontologically on the texts that express them, a fact that does not apply to non-literary works and that also affects the identity conditions of literary texts. The reason is not controversial. Indeed, it is generally accepted that the terms that constitute the vocabularies of different languages are not all equivalent. There are some that are so, but the majority of terms are not equivalent in meaning or function. Still, many people would hold that in a large number of cases, one can find formulas in one language that would get across the meaning of the terms used in other languages. My point is that this is possible in principle in the case of non-literary works, but that it can never be in the case of literary works. But why is this so? What are the differences between literary and non-literary texts and works that make literary works include the text, whereas this is not so for non-literary works?

There are many differences at stake here, but I refer to only three to make my point. Consider, first, the nature of the vocabulary used in literary and, say, philosophical texts, how that vocabulary is used, and how the meaning of that vocabulary is treated. And let me add that I choose philosophical texts because it is frequently argued that there is no distinction between philosophy and literature.[25] Philosophical vocabulary is overwhelmingly technical. This does not mean that the terms used in philosophy are not generally used in ordinary discourse, whether spoken or written. It means that even when terms that are commonly used are employed by philosophers, most of these terms acquire meanings different from those involved in common usage. Moreover, even when the meanings are not changed completely, philosophers circumscribe and limit the meanings of the terms they use. A word such as 'substance,' for example, which is commonly used in ordinary English, is a technical term in philosophy. Indeed, it is a technical term for most philosophers who use it, because they determine a particular sense in which they use it. The terms used in ordinary language, on the other hand, have meanings that are frequently open-ended both because there are no strict criteria for their use and because their connotations vary. So much, then, for philosophy.

The situation with literature is very different. In literary texts, terms are used primarily in an ordinary sense, and their open-endedness is usually regarded, and frequently intended, as a good thing. Writers of literature do not generally define their terms or explain to us what they mean. They thrive on suggestion and connotation, leaving much leeway for the audience. Indeed, as we saw earlier, some critics have argued that this open-endedness is precisely the essence of literature.

The order of the words is also very important in literature, because literature aims to cause a certain effect on audiences that does not consist in the pure cognitive grasp of ideas. Literature is highly rhetorical. Each language has developed certain syntactical structures that produce certain effects in the audience that speaks the language of the text, and that are impossible, or produce very different effects, in audiences unfamiliar with that language. The audience plays a very special role in the case of literary texts.[26] The Latin periodic sentence, the epitome of elegance in that language, is generally a failure in English. In Latin, it is not only a mark of elegance, but is intended to produce a certain effect. When one is reading these clauses and subclauses, not yet having arrived at the verb that puts it all together, one is supposed to develop a sense of anticipation that culminates in the grasp of meaning and in the relief one achieves when the verb is reached at the end. In English, it is impossible to put the verb at the end of a sentence in most cases, and the use of long periods of subordinated clauses, instead of causing anticipation, tends to produce confusion and frustration in audiences. A translation from Latin that tries to reproduce the Latin period in English is bound to have an entirely different effect on the English audience than the Latin had on the original Latin audience for which the Latin text was intended.

This brings me to style. Style is largely a matter of word choice, syntax, and punctuation. But style also depends very much on historical circumstances. Consider, for example, that a literary piece may be regarded as having an archaic style at a certain time but as not having it at another time. A book written in the twentieth century in the style of Cervantes is considered archaic, but a book Cervantes wrote in the seventeenth century is not considered to have an archaic style.[27] Style is always historically relative. It is also contextual insofar as it is relative to an audience. Now, style is of the essence in literature. The style of an author is fundamental to the consideration of the author and his or her work. But this is not so important, and some would say not important at all, when it comes to non-literary works. What matters in a philosophical work, say, is not the style of the author or the piece in question, but the philosophy, that is, the ideas the piece contains or, if you will, the claims it makes and the arguments with which it supports them.[28] In this sense, although a text of philosophy may have a certain style, generally the work has little to do with it. This is a reason why the elements constitutive of texts are not part of the identity conditions of non-literary works, whereas they are in literary works.

Of course, one may want to argue that since works are always expressed in texts, there is no way of avoiding style. And, indeed, there are some authors who have insisted that the only way to present philosophy or science is in particular stylistic formats. This was certainly the case with Plato, for whom the proper form of philosophical discourse was the dialogue.[29] And many other philosophers' writings can and are characterized stylistically, e.g., Russell's, Nietzsche's, and Hume's. Indeed, even those philosophers, like Aquinas, who appear to avoid stylistic peculiarities can be said to have a certain style that is clear or obscure, direct or indirect, learned or scholarly, and so on. Moreover, they use certain genres in their writing, such as the article, the *quaestio,* the commentary, and so on, and genre is bound up with style even if it is not the same thing. So it is difficult to argue that philosophy, and this goes for other disciplines as well, does not care for style, although one might argue that it does not care for a particular style.

Still, the point I am making is not that non-literary writing lacks style, or even that the style is always unrelated to meaning. My point is that non-literary authors do not generally think that what they are doing is essentially related to the style they use. Of course, not all non-literary authors have thought this way. The mentioned case of Plato is a clear exception. But this attitude is rather the exception than the rule.[30]

The Interpretation of Literature

The view of literature presented above has important implications for the interpretation of literary texts. If a literary text is a text whose work includes the text, then one would think its interpretation should take this into account. Interpretations$_1$, that is, the understanding of the meanings of these texts, should be more than just the cognitive grasp of propositions, for the work is not just a collection of propositions, but includes the text.[31] And interpretations$_2$, that is, texts used to cause the understanding of the meaning of a text in an audience, should also aim to produce more than just the mere cognitive grasp of propositions. An interpretation$_1$ of *Don Quixote* should be more than the understanding of the cognitive content of the work, and an interpretation$_2$ should do more than produce the cognitive grasp of those propositions. The identity of *Don Quixote* as a literary work requires that interpreters take account of the text in their own understanding and the understanding they may seek to produce in others. In this sense, the elements that make up the Spanish text of Cervantes' *Don Quixote* become essential: terms, order, rhythm, and so on.

This does not mean that authorial interpretations of literary texts are necessarily illegitimate, or that Freudian and feminist interpretations of literary texts are inappropriate. It is always a mistake to insist that only one kind of interpretation is legitimate or appropriate. Audiences can do with texts whatever they wish, and who is to tell them that they cannot, or should not? These interpretations of literary texts are legitimate and appropriate as long as two conditions are met: First, they are interpretations of *the literary text;* second, they have a definite aim. The first imposes further important conditions. Because a literary text is part of the identity conditions of the work it expresses, any interpretation of the text should take textual elements into account, otherwise it is not an interpretation of *the text,* but of *some other text.* A Freudian interpretation, for example, should take into account the choice of words, style, and so on, and these elements should be related in significant ways to the principles to which the Freudian interpreter seeks to relate the text in order to produce the interpretation. If this is not done, then the interpretation is not about the literary text in question, but rather about some other text that the interpreter abstracts from the literary one that he or she claims to be interpreting.

Suppose that a Freudian wishes to produce an interpretation of the text of *Don Quixote*. If in doing this he pays no attention to what makes the text of *Don Quixote* the text it is, then the Freudian's interpretation is not of the text of *Don Quixote*, but of some other text, whatever that may be. Say that the interpreter does not know Spanish and is basing the interpretation on an English translation. Is this an interpretation of the text of Cervantes' *Don Quixote*? Surely not! It is, rather, an interpretation of the English translation of *Don Quixote*, and the English translation is certainly a different text from Cervantes' Spanish text of *Don Quixote*, even if it tries to express the same work the Spanish text expressed. To say this, however, does not entail that, as some claim, Freudian interpretations of literary texts are illegitimate; it entails only that they should be interpretations of *the literary text* and not of *some other non-literary text*. One is free to give interpretations of whatever text one wants, but it is inadvertently confusing to pass the interpretation of one text as that of another, and it is dishonest to do so consciously.

The second thing that needs to be clear for any interpretation of a literary text to be legitimate is that it have a definite aim, even if that aim is precisely to be aimless. To fail in this is simply to preclude the possibility of judgment.

Literary Interpretations

But what, then, is a literary interpretation of a text? Surely, it has to be one whose aim includes a grasp of what is literary in the text. And we have seen that the literary in a text has to do with the inclusion of the text among the identity conditions of the work it expresses. This means that a literary interpretation must play up the text and its features. A literary interpretation of the text of *Don Quixote* will underscore the language Cervantes used, the style of the text, and so on. Its aim is to enlighten us as to those features of the text of Cervantes that make *Don Quixote* the work it is. This involves grasping two things: the propositional content of the text and the non-propositional aspects of the text. A literary interpretation, as opposed to a non-literary one, then, must satisfy two conditions. Whereas in a philosophical interpretation, say, it is enough to understand the propositional content of the text in question—and the same applies to the non-literary interpretation of Euclid's *Elements* or Gibbon's *History of the Decline and Fall of the Roman Empire*—in literary interpretations we need to go beyond this and grasp also certain characteristics of the text that are not propositional but nevertheless integral to the work the text conveys.

This may be accomplished in two ways by interpreters. In one way, they may aim merely to grasp the propositional content and the pertinent non-propositional elements of the text that make the literary work what it is. This yields what one might call a *meaning literary interpretation.*

In another way, interpreters may try to relate the text or its meaning to certain factors that they bring into the picture, such as psychological, socio-logical, cultural, and so on. This entails that the literary interpreter is seek-ing rather a *relational literary interpretation.* In this sense, for example, we can have a Freudian literary interpretation of the text of *Don Quixote.* This entails an interpretation that pays attention to the peculiarities of the text of *Don Quixote* and also tries to relate it to some Freudian principles.

This underscores a fact generally ignored by those who write on the hermeneutics of literary texts, namely, that literary interpretations can be meaning interpretations or relational interpretations. Indeed, most of the endless controversies about the interpretation of literary texts we have been subjected to for the past 50 years miss it.

So far, we have been speaking of the literary interpretations of literary texts, but what do we do with texts that are not considered literary? Can there be literary interpretations of texts that are not considered to be liter-ary? If non-literary texts have works that do not include their texts in their identity conditions, there appears to be no point for the interpreter to refer to the idiosyncracies of the texts when providing interpretations of them. If Euclid's *Elements,* considered as a work of science, has nothing do with the Greek text used by Euclid to express it, a literary interpretation of the text of the *Elements* would seem useless, if not misleading.

Well, perhaps it is! Can one really make sense of a literary interpretation of the text of Euclid's *Elements?* The answer appears simple in this case, but not all cases are so simple, for two reasons: First, works that consist funda-mentally in a propositional meaning, in ideas let us say, are of course ex-pressed through texts; and, second, many works of this sort use literary devices, such as stories and metaphors, in order to convey their propositional meanings more effectively.[32] Both of these reasons suggest that one can in-terpret the texts that express these works literally as long as one emphasizes the texts through which they are expressed and the literary devices they use to convey their propositional meanings. In some cases, as happens with Eu-clid's *Elements,* the literary interpretation might be pointless, but in texts like Aristotle's *Nicomachean Ethics,* it might not.

Literary Interpretations of Revelation

Let us turn now to the literary interpretation of revealed texts in particular. We might begin by asking whether it is at all important for the discussion of this issue to determine whether revealed texts are literary or not. In one way it appears important, for if revealed texts are literary, then clearly a literary interpretation of them is appropriate, and perhaps even necessary insofar as any interpretation of these texts should do justice to their literary character. The problem with this road is that even if one ignores other problems, it is quite difficult to argue that all revealed texts are literary or have substantial literary qualities. Surely, some appear to be. It would be difficult not to think of the Song of Songs or the Psalms as literary, for example. But there are other texts regarded as revealed that would be equally difficult to consider literary.[33] Works that contain genealogies or consist of legal codes fall into this category. It seems better, then, to set aside questions about the literary interpretation of revealed texts based on their literary or non-literary quality.

I propose instead to ask some questions based on the aims that one may pursue with the literary interpretation of revealed texts. But, even before we address these questions, we should ask whether the literary interpretation of revealed texts is at all possible. The answer poses no serious difficulties. Revelation, as we have understood it, consists of texts, and so it is always possible to provide interpretations of it that aim to produce an understanding of the peculiarities of the texts in addition to their cognitive meanings, whether the works expressed by them take texts into account or not. Even a legal code, like the Decalogue, which is presumably devoid of fine literary qualities and whose aim is simply to communicate a set of commands, can be interpreted literarily insofar as it is a text and in interpreting it we can refer to the constituents of the text. I can speak, for example, of the way the commandments are presented, or of the way the text expresses their character as commandments, and so on. Likewise, I can provide a translation that not only attempts to render the cognitive content accurately but also to reproduce as much as possible the features of the text.

Apart from the general question of possibility, there are other, more specific ones that have to do with the aims pursued by interpretations, so we need to review these aims. The general aim of interpretations is to be or to cause acts of understanding in relation to the texts under interpretation, but this is not all they are aimed to do. There are also other, more specific aims they may have. Some of these are consequent upon the fact that they are meaning interpretations and some upon the fact that they are relational.

The meaning interpretations that interpreters of revealed texts may want to have, or to produce, are six: the understanding of the meaning of a text considered independently of what authors intended to be understood, or what authors and audiences actually understood by them; the understanding of what the divinity understands; the understanding of what the divinity wishes us to understand; the determination of what the instrumental author of a text understood or intended by it; the determination of what particular audiences of texts understood by them; and the understanding of the implications of the meaning of a text—whether that meaning is taken as independent or not, of what the authors and audiences of the text understood by it.

The relational understandings that interpreters of revealed texts may want to have, or to cause, are as many as the possible factors to which they may wish to relate the texts or their meanings. We have already cited some examples of these in previous chapters, but let us add the following: understanding of authors and audiences (mind you, this is not equivalent to their understanding of the texts); identifying the sources of the views expressed by the texts and their influence on the views of others; grasping the causes that gave rise to the views expressed by the texts; and learning a lesson that may serve to guide actions.

Now, the specific questions we need to answer concerning the literary interpretation of revealed texts are three: (1) Are literary interpretations of revealed texts sufficient to carry out the aims we have outlined? (2) Are literary interpretations of revealed texts necessary for these aims? And (3) if literary interpretations of revealed texts are neither sufficient nor necessary for these aims, are they at least useful?

In the previous chapter we saw that, except for one (i.e., what the divinity wishes us to understand), no meaning interpretation of revealed texts makes sense. So it would be useless for us to review these in the context of literary interpretations. Moreover, the questions we have asked can clearly be answered negatively, without much reflection, in the case of some of the cited examples of relational aims. An interpretation whose only function is to take into account the literary qualities of a text is surely not sufficient, necessary, or even helpful for grasping the causes that gave rise to the views expressed by a text or for learning a lesson that may serve to guide our actions. But there are at least two aims, one meaning and one relational, that merit attention.

Understanding What God Wishes Us to Understand

Are literary interpretations, then, sufficient, necessary, or merely helpful in understanding what God wishes us to understand? Keep in mind that the general problem with divine intentional interpretations is that they are too formal and therefore empty. Our issue amounts, therefore, to establishing whether literary interpretations can supply something that would solve this problem.

That literary interpretations are not sufficient for this purpose is rather obvious. What is peculiar to literary interpretations is that they take into account certain characteristics of the text under interpretation, such as the rhythm, the style, the sound or appearance of the signs of which the text is composed, and so on. But none of this is sufficient to give us an understanding of what God means to convey to us through a text. Discussing or reproducing the parallel structure of the Psalms, for example, can tell us little, if anything, about what God wants us to know through them.

If revealed texts are supposed to convey facts from divinities to believers, even though they might also aim to produce certain non-cognitive effects on them (e.g., emotions), the analysis of the literary qualities of the texts is not enough to make believers understand the facts in question. It may satisfy someone interested merely in the literary qualities of the texts, or the non-cognitive effects of the texts on audiences, but certainly not someone who wishes to get at the presumed facts the texts are supposed to convey. This applies even if there is no divinity and therefore no revelation. For, even then, to understand a text *qua* revealed involves understanding a fact as if it were divinely presented.

Part of the reason why analyses of literary qualities are not sufficient for understanding revealed facts is that the peculiarities of revealed texts—their style, rhythm, and so on—do not by themselves signify anything relevant for believers. The revelatory character of the texts remains hidden. If in analyzing the Decalogue, the only things I mention in an interpretation have to do with style, and I say nothing about the presumably divine prescriptions it contains, I have certainly failed to convey what the text is all about.

What has been said concerning revealed texts can also be said about other texts, even literary ones. One could argue that grasping the literary qualities of a text is not sufficient for the understanding of whatever facts the text is intended to convey beyond certain non-cognitive effects on an audience. Paying attention only to rhythm and style, say, will not tell me all that Poe's *The Raven* is supposed to tell me. This is why literary interpretations aim beyond the grasp of literary qualities. They are intended also to get at the propositional meaning of the text, or to establish an understanding of that meaning in relation to factors brought into the process by the interpreter.

If not sufficient, then, could literary interpretations be necessary for understanding what God wishes us to understand? The answer is again negative insofar as the revealed message is concerned. This message concerns certain facts the divinity is supposed to wish believers to understand. And although the text is the means whereby these facts are conveyed, the text is not part of these facts. The need for the text is epistemic—believers need the text to understand the facts. But what believers understand is not that the text has a certain style or not, is elegant or not, and so on. They understand such things as that "God created the world," that "God is one," and that "Muhammad is God's prophet." The text is not ontologically part of the divine message conveyed by the text.[34] This, again, is very much like a microscope and bacteria. The text is like the microscope and the facts are like bacteria. We need the microscope to see bacteria, and the microscope in a sense controls and determines what we see. But the bacteria are not, and do not include, the microscope. If what the God of Abraham wishes for believers to understand, through the text of the Decalogue, is a set of prescriptions against certain actions, we need the text to get at those prescriptions, but the way the text is constructed is not part of the prescriptions. Keep in mind also that if literary interpretations were of the essence, then few believers other than those who know the language in which the revealed text is written would have access to the divine message. For the work would be untranslatable, and not even interpretations$_2$ of the text would convey what the original is supposed to convey.

Finally, if not necessary, are literary interpretations at least useful to the interpreter of revelation? It depends. If they lead to a misunderstanding of the message, then clearly they are not useful. But if they lead to a correct understanding of the divine message, they are. To the degree that taking into account the structure and style of a text, for example, leads to a better grasp of the divine message, a literary interpretation will be useful. Consider, for example, the parallel structure in the Psalms. Recognizing this should prevent interpreters from trying to justify different meanings for verses that appear to mean the same thing.[35] On the other hand, to the degree that literary interpretations draw attention away from the divine message, or confuse it, then they are not useful. This is why literary interpretations cannot be of the essence as far as revelation is concerned, and why to emphasize them may in fact be counterproductive in some cases.

Understanding Instrumental Authors or Particular Audiences

Understanding instrumental authors or particular audiences entails going beyond understanding the views that the authors or audiences understand through the texts under interpretation. Indeed, it may go beyond the views expressed by all the texts that an author produces and with which an audience of a text may be acquainted. Understanding instrumental authors or particular audiences of revealed texts involves seeing them as wholes, considering all the views they express or understand and those that they may not even express or understand, understanding other aspects of their identities that have nothing to do with the views they hold, and considering these authors or audiences in particular contexts that help to put them in perspective. The question for us is whether the exclusively literary interpretation of a text is sufficient, necessary, or helpful to carry out this task.

The answer is pretty similar in some respects to the answer given in the previous section: Literary interpretations are neither sufficient nor necessary, and they may be helpful or not, depending on the circumstances, for the understanding of authors and audiences, if that understanding takes into account only the message of the text. But a text uncovers other things beyond its message about its author. In a literary context, for example, it may tell us something about the talent for rhyme of the author, the linguistic skills of the author, and so on. So, a literary interpretation of a text can tell us much about an author, or an audience, that a non-literary one cannot. And this applies both to the divine and to the instrumental authors of revealed texts.

Conclusion

In short, the mark of the literary work is that it includes the text that expresses it. Consequently, literary interpretations are those that take into account elements belonging to texts, and this goes beyond purely propositional understanding.

Now, the function of revealed texts is to produce in believers the understanding of certain significant facts that the divinity intends for them to understand. These facts are not literary phenomena, nor can they be grasped exclusively through literary interpretations, although literary interpretations may help, depending on the circumstances, to grasp them. This is the reason that literary interpretations can be considered neither sufficient nor necessary for the interpretation of revelation.

Next, we turn to sociological interpretations, another popular way of approaching revealed texts today.

Chapter 5 ✦

Sociological Interpretations

Sociological interpretations are among the most popular relational interpretations today.[1] They are understandings, or texts aimed to produce understandings, of texts in terms of sociological factors, be they economic, psychological, cultural, political, or historical. These factors include "professional interests, struggles over professional chairs, wars, and mentalities," as a supporter of sociological interpretations in various fields puts it.[2] Like other texts, texts regarded as revealed can be understood in their social context rather than as conveyors of a divine meaning.[3]

The sociological approach to revealed texts has had much success recently. If one looks at departments of theology in the United States today, one finds that a large proportion of the members of these departments engage, sometimes almost exclusively, in sociological interpretations. Even in Christian denominations in which a generally conservative perspective has been dominant, such as Roman Catholicism, sociologism has made great inroads. It takes only a superficial look at the composition of departments or schools of theology in major Roman Catholic universities in the United States to see that many faculty members practice some form of sociologism. Indeed, in some ways, these departments look no different from departments of religion in secular universities, where the overall aim is to produce interpretations that are consonant with sociological principles rather than with religious beliefs. Sociology is frequently used as the main tool to understand revelation.

Traditional fields, like biblical scholarship and systematic theology, are on the wane, and instructors are being hired who adopt feminist, Freudian, historical, and even (or perhaps particularly) Marxist interpretive principles.[4] In some cases, representatives from other religious traditions are favored over those who practice traditional theology. It is not infrequent that departments of theology in Roman Catholic universities, for example, will lack experts in the thought of Augustine, Aquinas, and Suárez—theologians who dominated the Roman Catholic theological tradition until very recently—while having specialists devoted to the cultural, psychological, political, and feminist study of revealed texts. In short, revealed texts are studied not for what a divinity tried to convey through them, or for what their authors and contemporaneous audiences understood through them, but in order to fit them within certain conceptual parameters that interpreters bring to them. This is quite clear from the description of the sociological method given by the first exegete who coined the expression "sociological exegesis." According to Elliott, this involves "the employment of the perspectives, presuppositions, modes of analysis, comparative models, theories and research of the discipline of sociology."[5] Similar statements are frequently found in interpretations authored by proponents of this approach.[6]

Some of the conclusions reached in chapters 3 and 4 add support to the sociological point of view. If the only acceptable meaning interpretation of a revealed text is one that seeks to understand what the divinity wishes believers to understand, and this turns out to be an empty prescription because the texts themselves offer no guidance as to what that might be, then we might as well abandon the search for divine meaning and embrace other approaches. And since the literary approach is of no use in this regard, the sociological approach becomes an attractive alternative. A sociological analysis may provide what meaning and literary analyses cannot. But is this correct? And if so, to what extent should we embrace the sociological interpretation of revelation?

Three positions can be easily identified with respect to this issue: 1) Revealed texts should be interpreted exclusively in sociological terms; 2) the interpretation of revealed texts should exclude all consideration of sociological factors; and 3) there is a place for sociology in the interpretation of revealed texts but this place is not exclusive.

Versions of all three positions have been explicitly defended by interpreters of revealed texts, but my aim in this chapter will be to make a case for the third position. I argue that the role of sociology in the interpretation of revealed texts depends on the aim pursued. If, on the one hand, the aim is sociological understanding, then sociological considerations are essential, although still insufficient, to understand revelation *qua* revelation. If, on the other hand, the aim is to understand meaning—taken in any of the modes discussed in chapter 3—then sociological considerations play only an ancillary role in interpretation. In this case, although the consideration of sociological factors is sometimes factually necessary for the interpretation of revelation, they are not essential in the interpretation. This means that positions that argue for the exclusive use of sociology or for the exclusion of sociology in the interpretation of revelation commit the same kind of error: They do not do justice to the proper role of sociology in this regard.

I begin, then, by examining some arguments for and against the exclusive use of sociological factors. Then, I turn to the proper place of sociology in the interpretation of revelation.

The Case for Sociological
Interpretations of Revealed Texts

The backbone of the position that emphasizes the importance of sociological interpretations of revealed texts is constituted by three arguments. The first notes that all other positions are naive. The reasons why revealed texts are produced have nothing to do with divine revelation. Moreover, the views presented in these texts are largely, or even exclusively, presented because of factors that are part of the social context in which the texts were produced. For example, the reason for the rules that prescribe sacrifice offerings contained in the Old Testament is not to placate a God against whose will his people have transgressed, but simply to provide food for a priestly class fond of privilege and easy living. Likewise, religious regulations concerning eating have more to do with maintaining health in the population than with any wishes of a divinity. Interpretations of revealed texts that do not pay proper attention to sociological factors are, therefore, inaccurate, because they ignore the actual causes that produced the phenomena they aim to explain. To miss the real reasons for the practices of sacrifice and eating regulations is to misunderstand these practices and regulations.

The second argument points out that interpretations that try to account for religious phenomena in non-sociological terms assume the existence of deities whose existence has yet to be confirmed. Moreover, the identity and nature of these deities vary from religion to religion and often imply conflicts between the deities, contradictions among beliefs, and incompatibilities among practices prescribed for humankind. Whereas some deities are merciful, others are cruel; whereas some religions are monotheistic, others are polytheistic; and whereas some religions prescribe a life of chastity, others prescribe licentiousness. Who is right, then? The only common ground that can be used to explain religious phenomena is sociology.

Third, it is argued that religions, religious texts, religious views, religious arguments, and religious experiences themselves are social phenomena. They are the products of social individuals working within social parameters and subject to social forces. We could paraphrase Peckhaus and say that religion is the result of human activity in time.[7] Kusch is even more explicit when he notes that "entities like reasons, arguments, or theories *are* social entities; that is, they are social institutions, parts of social institutions, or dependent upon social institutions."[8] Religious reasons, arguments, texts, and views, argue some supporters of the sociological point of view, require sociological interpretations.[9] To treat such phenomena in non-sociological terms is to misunderstand their nature and to produce interpretations that have no credibility or accuracy. Applying what Peckhaus says about philosophy to the case of religion, we could say that a non-sociological interpretation of revealed texts is an illusion because of the temporality of religion as an activity and the social context of religion and religious practices.[10]

These are powerful arguments, indeed, and they require careful attention. Rather than addressing them individually at the outset, however, I turn now to some of the arguments that can be mustered against the use of sociological factors in the interpretation of revealed texts.

The Case against Sociological Interpretations of Revealed Texts

There are also three key arguments that can be used against the view that the interpretation of revealed texts must not be done in sociological terms. First, one may argue that in spite of many efforts, those who favor sociological interpretations have not yet succeeded in presenting a clear description, or illustration, of the method they propose. In other words, it is not at all clear what the sociological method, or a sociological interpretation of revealed texts, is. This can be easily illustrated with various sociological interpretations.

In the first place, there is a considerable degree of latitude as to what is considered sociological. Some accounts involve political forces; some accounts involve cultural factors; some accounts involve particular social factors; and so on. So which of these is truly sociological? In short, there is considerable variety as to the phenomena that are considered relevant in sociological interpretations, and it is not clear what the parameters of relevant phenomena are. This can be easily illustrated with the various accounts contained in a recently published volume on the sociology of philosophical knowledge. Some of these accounts involve political forces. An article by Matthew Chew is a good example. He explains the views concerning indigenous knowledge held by Chinese and Japanese philosophers in terms of the politics of the philosophical profession and the university in China and Japan. Other sociological accounts involve cultural factors, such as deeply rooted beliefs and attitudes. A good example of this is an article by Barry Sandywell in the mentioned volume, in which he attempts to show that theoretical discourse in ancient Greece is the result of the fundamental agonistic ethic that permeated Greek culture at the time. Still other accounts involve particular social factors. For example, Randall Collins argues that the attitude of philosophers toward ethics can be explained in terms of the fabric of the particular kind of social group formed by academics and intellectuals themselves.

There is, moreover, a considerable degree of generality and even vagueness in these interpretations. Some of these appear as if they were ultimately based on certain feelings and impressions, where an initial intuition dominates the discussion, leaving us in the realm of conjecture and speculation. David Bloor's characterization of Wittgenstein's thought on the basis of Karl Mannheim's categories could be used to illustrate this feature. Indeed, in this case it appears as if the account is ultimately based on certain feelings and impressions. Consider how Bloor himself describes his experience: "I was then *spontaneously and forcefully struck by what seemed* the evident similarity between the *Investigations* and what Mannheim said about conservatism. I *felt* that Mannheim *could almost have been* describing Wittgenstein's work. I will not be able, and will not even try, to recreate that experience in you, but I will identify for you some of the grounds for *this feeling of having, at last, identified the spirit, as it were,* informing Wittgenstein's work."[11] In all fairness, I should point out that Bloor then proceeds to substantiate his claims in various ways, some of which are quite enlightening. Still, the initial intuition dominates the discussion, and one could argue that much is left in the realm of conjecture and speculation.

Second, one can argue that even if revealed texts and the views they express are the result of social forces and, indeed, are themselves to be considered social phenomena, this is not sufficient (1) to discard other interpretations in favor of sociological ones, (2) to grant other interpretations a role secondary to sociological ones, or even (3) to regard sociological interpretations as being on an equal footing with other ones. One must distinguish between the context of the expression of a view and the view. This can be put in terms of a distinction I introduced earlier between the intensional and extensional historicity of a sentence. The extensional historicity of a sentence has to do with its historical context. In this sense, a sentence is historical when it is entertained or held by someone at a particular time and place in history. The intensional historicity of a sentence, on the other hand, has to do with what the sentence says. A sentence that says nothing temporal or historical is not intensionally historical. When I say 2 + 2 = 4, I have said something in time, and what I say is temporal and historical to that extent. But what I have said has nothing to do with time or history; it involves a relation between concepts that is completely atemporal. This, of course, is different from a case in which I say something like: My oldest daughter got married five years ago. In this case we have both an extensionally and an intensionally historical sentence, because not only have I expressed the sentence in time, but what I say is also temporal. Most views expressed by revealed texts and the rules according to which they are judged are not intensionally historical, any more than mathematical principles are, and therefore the kind of interpretation that sociological interpreters propose does not do them justice.

The third argument against the use of sociological interpretations in revealed texts points out that they are inconclusive. A sociological interpretation tells us that text T means P because, for example, P was a widely held view in the society S in which T was produced. But this does not explain why the author of T chose to hold P. Does not holding P have to do with the merits of P, or at least the merits that S saw in P? To say that T expresses P because S held P leaves open the question of why S held P. At this point the sociologist has two alternatives. One is to say that no further account can be given. But then, why go to S at all? Why not stop with T or its author? The move from T, or its author, to S appears gratuitous. And there is another problem, namely, that the step from T, or its author, to S relies on a questionable assumption: If S holds P, T must express it, or the author of T must hold it. But is this so with every view? Clearly not, for revealed texts frequently challenge the views of their societies. This leaves open the question of why texts sometimes express views widely held in the societies that produce them and sometimes do not. And how are we going to account for this sociologically?

The other alternative is to give another sociological account of why T expresses P, but this would in turn require a further account, and so on *in infinitum*. This procedure is unsatisfactory unless we come to a point at which the account consists in pointing out the merits of P. But if this is so, then why do we need to go to S in the first place? We could identify those reasons in reference to T and leave it at that.

The Role of Sociology in the Interpretation of Revealed Texts

Qua interpretation, the general aim of the interpretation of revealed texts is to be, or to cause, acts of understanding in relation to these texts, but this is not all they aim to do. Some aim also to be meaning interpretations and others to be relational. Hence, some other, more specific aims result from these. The six meaning interpretations that interpreters of revealed texts may want to have, or to produce, were discussed in chapter 3. The relational understandings that interpreters of revealed texts may want to have, or to cause, are as many as the possible factors to which they relate texts or their meanings. Examples of these have been cited in both chapters 2 and 3. Now, the question that we have to answer concerns the best, or the most appropriate, way interpreters may accomplish these aims in the case of revealed texts. Should they employ a sociological method exclusively? Should they employ non-sociological methods independently of sociological ones? Or should they employ a mixture of these methods, and, if this is the way, how should these methods be combined and what are their respective roles? Let us attempt to answer these questions in the context of seven specific aims.

Understanding What God Wishes Us to Understand

If the aim of the interpretation of revealed texts is to understand, or cause an understanding of, what God wishes us to understand, we need to ask: Are sociological analyses sufficient, necessary, or at least helpful to accomplish this aim?

Surely, the answer to this question is determined by the aim pursued: the understanding of what God wishes us to understand. But this already takes us out of sociology and into the realm of faith and theology. For, where else are we going to find criteria for determining how to proceed in the understanding of revelation? Only a believer, within a faith, can meaningfully ask such a question. For the non-believer, as St. Paul would say, the question makes no sense. Indeed, for the non-believer, the question must be translated into questions about the social factors that lead particular societies to believe that certain texts say something about a divinity, to believe in that divinity, and so on. This takes the religious element out of the discourse immediately, with the consequence that the question concerning the way to proceed in order to get the meaning God wants believers to get from revealed scriptures is transformed into a question about how society behaves. 'God' does not any longer mean God, but rather a certain belief about a deity held by a society. And 'revealed scriptures' does not any longer mean revealed scriptures, but rather texts that certain groups of people believe are revealed. Outside of a faith context and the theological principles accepted by a community of believers, the question that we are asking makes no sense. It makes sense only in that context, and therefore it is in that context that it should be answered.

This can be clearly seen if we consider the differences between the following two questions, where T is a text considered revealed by some community and X stands for any one person or persons:

1. What does God wish X to understand through T?
2. What does X understand through T?

The second question makes sense whether one believes that T is revealed or not. But the first makes sense only for those who believe in God, who accept that T is a revelation from him, and who have a set of theological principles that guide them in their understanding. If we accept that a certain text is a revelation from God, and the purpose of its interpretation is to try to understand what God wishes us to understand through it, then we may certainly ask a further question concerning the place of sociological interpretations in that process of understanding. But the further question comes only after, and in the context of, belief. This means that the ultimate arbiter of such a role is faith, that is, the religious beliefs of the community, together with their articulation into a theology. Clearly, we have a relational kind of interpretation here in which faith and theology provide a term of the relation on which the interpretation is based.

Under these circumstances the role of sociology in the interpretation of revealed texts cannot be settled across the board, but on only a case by case basis, that is, depending on the particular beliefs and theology in question. For some religions, sociological interpretations may have a place, but for others they may not. For example, in a religion in which the only source of understanding what God wishes believers to understand is through personal illumination, sociology has no place. If a religious epistemology is exclusively based on illumination, mystical insight, and the like, there is no room for sociological techniques. On the other hand, if a religion presents itself as a rational body of beliefs that are supported by natural knowledge, and in which illumination and mystical experience play only a part in a whole epistemological apparatus, then sociology can have a place. But again, the particular place it has depends on the specific principles of the faith and theology in question. Keep in mind, however, that in all cases, the role of sociological interpretations needs to be taken in the context of theology and cannot contradict religious beliefs or theological principles.

In short, if we want to know the role of sociology in the understanding of what God wishes us to know through revealed scriptures, it is only by accepting the religious beliefs of the community that regards the scriptures as revealed that the question can be answered. This does not mean that nonbelievers may not, in certain cases, be able to have such understanding.[12] It means that in order to do so, they must function as if they were believers; they must accept the primary role of the pertinent religious beliefs. To understand what God wishes us to understand, we must proceed as if we were part of the pertinent community of believers and accepted the religious principles of the community.

In this context, we must keep in mind a distinction between two senses of 'faith.' One is merely a body of doctrines or beliefs; another is a certain experience, phenomenon, or quality that affects only certain persons. In Christianity, the first is a set of doctrines such as that of the Trinity, of Providence, and the like (often called "articles"). The second is a supernatural gift bestowed on certain persons that transforms them and their relation to God. The faith that is required for theological understanding and that is accessible to persons who are not members of the pertinent religious community is the first. The second is available to only a few, and its results are spiritual rather than cognitive.[13]

So, the answer to our original question is that the sufficiency, necessity, or usefulness of sociological analyses in the interpretation of revelation—

when this aims at an understanding of what God wishes us to understand—
is that it depends on the beliefs of the community of believers. Independently of these, the value of sociological analyses cannot be judged.
Unqualifiedly, sociology is not sufficient, necessary, or even helpful for the
understanding of what God wants us to understand.

Understanding What Instrumental Authors
or Particular Audiences Understand

A second aim of the interpretation of revealed texts is to understand, or to
produce an understanding of, what instrumental authors or particular audiences understand.[14] There are substantial differences between understanding
what God wishes a group of believers to understand through a revealed text
on the one hand and understanding what instrumental authors or particular audiences understand on the other. The first task can take place only
within a theological context in which the interpreter accepts certain beliefs
at face value. Understanding what instrumental authors or particular audiences understand is quite a different matter, because here the interpreters do
not need to proceed by accepting certain theological principles and beliefs,
although they must be aware of the fact that the instrumental author of the
text and particular audiences hold them.[15] In this case, we are dealing with
persons who have a certain understanding of what is meant by a text they
composed, read, or heard. Consider again the two questions we raised in the
previous section. To ask "What does X understand through T?" requires no
religious standpoint on the part of the questioner, whereas to ask "What
does God wish X to understand through T?" does.

The task of understanding what the instrumental author and a particular
audience of a text understand through the revealed text is not different in
principle from the task of trying to figure out what Plato thought when he
wrote a particular Dialogue. To do this, interpreters do not need to adopt
the standpoint of a particular theology, or any theology at all, although they
do need to know what the instrumental author and particular audience in
question believe. Knowing this is necessary to figure out what they take the
text to mean. To this extent, this kind of interpretation differs from that of
a Platonic Dialogue, for the interpretation of the latter does not rest on the
understanding of a set of religious beliefs to which Plato adhered.

Is sociology, then, sufficient, necessary, or useful to understand what
particular authors or particular audiences understand through a revealed
text? It is clearly not sufficient by itself insofar as knowledge of the beliefs
and theological framework accepted by the author and the audiences in
question are necessary, even though it is not necessary that interpreters
themselves adopt, or act as if they adopted, these beliefs and theological

framework. But sociology is both necessary and useful insofar as a revealed text, its author, and its audience are immersed in a cultural context without consideration of which the understandings of the author and the audience would be impossible.

Understanding Instrumental Authors or Particular Audiences

Understanding what instrumental authors or particular audiences understand through texts regarded as revealed must also be distinguished from the task of understanding instrumental authors or particular audiences themselves. In the latter case, the understanding goes beyond the views the authors or audiences have in relation to a particular text. The task here is to consider all the views they express or understand and those that they may not even express or understand, understanding other aspects of their identities and considering these authors or audiences in particular contexts that help to put them in perspective. The understanding of instrumental authors or various audiences is contextual to a degree that understanding revealed texts by themselves may not be, and therefore the understanding that interpreters seek to have, or to produce, of them must likewise be contextual. The question for us is whether it is sufficient for this aim that they refer to them, whether the context in question is such that it requires reference to sociological factors, and how helpful such references might be.

Much of what was said in the previous section can be repeated here. But there is more to it than this, because the views of instrumental authors and particular audiences, in this case, are not restricted to those expressed by the authors in the texts. For this reason, interpreters must use other evidence to figure out what those views are, and this evidence is often found in the authors' and audiences' social context within which they are situated. Moreover, if what the interpreter wants to do is to understand something about authors and audiences that goes beyond their views related to a particular text, or even their views in general, then it becomes even more clear that we have to go beyond the texts to the social context of the texts, the authors, and the audiences we wish to understand. Sociological interpretations, then, play a particularly important role in the understanding of instrumental authors and particular audiences. Indeed, the overarching task here is sociological. But we must keep in mind that such an understanding must include an understanding of the author as author of a revealed text, and of the audience as believers in a divine message. This means that the beliefs of the author and audience, and the theology into which those beliefs are articulated, have to come in to help interpreters, even if, as in the previous case, it is not required that interpreters proceed as if they accepted them.

Understanding the Meaning of a
Revealed Text and Its Implications

One of the aims of the interpreters of revealed texts is to understand, or to produce an understanding of, the meaning of these texts when this meaning is taken in the various ways we explored earlier. Of course, it makes no sense to speak about some of these alternatives when the divinity in question is regarded as omniscient and omnipotent, as the Judeo-Christian God generally is, and we have already discussed understanding what God wishes believers to understand, and what instrumental authors and particular audiences understand. The question here concerns only the meaning of the text when understood to go beyond these. Can sociology, then, be sufficient, necessary, or merely helpful, if at all, to understand the meaning of revealed texts considered independently of what their authors and particular audiences understand by them? Even a cursory consideration of the situation indicates that sociology is not *de jure* necessary for this enterprise, although it might be very helpful and even factually necessary for the task. Let me explain.

If the aim interpreters have in mind is to understand, or make certain audiences understand, the meaning of a revealed text, such an understanding must be based on the awareness of the relations among the religious views expressed by the text, for to understand the views expressed by a text is fundamentally to understand how the religious views it expresses are related to each other. But sociology contributes nothing to this. Only within a theological context do we get what we need.

Theology here, as in the aims discussed in the two previous sections, need not be accepted by the interpreter at face value; it need only be taken as presupposed by revelation. On the contrary, sociological factors are not *de jure* necessary to the extent that it is logically possible to understand the views expressed by a revealed text, and the relations between those views, without understanding the sociological factors that may have contributed to their formulation. For example, it appears possible to understand the claim that God created the world in six days without knowing much about Hebrew culture and society at the time Genesis was written.

Of course, sociological knowledge is useful, and in certain cases factually necessary, to the task of the interpreter of revelation for at least four reasons. First, revealed texts are composed of language, and language is a cultural phenomenon for the knowledge of which we need to take into account the society that produced it. Second, the very concepts expressed by revealed texts are developed by, or at least based on, widely accepted concepts current in the societies in which the authors of those texts lived, so that in order to grasp them one must in some cases grasp the social conditions under which they arose. Third, social factors do influence, and often determine, the views authors express in texts, and, therefore, knowledge of them can aid in understanding those views. And, finally, certain sociological research can provide evidence for what an author knew or could have known and thus help to explain gaps in a text.[16]

We might say, then, that sociology is neither sufficient nor necessary in principle for the understanding of the meaning of revealed texts, although sociology is useful for this task and may even be factually necessary insofar as, without knowledge of it, the task of the interpreter may be impossible. Sociology functions as a handmaiden, an aid; it helps the interpreter to figure out the meaning of words and the limits of concepts, both propaedeutic tasks to the understanding of the views expressed by the text.

Let me put it this way. The interpreter wants to understand, or to cause an understanding of, a revealed text T in an audience. To do this, the interpreter has to understand, or say, that T means M. This involves the explanation of the relation among the concepts expressed in T, including the analysis of the views it expresses, all of which constitutes a non-sociological account. But in order to produce this account, the interpreter also has to know, for example, how the words in T were used at the time in which T was produced, the semantic import of certain syntactical arrangements, and so on. This sociological knowledge is not part of the interpretation properly speaking, but it helps to produce it.

Theology, on the other hand, is necessary to the extent that much of what a text means is contingent on beliefs that are not expressed in the text but are taken for granted. Outside the theological context, these revealed texts can tell us little or nothing about what they purport to say and about what those who regard them as revealed think they are concerned with.

Determining Sources and Influences

Another aim that interpreters of revealed texts often have is to determine sources and influences.[17] In principle, we should distinguish between the sources and influences of a revealed text and the sources and influences of the views of an instrumental author, as well as between sources and influences themselves. But in fact we can dispense with these distinctions for our limited purposes here.

Concerning an instrumental author, we should consider at least two cases for purposes of illustration. In one case, interpreters wish to settle whether a particular instrumental author A_1 borrowed view P_1 from another author A_2, who also held view P_1. In another case, interpreters want to explain how an instrumental author A_1 derived view P_1 from view P_2 that was held by A_2. Both cases require interpreters to engage in considerations that involve language and other sociological factors. Take the case of an instrumental author whose native tongue is different from that of the author from whom she is supposed to have borrowed or derived a view. Obviously, it is important to know whether the alleged borrower knew the language of the earlier author or not, or whether she had access to only a translation of the work in which the view was propounded. These considerations are sociological insofar as they involve reference to social phenomena, but they are nonetheless important for the interpretive task.

It should not be forgotten, however, that a prerequisite of explaining the relation of dependence between views is understanding the views in question and how they are related. Suppose that the views are not expressed in exactly equivalent language, or that they are so expressed that one looks like the logical consequence of the other. In order to show how in fact this is so, interpreters must understand the views and establish the relations among them, and this makes sociology dependent on theology insofar as the key to those views and relations might be found in theological doctrines held by the authors of the texts. Theology may provide the missing links between the different views and explain why they were adopted. Determining sources and influences for the most part presupposes understanding the meaning of revealed texts, and these in turn require taking into account theological contexts. This means that sociology is not sufficient by itself to determine sources and influences, although it is both necessary and useful for it.

Identifying Causes

Another aim of the interpretation of revealed texts is to identify the causes that give rise to views expressed by them or, paraphrasing Collins in a more general context, what determines the creativity of authors and the topics they choose.[18] This is an important aspect of the interpretive task, for the core of all understanding is the explanation of why something occurred, and the answer to this question generally identifies the cause(s) of it. A full interpretation must include the description of causes. For an understanding of revealed texts, this explanation involves establishing the causes that gave rise to the views expressed by them.

It is here that the greatest disagreement occurs concerning how the interpretation of texts in general is to be carried out, for in most cases different causal analyses can in principle be given of the same fact, and different interpreters favor different approaches. In answering the question Why does text T say P? a culturalist, for example, will say that it is essential to refer to the cultural context in which T was produced. The argument for this is that a revealed text is a cultural phenomenon and, therefore, requires a cultural explanation. In order to understand why T says P, it is necessary to know the surrounding cultural context and to see how that context relates to T and to P.

Someone who favors socially oriented interpretations will argue in a similar fashion: The answer to why T says P makes no sense unless one looks at the society in which T was produced, because humans are social animals who live and interact with each other and whose actions and views are regulated and determined by those social relations. Therefore, this answer needs to include a reference to the author of T, to the social context in which the author produced T, and to the relation of that social context to T, the author, and P.

The interpreter who favors political explanations will produce a similar argument. The answer to why T expresses P requires that we look at the political situation under which the author of T worked. An author's views are subject to political pressures, and so their appearance or disappearance must take those pressures into account.

These and other types of sociological accounts are considered essential for the explanation of the views expressed in texts, including revealed texts, by those who favor a sociological approach. Understanding revealed texts requires understanding the cultural, social, political, and other similar causes that surrounded the authors who produced them and that, it is argued, are responsible to a large extent, if not exclusively, for those views. A non-sociological explanation of why a revealed text expresses certain views is not adequate and is in fact, according to many of those who favor sociological explanations, inaccurate. For the real reasons why these views are expressed have often nothing to do with their worth and the evidence that is mustered in their favor. The real reason they are held is that they respond to cultural biases, social relations, political pressures, biographical events, and so on. We already heard echoes of this argument earlier.

But are sociological explanations relevant to the interpretation of revealed texts? Is the interpreter of revealed texts searching for causal analyses that explain why an author composed a text that expresses a particular view on the basis of cultural, social, political, biographical, and similar phenomena? Or is the interpreter searching for something else?

Interpreters who seek to understand, or to produce, a religious understanding of revealed texts answer yes to the last question. Sociological explanation is not the kind of explanation appropriate in the interpretation of revealed texts because it does not explain why the instrumental authors in question expressed the views presented in the texts they produced. One may be able to identify various sorts of sociological factors that played a role in the production of the texts. What Peckhaus says about philosophy is also true, *mutatis mutandis,* about theology: "Philosophical work is not only determined by the progress in the thoughts of the working philosophers but also by the heuristic which they follow, which may, however, not be explicitly formulated. It is determined by their tacit knowledge, accepted at their time, or by external factors to autonomous thinking like the discussion within the discipline or the reception of preceding or competing conceptions of treating a topic."[19] The interpreter of revealed texts, *qua* interpreter of *revealed texts,* however, is not interested in those factors but rather in the religious reasons that explain why the author of the text expressed the views he or she did. And this is so because those are the factors that would have, should have, or actually have influenced the author when the author was acting as an author of a revealed text.

The point that needs to be stressed is that in order to understand why the author of a revealed text makes a claim, it is essential to refer to the bona fide reasons the author gave for them, but not just in the sense that we impute them to him or her, but in the sense in which he or she held them. To do this involves no sociological account, although the particular choice of reasons and evidence used by the author to support his or her claim could be explained sociologically.

Consider the following situation: An interpreter of a revealed text wants to explain why author A held Q. Many explanations are possible, but let us consider five:

1. A held Q because:
   a. A knew that $P \supset Q$, and
   b. A knew that P, and
   c. A knew that $[(P \supset Q) . P] \supset Q$.
2. A held Q because:
   a. A was part of group S (e.g., a society, a religious community), and
   b. S encouraged belief in Q.
3. A held Q because:
   a. A wanted to get X, and
   b. holding Q was a way of getting X.
4. A held Q because:
   a. God revealed Q to A.
5. A held Q because:
   a. A believed that God revealed Q to him.

The differences between these five explanations of why A held Q should be quite clear. Account 1 reveals the relation between A's view that Q and other of A's views; account 2 reveals the relation between A's view that Q and the social group of which A was a part; account 3 reveals the relation between A's view that Q and A's wants; account 4 identifies a divine cause for A's view; and account 5 points out a relation between A's beliefs and the view A held. Account 5 is in fact a particular case of account 1. Now, my contention is that although different interpreters of revealed texts may be searching for different accounts, those who believe the texts are revealed, and for whom the texts are presumably intended, primarily search for accounts of the fourth type. This makes theological interpretations essential for the understanding of these texts not just for believers, but for non-believers as well. The reason is that even non-believers need to understand the nature of the texts.

Revelation is supposed to be the product of a divinity's attempt to communicate his or her wishes primarily to those who believe in him or her. To understand a revealed text as nothing like this is precisely to misunderstand what it is about; it is to try to understand the text outside its accepted social function and, therefore, to misunderstand its message. Indeed, it would be very much like trying to understand a philosophical text non-philosophically. Let me dwell on this point a bit further and use the case of philosophy as an illustration. In this way, it will become clear that the situation with the interpretation of revealed texts is not idiosyncratic but has parallels in the case of other kinds of texts.

Philosophy is supposed to be a conscious, deliberate activity, the search for views supported by reasons. Certainly this position has been dominant in the West—otherwise, much of what Western philosophers say would make little sense. To ignore, then, the reasons that philosophers claim determine their views, whether in fact they do or do not, in favor of causes that they do not acknowledge is to miss an essential aspect of the enterprise in question. The problem with exclusively sociological histories of philosophy is not that they are not philosophical, but that they are inaccurate, for they neglect to give proper weight to factors that philosophers claim are most important for their views. In doing so, they fail to provide a proper explanation of philosophical facts.

Consider the case of Wittgenstein. Bloor argues, in an article to which reference has already been made, that Wittgenstein's conservative views are better understood in terms of the conservative views of the society in which he lived.[20] The argument is not just that Wittgenstein shared conservative views with the society in which he lived, but also that Wittgenstein held those views because he was a member of that society (something like account 2 above). Now, let us assume that this is true, although the explanatory jump here is rather large, as should be obvious (there are all sorts of assumptions about the argument that are not made explicit or defended). Still, Bloor's explanation does not allude to the most important element for anyone who wants to understand Wittgenstein's philosophy, namely the reasons Wittgenstein gave for holding the views he held. Now, one may argue that those reasons were not in fact the causes of his holding those views. And one may argue further that those reasons were mere rationalizations, or that they were ideological, or whatever. But the fact is that these were reasons given by

Wittgenstein, and given as philosophical reasons, and interpreters of philosophical texts should pay attention to them when they are trying to present an account that explains why the views in question were held. The reasons should be looked at and judged for the account of the philosophical thought of Wittgenstein to be complete or even intelligible.

Unfortunately, this fact does not seem to impress many of those who favor sociological accounts. Indeed, some go so far as to offer explanations that contradict the author's explicitly stated views. For example, Cristina Chimisso argues that Bachelard has been made into a mythical figure, through the manipulation of various symbols available to the culture, by a cadre of followers from diverse backgrounds who view this constructed image of Bachelard as essential to the understanding of his significance.[21] This, she accurately notes, contrasts with Bachelard's own explicit views, for he carefully separated the scientific, rational, objective, and anti-mythical from the biographical, imaginative, social, subjective, and mythical. Yet, in a paradoxical move characteristic of sociological accounts, Chimisso concludes that Bachelard himself contributed to this myth by creating a myth when speaking of the rational and disinterested scientist: "the myth of the absence of myth." Now, since this conclusion contradicts Bachelard's explicit views, what help can it give us in understanding Bachelard himself, from his own point of view, as it were? Does it help us see what Bachelard saw or thought he saw? Does it help us understand how, on his own grounds, he arrived at the conclusions to which he arrived? Does it aid us in grasping the relations between his views and the reasons he gave for them? The sociological account Chimisso gives does help us understand how others saw Bachelard and why he has become a kind of cult figure, but it does not help us understand Bachelard himself. And understanding Bachelard himself is essential for the historian of philosophy.

The neglect of arguments and reasons explicitly offered by philosophers for their views seems often capricious and based on the prejudices of sociologists, who often do not appear to understand the philosophical *modus operandi*. Consider the case of John Duns Scotus's views on individuation. His discussion of this topic is contained in the *Ordinatio* and covers more than 60 pages, which are devoted almost entirely to tightly constructed arguments against views he opposes and for the view he supports.[22] The issue that concerns him is the cause or principle of individuation, that is, what makes something individual (e.g., this cat) as opposed to universal (e.g., cat). Scotus considers and rejects all the views of his predecessors: individuation by form, matter, accidents, existence, and so on. He charges that these views are inadequate to explain what makes something individual and proposes that the principle of individuation is something *sui generis*, a decharacterized formality he called, for lack of a better name, *haecceitas* (i.e., thisness). Now, a typical argument of Scotus against the views he rejects is that the view in question is contradictory. For example, he argues thus against accidental views of individuation: An accidental view of individuation relies on the distinction between substance and accident and the view that accidents depend on substance for their being. But the view that accidents individuate implies that substance depends on accidents for its being, for the individuality of the substance is due to the accidents. Therefore, the accidental view of individuation is contradictory.

Yet, the sociological interpreter would have us believe that we should take Scotus's enormous argumentative effort with skepticism and concentrate rather on sociological factors such as the power struggle between religious orders in the university, the hostilities between Franciscan Spirituals and those opposed to them, the rivalry between the papacy and secular governments, and other sociological phenomena of the later Middle Ages. The correct explanation of Scotus's view on individuation, from the sociological perspective, does not consist in the reasons he gave for it, but rather in the fact, for example, that he was a Franciscan and wanted to uphold the Order's traditional doctrines. (Of course, this does not explain why Scotus went against traditional Franciscan doctrines many times.[23]) The real reason he rejected an accidental view of individuation is not that such a view was contradictory within the Aristotelian framework he largely accepted, as he explicitly claimed, but rather some other reason that had to do with medieval society or his own particular situation.

Does this make sense? Shouldn't an interpreter take account of something that we know actually happened, such as the reasons Scotus gave for his views, rather than second-guessing him in terms of claims about "sociological" factors whose connection with his views are highly speculative and based on certain methodological assumptions? And what do all these sociological factors really have to do with Scotus's theory of *haecceitas?* I challenge sociological interpreters to explain sociologically, on purely sociological grounds, why Scotus held *haecceitas* rather than accidents, for example, to be the principle of individuation. When I see that done in a credible way, I will begin to take more seriously the claims of sociological interpreters of philosophical texts.

But there is even more than this. For, even if the sociologist were successful in explaining that Scotus in fact rejected an accidental principle of individuation because of some sociological factor, this would not make clear the inconsistency he said he saw, as a philosopher, in the view he criticized. As an interpreter of philosophical texts, I need to understand the inconsistency Scotus saw in this position. And this inconsistency is not made evident to me by sociological analyses, but rather by an investigation of the relations among ideas.

The exclusivist sociological point of view, if carried to its logical conclusion, has even more alarming consequences for religion than for philosophy. Indeed, an exclusively sociological point of view implies that revelation is a grandiose hoax and that the instrumental authors of revealed texts and religious believers are malicious hypocrites or stupid dupes, for their views are not held because of the value they see in them and the reasons they explicitly give for them. Well, even though this is so in some or perhaps in many cases, it hardly justifies the conception of revelation as a whole in exclusively, or even primarily, sociological terms.

Learning a Lesson

The last aim of the interpretation of revealed texts to which I shall refer is to learn from them. Adapting Brentano's well-turned phrase about philosophy to this case, we could say that the ultimate aim of revelation must always be the exposition of divine truth. This is a common reason that interpreters identify for engaging in the interpretation of revelation. I am not going to question whether in fact this is a bona fide reason or even whether it is an acceptable one. For my purposes, it suffices to point out that it is frequently given, and accepted: One of the aims of interpretation of revelation is to learn divine truth.

If we accept this, we must also grant that the interpretation of revealed texts must be done in such a way that we can learn a divine message from them. But then, we may ask, what can we learn about these texts from exclusively sociological accounts? One thing we can learn, of course, is to be on our guard against rationalizations based on sociological and ideological pressures. Understanding that sociological forces have an impact on believers can help believers be more deliberate and conscious of how and why they think the way they do. Moreover, the sociological interpretation of revealed texts can make everyone more honest and modest interpreters by bringing attention to the limitations of the procedures used.

All this is useful, but none of it is a positive contribution to the interpretive task, for we cannot learn divine truth from sociological analyses; we can learn only sociological truth. This is another reason why the interpretation of revealed texts must be done in a way concordant with their function as revealed, and why sociological analyses do not have the same interest for believers as theological analyses of revealed texts have. The interpreter of revealed texts must engage in judgments of theological value in order to teach us about the religious significance of the texts. By contrast, the sociologist cannot, *qua* sociologist, make judgments of theological value. Sociologists can only describe the sociological factors that give rise to a view, but they cannot in good conscience, as sociologists, tell us whether a view is theologically good or bad, or whether an argument offered in its favor is sound or not. Only the believer, or perhaps someone who adopts a believer's viewpoint, can do this. Therefore, only the interpreter who does the interpretation of revealed texts theologically can truly understand these texts and help an audience learn from them what they are supposed to teach.

Answer to the Arguments for and against Sociological Accounts

What has been said means that I find value in some of the arguments offered earlier in favor of sociological interpretations of revelation as well as in some of the arguments offered against their use. It also means that my position will not satisfy ideological purists on either side of the controversy.

With respect to the arguments in favor of sociological interpretations, I agree, first, that the reasons some authors hold certain views have often very little to do with the reasons they give and can be traced to sociological factors of various sorts. But I disagree that because of this, sociological factors are always essential to the interpretation of revealed texts. There is no logical requirement to refer to them in the interpretation of these texts, although they can be very helpful in the ways I have stated.

With respect to the second argument, it is not true that all non-sociological accounts of revealed texts assume the existence of deities and the truth of unproven doctrines. Certainly philosophical interpretations do not. But it is true that theological interpretations do, although this is to be expected and is even, as I have argued, of the essence if the interpretation of revealed texts is to have any theological significance.

Finally, it is obvious that religious views and reasons belong to social beings engaged in social relations. To deny this would be absurd. But this does not entail that religious views and reasons are not related in non-social ways or are exclusively the product of social factors. Sociological interpreters go too far when they try to reduce theological relations to social ones.

The arguments given against sociological interpretations also go to extremes. It is true that there is considerable latitude on what sociological interpreters consider sociological explanations, but this certainly does not preclude the possibility of a common core to all or most sociological explanations. Nor does the vagueness and generality of some sociological interpretations imply that all of them are or must be so.

I agree entirely with the second and third arguments given earlier against the use of sociological interpretations in the understanding of revealed texts, but these arguments affect only views that either entirely exclude theological ones or try to blur the distinction between sociology and theology. For reasons I have already stated, I disagree with both strategies. A purely sociological interpretation of revealed texts is necessarily incomplete. And the attempt to blur the distinction between sociology and theology by reducing theology to sociology is as misguided as that of reducing sociology to theology. Both attempts beg the question and do not do justice to the disciplines or their histories.

Conclusion

In sum, sociological analyses have a place in the interpretation of revelation, but their role depends on the aim of the interpretation and in most cases is propaedeutic and ancillary. Sociological analyses are useful in that they help determine the views expressed in texts by instrumental authors and understood by particular audiences, and the influences and sources of those views. Moreover, in some cases, such analyses are factually necessary insofar as only through them can we have access to certain views and explain why they have been held or entertained. This is the role sociological interpretations should appropriately play, but to extend such a role beyond these parameters and give sociological analyses priority over theological ones, or even to place them at the same level as theological ones, is a serious mistake.

The mistake of those who inordinately favor sociological interpretations of revealed texts is threefold: They mistake the proper role of sociological explanations; they improperly privilege sociological explanations over other explanations, including theological ones; and they tend to forget the essential role of theological explanations in the interpretation of revealed texts. These mistakes can be traced to a misunderstanding of the natures of theology and sociology. I have discussed sociology in this chapter, so now I must turn to theology.

Chapter 6 ❧

Theological Interpretations

In addition to meaning, literary, and sociological interpretations, the other relational approach to the interpretation of revealed texts I wish to discuss is theological. This is a traditional approach that has lost impetus in recent years, although there are some theologians who still both favor and practice it.[1] As we saw, meaning, literary, or sociological interpretations do not do full justice to revelation. The only kind of meaning interpretation that makes sense aims at an understanding of what God wishes believers to understand, but this turns out to be empty. And literary and sociological interpretations, although helpful in some cases, are clearly insufficient in every case to carry out the understanding of revealed texts, *qua* revealed; they are unnecessary in some cases; and in some others they are even unhelpful. The question for us now is whether theology can do the job these interpretations cannot do adequately.

The proposal I make in this chapter is controversial for two reasons: First, theological interpretations of revelation are in general out of favor today; second, I claim that theological interpretations are relational. Most of those few interpreters who still cling to the theological interpretation of revealed texts think of them as meaning interpretations of the authorial kind. Their view is that theological interpretations provide an understanding of what the divinity wishes believers to understand. I claim, on the other hand, that the only interpretation that makes sense for texts regarded as revealed is theological, but that this kind of interpretation is relational rather than authorial.

The discussion of theological interpretations requires at least a working notion of theology. To develop such a notion is by no means easy insofar as there has been fundamental disagreement on the nature of theology from the very beginning. The proposal that follows should be regarded as a modest attempt within the limited parameters of this book.

Theology

In a most general sense, we speak of theology in two ways. In one way, we speak of it as something we have, hold, study, develop, adopt, commit ourselves to, discover, admire, believe, formulate, and state. In another way, we speak of it as something we do, practice, engage in, and carry out. When we speak of theology in the first sense, generally we are thinking of it as a view.[2] The first condition necessary for theology in this sense is that someone hold or may hold it. I say "may hold" because there are theological views probably no one would hold, or could consistently hold. There is no reason why we cannot think of a theological view that not only has never been held but will never be held by anyone. We might examine such a view, consider why it is untenable, and argue against it, even though it will always remain a straw figure.

To be a view is, of course, not enough to qualify something as theology. For one, the view in question must also seek to be accurate, consistent, and supported by sound evidence.[3] Note that I do not say that it is or must be so. Theological views can be inaccurate and inconsistent or have no sound supporting evidence, and yet this does not disqualify them from being theological, just as being bad literature does not disqualify something from being literature, or being a bad person does not disqualify someone from being a person. In order to qualify as theological, a view need not be accurate, consistent, or supported by sound evidence, but it does need to seek to be so. It must seek to be accurate in the sense that it must aim to be faithful to experience understood broadly to include both empirical experience and non-empirical intuitions. It must seek to be consistent because it must attempt to avoid contradiction. And it must seek support in sound evidence because theological views aim to have the status of knowledge, and views without sound support are matters of opinion, rather than knowledge.[4]

The second understanding of theology is as something one does, practices, or engages in. In this sense, theology is an activity rather than a view. It appears at first that the activity in question may be of two sorts. One is the activity whereby a view is produced; another is the activity whereby one seeks to develop the formulation, explanation, and justification of rules according to which the production of such a view must proceed. But clearly the latter activity also involves the production of a view, although in this case it is of proper theological method. Therefore, strictly speaking, it should be subsumed under the general heading of theology. In essence, there is no fundamental distinction between these two sorts of activities.

The notion of theology as an activity generates another, quite widespread conception of theology. Repeated activities create in the subjects who engage in them a certain skill or disposition that Aristotelians call *habitus*.[5] So, in addition to a view and the activity whereby it is developed, we can speak of the disposition or skill of someone who regularly engages in the activity. This is a person who can, unlike others, develop views of the sort sought.

The last two conceptions bring to the fore still another general way in which we speak of theology, namely, as a view concerning theological method.[6] In this sense, a theology consists of the set of rules that must be used to guide the activity that yields theological views; it is a procedure that must be followed to achieve theological knowledge, although its character is also associated with the activity involved in the implementation of rules. Obviously, a theology, understood as a set of rules, can be subsumed under the notion of theology as a view. Still, it is convenient to keep it separate because of its peculiarity and in order to prevent confusion. We have, then, four different general ways in which we speak of theology:

1. A view that seeks to be accurate, consistent, and supported by sound evidence
2. The activity whereby 1 is developed
3. The skill, disposition, or capacity present in those who regularly engage in 2
4. The rules that are to be followed in the formulation of 1

Obviously, 1 takes precedence over the others, for it is the aim of all the others and presupposed by them. None of the others makes sense apart from it, even if 1 cannot be developed without the others. If we were speaking in Aristotelian terms, we could express the point by saying that 1 is the final cause, the goal of 2, 3, and 4.

What has been said about theology thus far is not enough to distinguish it from other disciplines. Indeed, we could also speak of philosophy, for example, as a view that seeks to be accurate, consistent, and supported by sound evidence, as an activity whereby this view is developed, as a skill, disposition, or capacity present in those who regularly engage in this activity, and as the rules that are to be followed in the formulation of such a view.[7] So we must next inquire as to what gives theology its distinctive character.

Although philosophers and theologians have often differed on this point amongst themselves, one can easily discern four different positions as well as various ways of integrating them. One position distinguishes theology on the basis of the object with which it is concerned. This is well exemplified in various other disciplines of learning. For example, astronomy is concerned with celestial bodies, ontology is concerned with being, and human anatomy is concerned with the human body. If we adopt this approach, we should be able to point to an object, group of objects, or kind of object with which theology, and only theology, is concerned.

A second position finds the distinguishing characteristic of theology in its method. Again, other fields of inquiry serve as support and illustration of this approach. For example, it is customary to distinguish chemistry from physics based on the different methods each uses, rather than the objects with which they are concerned, for these objects can be, and often are, the same.

A third position finds the distinguishing difference of theology in its aim. As in the previous cases, there are similarities with the way other disciplines are distinguished that support this claim. For example, one may point to the fact that the difference between ethics and politics concerns their aims: In ethics, it is the good of the individual; in politics, it is the good of the state. Or one may cite the cases of medicine and veterinary science, whose aims are the health of human and non-human animals respectively.

Finally, a fourth position identifies the difference that sets theology apart from other disciplines with the kind of knowledge it yields. Often, this is understood in terms of propositions (or statements, sentences, or judgments, depending on the theologian). Authors who distinguish theology in these terms point out that theological propositions are different from the propositions of other disciplines. And, indeed, even a simple inspection of theological propositions indicates that this may be so. A proposition such as "Christ is God" is quite different from the propositions we find in the works of physicists and psychologists.

It is not often that we find authors who exclusively and explicitly argue in favor of one of these approaches and against the others. Most often we find that authors argue for one of them and either neglect the others or subordinate them to the one they favor. Moreover, many attempts have been made to integrate two or more into one.[8]

We need not search much in history to find these various approaches at work in the general classification of human knowledge. One of the earliest attempts to make distinctions among our views based on their objects is illustrated by Plato's divided line in the *Republic*.[9] The purpose of this line appears to be to distinguish among various kinds of knowledge on the basis of their objects. Knowledge properly speaking is only of intelligible entities, whereas opinion concerns only sensible objects. The kind of object, then, determines how we can know it and what we can know about it.[10] Naturally, because this view can be used to distinguish among various kinds of knowledge, it in turn gives rise to the position that the object determines the kind of knowledge. Often, those who adopt this perspective speak of the subject or subject matter of knowledge, rather than its object.[11] There are several reasons for this terminology: Some think in terms of a subject in which features or characteristics inhere; others think of subjects of predications in sentences; and still others conceive the subject as the object considered in relation to a knower or under a certain perspective, whence the use of the term 'formal object.'[12] Moreover, they contrast these with the objects toward which mental or perceptual faculties are directed.[13]

Aristotle's attempt to develop criteria of scientific knowledge in *Posterior Analytics*, on the other hand, may be taken as illustrating a different approach, which holds that method distinguishes among different kinds of knowledge.[14] For Aristotle, scientific knowledge is characterized by the use of demonstrative reasoning. Demonstrative reasoning is deductive reasoning known to be valid and based on true premises that are known to be true because they are not themselves mediated through other knowledge. If Aristotle had ended with this, one could say that, contrary to Plato, he distinguished scientific knowledge exclusively on the basis of the method by which it is attained.[15] But Aristotle went further and added that scientific knowledge must be knowledge of the universal and of what is real, and that the premises of the reasoning that yields scientific knowledge must be related to the conclusions as causes are to effects.[16] Obviously, these conditions go beyond method and concern the object of knowledge itself.

The aim has also been used to distinguish among different kinds of knowledge. Aristotle's own distinction between theoretical and practical sciences illustrates the point.[17] What distinguishes these sciences is that the former have knowledge as their aim, whereas the latter are intended to guide action.

Finally, the kind of knowledge, or the kind of proposition, has also been used to distinguish disciplines from each other. There are antecedents of this attempt in the Middle Ages. Ockham's view that sciences are distinguished by the subjects and predicates of the propositions of which they are composed sets an important precedent.[18] But it is with Kant's characterization of metaphysical and mathematical judgments as synthetic *a priori* that this view entered the mainstream.[19] This idea was adopted by the logical positivists, who considered metaphysical and theological propositions a particular kind of nonsense, and ethical propositions as expressions of feelings.[20]

Naturally, there have been intermediary positions and positions that combine two or three of the mentioned ways of distinguishing the disciplines. For example, Aquinas, although emphasizing the object, argued that it is that object considered under the formal aspect under which it is studied that yields differences. Clearly, this is a way of recognizing the importance of method (that is, how the object is viewed or approached) as well among the distinguishing factors of a discipline.[21]

Theology comes in two main varieties: natural and revealed.[22] The first is based on the consideration of nature through natural means exclusively; the second is based on the examination of revelation based on faith.[23] In this book, the concern is exclusively with revealed theology. The question at hand, then, is how theology, understood in this sense, can be distinguished from other disciplines. Is it the object, method, aim, or the propositions of which it is composed that distinguish it?

It would make sense to choose the object as the distinguishing mark of revealed theology if an object could be found that is its exclusive concern, but this is not easy. God is most often identified as the object of revealed theology.[24] After all, the very etymology of the term 'theology' suggests it. However, natural theology and metaphysics are often also taken to be concerned with God, and yet very few natural theologians and metaphysicians would agree that what they do is revealed theology. Moreover, revealed theology is not exclusively concerned with God. Indeed, in many ways it is concerned with everything in the universe, for theologians want to know not just about God, but also about human nature, and indeed about everything that surrounds them. Some theologians try to account for this expanded object of theological interest by arguing that revealed theology deals with God primarily and with other beings only secondarily insofar as they are related to God.[25] This makes some sense, but it does not quite sharpen the edges of the discipline sufficiently.

The method also could be used to distinguish revealed theology from other disciplines, if revealed theology used only one method and this method were exclusive to it. And, indeed, some have argued that the method based on divine authority gives revealed theology its distinctive character, separating it from all other disciplines of learning.[26] This would require that all claims made in revealed theology would have to be based on appeals to authority. Thus the arguments made would have to have the form 'P is true because authority X says so.'

This, however, does not work for at least two reasons. First, revealed theology does not use the method of authority exclusively, but also uses methods developed and employed in other disciplines, such as exegesis, analysis of language and arguments, observation, and so on.[27] Not every claim made in theology refers directly back to what an authority says. Even arguments that take the form 'P is true because it is implied by Q, which is found in the authoritative source M' require more than authority to be established. Indeed, they rely on such notions as implication, which is part of logic, not revelation. Second, the method of authority is used in other disciplines to some extent as well, even if the source of the authority in question is different from that used in revealed theology. Indeed, there is no discipline in which authority does not play some role. What counts as scientific discovery, philosophical contribution, or artistic achievement is generally accepted as such on the basis of the authority of experts in the pertinent fields. One could object, however, that in science, for example, it is not the authority of the expert that ultimately counts, but rather the evidence that backs it up and the truth that the position proposed by the authority reveals. This ob-

jection, however, does not work insofar as the same could be applied to revealed theology: Ultimately it is not the authority of the theologian, or even
of a text, that counts, but rather the fact that God has revealed certain truths.

The nature or identity of the propositions that constitute a theology
could also in principle be regarded as the source of the distinction between
theology and other disciplines. It makes sense to say that theology is distinguished from physics, for example, because theology is composed of propositions X, Y, and Z, whereas physics is composed of propositions P and Q.[28]
The problem with this view is that it does not explain the ultimate bases of
the distinction. Why does one discipline not have the same propositions, or
the same kind of propositions, as another?[29] Surely the propositions are different because of some, more fundamental, distinction, and if this is so, what
ultimately distinguishes the disciplines is not the propositions themselves,
but rather what determines which propositions belong to them.

Finally, we come to the aim, and here is where we find the key to the
problem of how to distinguish revealed theology from other disciplines. But
we must be careful. Clearly there are some aims that do not make it possible for revealed theology to be distinguished from other disciplines. To say,
for example, that the aim of revealed theology is the understanding of the
world, or the truth, or some such general aim, is not helpful, for this is what
all disciplines purport to be trying to achieve. The key to getting the aim of
revealed theology right, and therefore to separating it effectively from other
enterprises of learning, is to realize we are dealing with *revelation,* so the understanding pursued by revealed theology must concern revelation. One
could hold, then, that the aim of revealed theology is to develop a view of
the world, or any of its parts, that seeks to be accurate, consistent, and supported by sound evidence based on revelation.

Even this formula is not quite clear, or perhaps it is not even quite right,
for it seems to suggest that the evidence considered by revealed theology is
exclusively restricted to revealed texts. And, indeed, many theologians have
claimed just this.[30] But nothing could be further from the truth. It is true
that most practitioners of revealed theology give revealed texts a special status. These texts are supposed to have been given to a group of believers in
order to provide them with a divine message; so their importance can never
be overstated. But this does not invalidate other sources of information and
truth that theologians may have at their disposal. Indeed, theologians come
to revealed texts already equipped with a body of knowledge built on the
human natural powers of observation and reasoning, that is, with a body of
knowledge based on common sense, experience, and science. And it is not
required of theologians that they reject this body of knowledge, or even
question it. Indeed, this knowledge, and the exercise of the powers on which
it is based, is essential to the theological task. No theologian can accomplish

the aim of understanding revelation without using the senses, reason, and experience, and this opens automatically the doors to the body of knowledge already built on these that theologians bring with them when they approach revealed texts.

This has important implications for the object with which revealed theology is concerned and the propositions of which it is composed, but most importantly for the method that it is supposed to use—for the first because the object of revealed theology is in fact everything; it does not have to be God, or the world, or anything in particular, although this does not prevent the understanding produced in revealed theology from establishing an order of importance and value among things.

There are also implications for the propositions that compose revealed theology. As expressions of views based on revelation, but not reducible to revelation, the sum total of the propositions of revealed theology will be different from those of other disciplines, although there is no reason why some of the propositions of revelation may not also be found in other disciplines. For example, the proposition 'God exists' may be found in revealed texts and in texts of natural theology, and the proposition 'St. Paul was a Roman citizen' may be found in revealed theology and in history. But there will be propositions in revealed theology that will not be found in any other discipline, such as 'Christ is God.' Keep in mind that by 'found' I mean "used" and asserted, not just "mentioned" or denied. The proposition 'Christ is God' may be mentioned by historians of Christianity in a sentence like 'Christians believe that "Christ is God."' And it may be said to be false by a non-believer who states 'It is false that Christ was God.' But the proposition 'Christ is God' cannot be used and asserted in any inquiry except Christian theology, for it is only a Christian believer who regards it as true.

For theological method, the implications of what has been said are substantial insofar as the fundamental basis of theological understanding is revelation. The appeal to authority, then, is essential to the method of revealed theology, although this does not rule out other methods as long as these are compatible with and subservient to authority.[31] Remember that revealed theology is a view that seeks to be accurate and consistent, and these aims open the doors to evidence other than scriptural, namely experience and reason. Still, authority is primary in the understanding of revelation. But what exactly does it mean to say that authority is primary in the understanding of revelation, and how exactly do theologians proceed?

The Method of Theology

Theologians come to revelation with an already formed body of knowledge based on personal and social experiences, common sense, cultural views, and scientific theories. This knowledge is vast, even in cases in which the theologians live in societies that appear to be relatively simple. The task of theologians is to bring together into a consistent body of knowledge the divine message contained in revelation and the body of knowledge that they derive from their experience and understanding of the world independently of revelation.[32] This task is not easy because usually neither the divine message nor the body of knowledge independent of this message is simple. The greatest difficulty does not lie here, however, but rather in the conflicts that appear between these two bodies of knowledge. What are theologians supposed to do when they encounter a contradiction between revelation and science, for example? Consider the following two propositions:

From revelation: God created the world in six days.
From science: The world took its present form in a process that lasted millions of years.

In order to see exactly whether and where there is a contradiction between these two propositions, we must subject them to analysis. The claims made, or assumed, by the first could be broken down as follows:[33]

R1: God exists.
R2: The world exists.
R3: God is the creator of the world.
R4: The world was formed in six days.

Now let us look at the claims made, or assumed, by the scientific statement:

S1: The world exists.
S2: The world was formed in millions of years.

If we put together these two sets of sentences into one set, it becomes clear that the set is consistent except for the contradiction between R4 and S2. No sentence of S says anything about God, or about the causes of the world, so there is nothing in the set of scientific sentences that contradicts sentences R1 and R3 of the set of revealed sentences. But the contradiction between R4 and S2 is sufficient to generate a problem for the theologian, who is trying, *qua* theologian, to develop a consistent view of the world based on revelation. What can the theologian do?

Two alternatives suggest themselves and have often been adopted at various times in the history of this controversy: to reject revelation[34] or to reject science.[35] The first alternative is unacceptable because it entails that believers give up their beliefs, rejecting most of what imparts meaning and structure to their lives. Moreover, it invalidates deep personal experiences and entails that religion is a hoax, or a superstition, based on deception. This seems *prima facie* unacceptable even to the objective non-believer who is trying to understand religion. It makes no sense simply and dogmatically to reject religious experience and belief because it conflicts with science, particularly when science is often found wanting and has a long history of mistakes. Let us not forget phlogiston.

The second alternative, to give up science, is not more appealing; for it entails a surrender of our most basic tools for checking opinion and developing knowledge. To give up science is to give up reason, and to give up reason is to open the doors to everything that is whimsical and arbitrary; it is, in fact, to surrender a fundamental part of our humanity.

A third alternative tries to find a middle ground between these two extremes. At least two possibilities open up. One is to say that the conflict between revelation and science is apparent because in fact the statements in each case deal with different subject matter.[36] This position makes sense in some cases, but unfortunately not in others. The example given above is an instance of those in which it does not (R4 and S2 are about the same thing). More than this is required to avoid contradiction. This brings us to another possibility, also favored historically: to reject the apparent meaning of revelation in favor of a deeper meaning concordant with non-revealed knowledge. This entails developing a view in which revealed texts can have at least two levels of meaning—one apparent and one real. The apparent meaning is simply a metaphorical way of grasping the real meaning. In the example we have been using, the apparent meaning of R4 is exactly what the sentence says, namely that the world was formed in six days. In this way, terms used in the sentence are taken to mean what they mean in ordinary speech: 'six' means six, and 'day' means day. By contrast, the real meaning of R4 does not have to do with days taken in the ordinary sense of the term. What it means exactly is, of course, a matter of debate and can be settled only within a particular hermeneutical framework of revelation. This is a primarily epistemic task that is beyond the parameters of the discussion in this book.[37] For our purposes, it is enough that it could mean something concordant with S2 and, therefore, eliminate the apparent contradiction between the revealed truth and the scientific truth.

This way of eliminating contradictions between revelation and science has been favored by many theologians from mainstream Western religions such as Christianity and Islam.[38] The question that remains concerns both the statements of revelation to which this procedure should be applied and the extent to which it should be applied. Is every text of revelation that contradicts a statement of science to be understood metaphorically? Or are there some statements of revelation that are to be taken as having only one meaning, even if that meaning contradicts the claims of science?[39]

But there is more to it than this, for revelation consists of texts, and these texts are understandable to us because they are about the things we know and experience. So knowledge and experience of these things is essential for this understanding. If revelation uses a metaphor of a tree to illustrate some religious truth, in order to grasp the truth we need to know the pertinent aspects of the tree on which the metaphor is based. And the same can be said about other images and concepts used in revelation. Moreover, revealed texts are physical objects and this presupposes certain powers of observation on the part of those who try to understand them. And these texts are rendered in natural languages, composed of terms with particular meanings and governed by particular grammatical rules.[40] Knowledge of all these is essential for the understanding of the texts. Revelation does not occur in an epistemological and ontological vacuum; on the contrary, it occurs in the world of human knowledge and experience.

Consider, for example, the Christian doctrine of the Trinity. Here we have a case of a doctrine that attempts to make sense of several texts of the Christian scriptures. None of these texts presents the doctrine as formulated by the Councils of the Church: There is one substance and three persons, the Father, the Son, and the Holy Spirit. In trying to understand the statements made in the Scriptures and integrate the resulting understandings into a consistent view, theologians borrowed the language of philosophy current at the time. God becomes one substance but three distinct persons. This is a clear appropriation of Greek philosophical terminology and concepts into Christian theology. The doctrines expressed by the Scriptures are articulated into a coherent doctrine in terms of the knowledge available at the time.

This attempt at understanding faith through reason illustrates how the interpretation of revelation relies on already accepted knowledge and conceptual frameworks. Scriptures can speak only in the context, and with the help, of what is already accepted on the basis of reason and experience. Indeed, if we were to look further, we would find that most scriptural interpretations, whether Christian or not, depend on already established conceptual schemes and extensive views about the world based on science, common sense, and experience. Revelation speaks to believers precisely through the means they understand, and these means are not themselves always based on revelation, even though they often rely on definite views about the divinity and the world. Moreover, the very task of theologians, even of those who are adamant about not mixing revealed truths with natural knowledge, requires this natural knowledge. Consider that some theologians argue that the task of the interpreter of revelation is merely to draw out inferences from revealed truths, making explicit through deductions what is implicit in them.[41] But this very task is impossible without the use of natural knowledge, such as logical rules of inference, logical principles such as the principle of non-contradiction and the principle of identity, knowledge of languages, and so on. So, it makes no sense to speak of revelation outside these parameters.

To this some have responded by making a distinction between two ways of understanding reason. One is merely as the capacity of intellectual apprehension in general, and the other as the knowledge derived without revelation.[42] Most theologians accept the first, but the second is controversial. Some argue that because of the current imperfect state of human reason in the first sense, reason in the second sense is unreliable. My view is that this division is artificial and unsustainable. Human natural capacities cannot be acceptable while their product is not. So we must take reason as one, namely, as the human natural capacity to know and as the product of that capacity, whatever that may be.

Finally, let me make clear that the claim that reason, understood broadly to include both human natural powers and the knowledge these powers yield, is necessary for the understanding of revelation and thus an essential part of theology does not imply that faith is the same as this understanding. Reason is a condition of faith, but faith is not reducible to reason.[43] Faith involves much more. In Christian theology, faith is primarily conceived as a spiritual, supernatural gift bestowed on some, who as a result are not only enlightened in some ways unavailable to those who do not receive it, but are also saved. Christian theologians frequently disagree as to what this means exactly. Some tend to view it as a personal encounter with God,[44] whereas others conceive it as a kind of knowledge. It is in the latter sense that theologians speak of articles of faith, that is, fundamental doctrines of the Christian Faith.[45]

Let me summarize, then. Revealed theology can be taken in three ways:

1. A view that seeks to be accurate, consistent, and supported by sound evidence founded primarily on revelation and integrated with views developed by science and those generally accepted and based on common sense and experience
2. The activity whereby 1 is developed
3. The skill, disposition, or capacity of those who regularly engage in 2
4. The rules that are to be followed in the formulation of 1.

Of course, 1 has priority over 2, 3, and 4, and its aim, paraphrasing the well-known Anselmian formula, is the understanding of revelation. Now we can turn to theological interpretations.

Theological Interpretations

In chapter 2, two kinds of interpretations were introduced: understandings (i.e., interpretations$_1$) and texts aimed to cause understandings (i.e., interpretations$_2$). In principle, then, there are also two kinds of theological interpretations of revealed texts: the understanding of revealed texts and texts that aim to cause an understanding of revealed texts. An example of the first would be the acts of understanding that a theologian, or someone else working within a religious tradition, has when he or she tries to understand a revealed text. An example of the second would be a commentary on a revealed text, such as Augustine's *Literal Commentary on "Genesis."* For our present purposes, however, this distinction is not important. Most of what will be said here about the theological interpretation of revealed texts applies to both interpretations$_1$ and interpretations$_2$.

A more pertinent distinction for our purposes is that between meaning and relational interpretations. The function of meaning interpretations is the understanding of the meaning of a text in any of the ways we saw that meaning can be taken. The function of relational interpretations is the understanding of a text in terms of something the interpreter brings into play.[46] An important question for us, then, is whether theological interpretations of revealed texts have the first, second, or both functions. I have assumed earlier in this book that they have the second function, but now I must offer some evidence in support of this claim.

The issue is highly controversial, because most religious traditions and theologians claim that their tradition correctly understands what the divinity wants them to understand through the text, what the text means, or the text's meaning and its implications. Moreover, they argue that those who do not understand the text as they do, do not because they misunderstand it, or because they bring into play interpretive elements and principles that should not have been brought into the interpretive process. This amounts to accusing others of providing relational interpretations and passing them as meaning ones, while appropriating meaning interpretations for themselves.

This is the kind of argument that leads nowhere, because it begins by begging the question in a rather brazen way. My interpretation is a meaning interpretation and correct; yours is incorrect and therefore not a meaning interpretation. I am right because I am seeking the meaning of the text; you are wrong because you are seeking to understand the text in terms of elements extraneous to it.

If we are going to grasp at all how theological interpretations work and on what bases they are to be judged, we must put this kind of polemic aside and look at what theologians actually do when they engage in the interpretation of revelation. One thing is quite clear: Theologians always begin within a theological tradition, be that Roman Catholic, Lutheran, Reform Jewish, Shi'ite Muslim, or whatever.[47] No theologian is a theological *tabula rasa*. Moreover, the theological tradition often includes hermeneutical principles that are used in the production of the interpretation. Consider, for example, the case of a Roman Catholic theologian. Her job is to understand revelation in terms of Roman Catholic established theology, that is, the prior interpretations of Fathers, Doctors, and sanctioned theologians of the Church, including papal encyclicals and Catholic dogma. For a Roman Catholic theologian to say that her interpretation is a meaning interpretation is really quite misleading. Perhaps she can say that ultimately what she wishes to do is to understand what God wishes believers to understand, or that she wishes to understand the meaning of a revealed text and its implications. But in fact she is working within preestablished parameters of Roman Catholic theology as context, and she rules out any understanding that contradicts any part of that theology that is considered essential (e.g., dogma). Her interpretation of the revealed text is guided, and affected, by the Roman Catholic theology she brings to the interpretive process.

A distinction introduced in chapter 2 between nominal and real meaning interpretation helps us understand the situation. The Roman Catholic theologian aims to produce a meaning interpretation of the authorial type. She wants to know what God intends for believers to know. But in fact she produces a relational interpretation insofar as God's intended meaning is determined by theological principles the interpreter brings into the picture. Note, moreover, that the dependence of the interpretation on theology is not merely epistemic—as, for example, an interpretation of a Greek text depends on the interpreter's knowledge of Greek. The dependence is ontological, or we might say normative, for what God wishes believers to understand is deemed to have to be in accordance with the theological principles brought into the interpretive process. God means what he ought to mean as judged by Roman Catholic theology.

Now, it is logically possible—indeed, it is expected—that the interpreter will in fact understand what God wishes believers to understand, or that she will understand the meaning of the text or its implications in her efforts to understand the text within the context of the Roman Catholic theological tradition. But this does not contradict the fact that what she has actually done is to understand the text in terms of Roman Catholic theology, and her understanding is inextricably tied to this. The understanding that the Roman Catholic theologian achieves, regardless of its ultimate coincidence with some meaning understanding of revelation, is in fact relational.

Consider two further points in support of this conclusion, one epistemic and one ontological. First, even if it turns out that the theological interpretation coincides with the understanding of God's intended meaning, how can one possibly know this except by appealing to theological principles? Indeed, even if one were to argue that some kind of experience vouches for it—say a mystical vision—how could one accept the trustworthiness of this vision without a theological context that validates it? The vision could be trusted only to the extent that it is supported by a set of doctrines that serves to distinguish it from visions that are not to be trusted, such as hallucinations. Second, the theology the interpreter brings into the interpretation of revelation establishes parameters for it to such an extent that it even rules out some possible interpretations. For example, for a Roman Catholic, no interpretation of revelation could possibly contradict established dogma. Indeed, for Christians in general, no possible interpretation of the scriptures could deny the Trinity and the existence of God, or claim that God is cruel and the Christian scriptures constitute a grand hoax.

The conclusion that the understandings Roman Catholics achieve of revelation are in fact relational, should be acceptable to them insofar as Roman Catholic hermeneutical doctrine grants that revelation must be understood in the context of tradition.[48] Indeed, Roman Catholicism appears to argue that precisely because Roman Catholic interpretations of revelation are relational, the results accurately reveal what God wishes believers to understand through revelation; for there is no wedge between what God wishes believers to understand in a revealed text (or the meaning of the revealed text and its implications) and what believers understand when they understand revelation in terms of Roman Catholic theology.

Other religious traditions, however, might not so easily accept that they are actually engaging in a relational interpretation when they claim they are pursuing a meaning one. Consider, for example, those Christian denominations that adopt as their fundamental principle of scriptural interpretation a very strict understanding of Luther's "*sola Scriptura.*" This would appear to preclude that they be regarded as giving relational rather than meaning interpretations, for their hermeneutical principle prescribes for them a method that appears to be completely non-relational: The task of these interpreters is to understand the Scriptures based merely on the Scriptures.[49] Indeed, this method was first put into place precisely in reaction to the Roman Catholic view that the Scriptures make sense only when understood in a theological context in which tradition plays an important role.[50] For those Christian denominations that strictly apply the method guided by this principle, the interpretation of revelation should not bring into play any theological context. The Scriptures are to be understood on their own terms. The aim of the interpreter is not to understand how they fit, or are related to, something other than the Scriptures, but rather to understand either what God wants believers to know through them or what they mean. (Some might even deny that this understanding should include the implications of the meaning or what

God wishes believers to understand.) In short, the claim is that theological interpretations of revelation are meaning, rather than relational, interpretations, provided proper hermeneutical procedure is followed.

Upon examination, however, this claim can be shown to be unwarranted for various reasons. First, what appears to be a rather innocent hermeneutical principle—*sola Scriptura*—turns out, upon analysis, to be anything but innocent. Indeed, it is quite deceptive insofar as it hides much hermeneutical theory that involves theological commitments of a rather significant nature. If the principle were as innocent as it appears, then the only context that one could use in order to understand a revealed text would be the one in which the revealed text was produced, for that is the only context that presumably played a role in establishing its meaning. Why? Because the very notion that the meaning extends beyond the original understanding is a view about what the text means. In the case of the Judeo-Christian scriptures, this context would have to do with the language in which the text was produced, the historical circumstances that surrounded its production, the instrumental author of the text, and so on. Of course, the interpreter would also be allowed to bring in exegetical, historical, and logical tools in addition to those that have to do with language and writing. These would be allowed because they are either used for the interpretation of all texts of the period in that language or constitute prerequisites of all understanding. Moreover, the aim of the interpreter would not be to understand how the text relates to them, but rather to understand the text by means of them. Going back to the example of the microscope, when I use a microscope to see bacteria, my aim is to see the bacteria, not to understand the relation of the microscope to the bacteria, even though that relation is essential to my seeing, and in fact affects what I actually see. Similarly, when I use my knowledge of history, language, and logic to understand a text, my aim is to understand the text rather than the relation of the text to my knowledge of history, language, and logic, even when the text is intended to be relevant to me. This is the claim.

However, the context that is brought into play by the interpreter committed to the principle of *sola Scriptura* contains much more than this.[51] One thing that it often contains is the view that the Scriptures are to be taken literally.[52] If the Scriptures say, for example, that the world was created in six days, this means that the world was created in six days and did not evolve through many millions of years. But clearly, this is a very strong criterion of interpretation. It is so strong that it creates conflicts between scriptural interpretations and science. Moreover, the rival position to this, according to which the Scriptures should not be interpreted literally but need to be taken in other ways, assumes as much theologically as its opposite.[53] And the same is true of the position that combines these two, which is the most common view not only among Christians but also among those of other religions. For who is the arbiter of the texts that should be taken literally and those that should not? Certainly the believer who acts in accordance with the articulated beliefs of the religion in question. But even if we were to suppose that, for purposes of interpretation, divinely revealed texts are to be treated as other texts in the languages in which they are presented, these texts do not fall into the easily identifiable categories (e.g., literary, historical, legal, scientific, poetic, and so on) we use to determine the ways of going about their interpretation. As a result, it is not clear how revealed texts should be treated and what hermeneutical techniques should be applied to them. Indeed, the fact that believers frequently treat them differently than non-believers confirms their especial status.

Another assumption that the hermeneutical doctrine of *sola Scriptura* often contains is the principle of scriptural inerrancy: The Scriptures contain no errors.[54] But this again is a very strong principle, so strong that it creates conflicts with historical knowledge. So, purely from a hermeneutical standpoint we see that the supposed meaning interpretation of the Scriptures is actually subjected to very strong interpretive criteria that are not applied to other texts and that are not found in the Scriptures themselves. For, where does it say in the Judeo-Christian scriptures that they are to be taken literally and that they are inerrant? There are no such statements in them.[55] But again, even to say that some scriptures are to be taken literally and some others are not, also involves theology. All of this indicates that interpretations based on the principle of *sola Scriptura* are not meaning, but rather relational, interpretations. Indeed, the very canon of the Scriptures to which this principle is applied is not contained in the Scriptures, as some authors explicitly acknowledge.[56]

A third hermeneutical principle that is often associated with the notion of *sola Scriptura* is that the Scriptures must interpret themselves.[57] But again it is difficult to show that this principle is contained in the Scriptures or can be inferred from what they say. The most that can be done is to show that the principle is used in some scriptural texts. But surely this is not enough to justify the stronger claim. Curiously, those who support the principle usually refer to non-scriptural texts for its support, a fact that gives further credence to my claim.[58]

Moreover, the context in question does not include only hermeneutical principles. Indeed, contrary to what proponents of this view might argue, there are theological doctrines and principles that steer the interpretation in definite directions and are brought into the process by the interpreter. Consider, for example, that the very fact that a text is regarded as revealed by a divinity already puts the text on a different footing, taking it out of its historical context and placing it in the context of a set of religious beliefs. These beliefs are then used by the interpreter to understand the text. Some of these concern the divinity itself, who is supposed to have provided the revelation. Among most Christians, for example, this entails that God is one and three, that Christ is God, and so on.[59] Some of these views can be derived, with more or less difficulty, from the Scriptures themselves, but some are not easily derivable and can be explained only in terms of interpretational traditions that take into account more than the Scriptures. Note that my claim is not that the principle of *sola Scriptura* is to be rejected; my claim is that it depends on a theological viewpoint.

Consider also that there is a textual context to a text, and that context is determined by a theological tradition.[60] Take, for example, the Christian scriptures. These scriptures are composed of many different texts, written at different periods of time and under different circumstances. When these texts are put together into a set, the Bible, they become something different than they were, and their interpretation necessarily changes, for the latter must take into account the new textual context. It is one thing to understand Genesis by itself, another to understand it as part of the Pentateuch, and still another to understand it as part of the Christian Bible. Such differences in fact can give rise to different religions, as is the case with Christianity and Judaism. Changing the textual context of a text changes its meaning and effects.[61]

Finally, we come to a most important point: Texts are silent outside of contexts. Texts are marks on a page, sounds uttered, or mental images used to convey meaning. By themselves, the entities that constitute texts have no meaning and have no power to communicate anything.[62] These entities can be used to convey meanings because there are authors and audiences who share contexts that serve to tie meanings to them. In the case of all texts produced within the same linguistic community, this context involves elements common to the members of the community in which they are used.[63] But in the case of texts regarded as revealed, there are also elements that are not common to all members of the linguistic communities and that are supplied by only those within the communities who share particular religious beliefs. These religious beliefs, when organized and systematized, constitute theologies, and it is in the context of these theologies that revealed texts are interpreted. Indeed, texts are regarded as revealed only by those who have certain beliefs, and religious communities use them to deepen their theological understanding. It is also for this reason that all theological interpretations must be regarded as relational.

Some theologians respond to this with the notion of scriptural perspicuity. Indeed, this was one of the major bones of contention between Protestants and Roman Catholics during the Reformation. Roman Catholics argued that the Scriptures are obscure and therefore need to be interpreted by authorities within the bosom of the Church and its tradition.[64] Protestants argued that the Scriptures are perspicuous and accessible to everyone.[65] Roman Catholics responded by pointing to the frequent disagreements among scriptural interpreters. And Protestants responded with a distinction between an internal interpretation (or judgment) and an external one.[66] The internal is the interpretation of the individual person, and it is sufficient for individual needs and salvation.[67] Each believer can, with the help of the Holy Spirit, reach this understanding without the help of authorities.[68] The Scriptures are perspicuous in this sense to everyone who has faith.

The external interpretation concerns a general understanding of the Scriptures that goes beyond individual needs and salvation. Here the interpretation needs to be public and "settled among Christians," as guided by the Holy Spirit and based on the Scriptures. The Scriptures are also perspicuous in this sense, and if there are disagreements and misunderstandings, they are the result of a depraved nature and a faulty faith. The Scriptures are clear in themselves and only obscure to those who are not guided by the Holy Spirit, but by Satan.[69]

It is not my place here to adjudicate who is right and who is wrong with respect to the particulars of this controversy between Roman Catholics and Protestants. Nor is it important for me to dwell on the details of how each of these positions has been understood throughout the history of the Christian Church.[70] My aim is rather to point out that both sides of the controversy rely on certain, and rather obvious, theological views. For example, Roman Catholics rely on the view that the Church, its authoritative bodies, and its tradition, are the final arbiters of scriptural interpretation. Reformation Protestants rely on the view that individual persons and the Church as a whole are the final arbiters of scriptural interpretation when enlightened by the Holy Spirit. Both rely on a certain view of the divinity, the nature of revelation, and the texts that count as authoritative, to mention just a few. And this is not just theology, but a particular kind of theology. Indeed, the variety of views concerning the Scriptures and their interpretation displayed in history supports the point that it is in the theological views brought into the interpretive process by interpreters that we find the differences in interpretation.[71]

But one might still want to ask how the theological interpretation of revelation is different from the interpretation of other texts, such as Jonathan Swift's "A Modest Proposal for Preventing the Children of Poor People from Being a Burden to Their Parents or the Country."[72] Either one accepts that in both texts the search is for the understanding of an authorial meaning—God's in the first, Swift's in the second—or for a relational meaning. If the first, my claim that theological interpretations are relational is undermined, and if the second, the distinction between relational and non-relational interpretations is undermined. In both cases my view suffers irreparable damage.

In order to answer this charge I need to show that an authorial interpretation of Swift's tract is not relational, whereas an authorial interpretation of revelation is. Of course, according to my theory, relational interpretations of "A Modest Proposal" are quite possible, but this is not the issue at stake. The issue that concerns us is whether theological interpretations of revelation can be authorial, and my answer is that they cannot. Now, why is it that an authorial interpretation of "A Modest Proposal" is not relational? Because Swift's understanding or intended understanding is not contingent on any thing we bring to the interpretation, including certain knowledge we might think pertinent. Indeed, it is possible that the understanding is actually quite contrary to what we think it is, based on the evidence we have. As unlikely as it may seem, it is possible that Swift could have meant his proposal literally to solve the problem of hunger. On the other hand, why is it that theological interpretations cannot be authorial? Because the divinity's intended understanding is contingent on what the religious community believes, so that the understanding of revelation cannot go contrary to the fundamental beliefs of the community. The reason is not that the community believes them, but rather that they are, one might say, part of the religious package. Thus, for example, it is impossible for the Christian God to contradict Christian doctrine through revelation; revelation makes sense only within the context of those doctrines and considered in relation to them, and this is not the case with Swift's text.

Now, if theological interpretations are relational and contexts are always specific, reflecting a particular view, then there can be no theological interpretation that is not specific. This is to say that all theological interpretations assume a specific theology, be that Roman Catholic, Lutheran, Calvinist, Greek Orthodox, Reform Jewish, Shi'ite Muslim, and so on. Therefore, when theological interpretations of revelation differ, the differences most often do not arise from the texts under interpretation, but rather from the theological assumptions that interpreters bring into their interpretations and according to which they understand the texts. The disagreement between Roman Catholics and Lutheran interpreters of the Christian scriptures is not so much about what God wishes them to understand through a text that both communities regard as revealed, but rather about the theological principles to which they relate the texts and in terms of which they seek to understand them. The disagreement about the meaning of the texts is, in a sense, secondary and derivative. To argue about it, as some theologians from different theological traditions do, is generally a waste of time. And agreement, if ever reached, will most often be minor, accidental, and precarious.

This is a major reason why ecumenism has failed in the past and will probably continue to fail in the future. No fundamental agreement and resolution concerning the interpretation of revelation can be reached until the theological differences between those seeking agreement are resolved. And these theological differences cannot be resolved by just looking at revealed texts: They can be resolved only by identifying the sources of theological disagreement and addressing them. To do otherwise is like trying to compare and reconcile Freudian and non-Freudian interpretations of a text. No reconciliation is possible in terms of the texts themselves, because the source of disagreement is to be found in the theoretical framework used to interpret the texts, rather than vice versa.[73] A theological interpretation, just like a Freudian one, seeks to understand a text in terms of a conceptual framework that is external to the text and is not shared by all members of the linguistic community within which the text is produced, but rather is particular to only some members of that community.[74]

The Problem of Circularity

The nature of theology and the conditions required by the interpretation of revealed texts seem to generate a serious problem of circularity.[75] A theology is a view that seeks to be accurate, consistent, and supported by sound evidence derived primarily from revelation and integrated with views developed by science and those generally accepted and based on common sense and experience. But we found that revelation cannot be interpreted except in a theological context. So we appear to have a situation in which theology is supposed to be based on something for which it itself is required. For religions that accept divine revelation, there cannot be theology without the interpretation of revelation, and there cannot be interpretation of revelation without theology.

Different religious traditions respond differently to this problem, although many do so only indirectly and do not explicitly raise the issue. Those that respond satisfactorily, or have the elements of a satisfactory answer, do so by introducing sources of theology other than revealed texts. Scriptures are not the exclusive means through which God reveals.[76] Three of these are most frequent. First, a mystical experience with the divinity; second, an encounter with a prophet or religious authoritative figure other than the divinity; and third, a tradition of either practices or beliefs. The first yields an understanding that can then be used to articulate the theological doctrines and principles required to interpret revealed texts. The second teaches believers what they need to know to approach revealed scriptures. And the third provides a context of beliefs and practices within which revealed texts are interpreted. For some religions, these sources of theology are given to any believer, but more often than not they are given to select persons in the community or are claimed to be given to the community as a whole. Moreover, for some religions, these lay the foundation of the theological principles required for the interpretation of revelation.

There is, therefore, a way out of the vicious circle, but the way out requires a source of divine truth other than revealed scriptures. Those who reject any source other than these find themselves in a serious bind, a Hermeneutic Circle they cannot break.[77]

The Function of Theology
in the Interpretation of Revelation

In chapters 3, 4, and 5, we asked whether meaning, literary, and sociological interpretations are sufficient, necessary, or merely useful, if at all, for the varied purposes pursued in the understanding of revealed texts. And the answer was that literary and sociological interpretations were not sufficient, even in cases in which the purposes of the interpretations were literary and sociological. The case for the understanding of meaning as what a divinity wishes believers to understand is, of course, stronger. Moreover, the necessity attached to them depended on circumstances and was often epistemic rather than ontological. Moreover, we did find that, again depending on circumstances, the consideration of literary or sociological factors could be helpful or unhelpful.

Now it is time to raise these questions explicitly with respect to theological interpretations: Are these kinds of interpretations sufficient, necessary, or merely helpful, if at all, for the purposes one may pursue in the understanding of revelation? Among these purposes, as noted in earlier chapters, are the following: (1) understanding what a divinity wishes believers to understand; (2) understanding what instrumental authors and particular audiences understand; (3) understanding instrumental authors and particular audiences; (4) determining sources and influences; (5) identifying causes; and (6) learning a lesson.

From previous discussions, we already know that theology is necessary and, therefore, helpful to achieve every one of these aims but that in some cases it is not sufficient. It is necessary for (1), (4), (5), and (6) because in all these it is essential to understand the meaning of the text taken as what the divinity wishes believers to understand, and this cannot take place outside a theological framework. Even to raise the question of understanding what a divinity wishes believers to understand makes no sense outside a theological context. How could it, when the very notion of a revealing divinity, a revealed text, revelation, and a believer make sense only, and arise, within a theological context?[78] These are notions that are satisfactorily defined only within a theological framework. Determining sources and influences presupposes understanding what believers are intended to understand by the divinity. Identifying causes presupposes that we know the reasons why a text presents a particular view, and for this again theology is essential insofar as the texts themselves often do not make these reasons explicit. And learning a lesson requires a measure of value that again is external to the text and provided by theology.

With respect to (2) and (3), theology is necessary insofar as the instrumental authors of these texts and the audiences for which they are intended are believers who work within a religious framework, or nonbelievers who are presumably acquainted with the religious beliefs in question. Hence, the understanding of the theological framework is essential both for the grasp of what these authors and audiences understand by the texts in question and for the larger understanding of the authors and audiences themselves.

Apart from these reasons, theology is necessary for the interpretation of revealed texts because it provides the very hermeneutical principles according to which they are to be interpreted. Without this guidance, the interpretation of revelation is like a ship without a rudder. One can choose and offer interpretations of it, but the interpretations will have nothing to do with the texts considered as revealed. These interpretations would not be interpretations of revelation at all. Theology supplies not just the conceptions of a revealing divinity, revelation, the author of revelation, and believer. It also determines the canon of revelation, the principles of interpretation of these texts, the relative importance of the texts and their messages, and the criteria for judging the adequacy of interpretations. None of this is given in the texts themselves, and none of it can be supplied by the literary critic or the sociologist. Only the theologian, working within a theological framework, can do it.

But theology is not sufficient for any of these purposes, in some cases because of ontological reasons and in others because of epistemological ones—ontological in the cases in which the aim goes beyond the understanding of what a divinity wishes believers to understand, as is the case with (2)-(6); epistemological because in all cases revelation consists of texts, that is, linguistic artifacts produced by human beings in particular historical and cultural circumstances, and knowledge of all sorts of things beyond theology is necessary for the understanding of these texts. Here is where literary and sociological analyses play a part.

Finally, theology is necessary but not sufficient for faith. One needs to believe in something in order to have faith, but one can understand the theological underpinnings of a religion and still not have faith in it.[79] But this, of course, is not an issue we set out to discuss in this book.

Conclusion

In sum, a theological interpretation of a text aims at an understanding of the text that is concordant with, and framed in terms of, the theological tradition within which the text is regarded as revealed. Because of this, theological interpretations are always relational and established within specific theological parameters. Although, nominally, interpreters might claim their theological interpretations are meaning interpretations, in reality they are always relational. The root of interpretive disagreement, then, is more often than not to be found in the theological tradition of the interpreter rather than in the exegesis of texts.

In previous chapters I claimed that the most common kinds of interpretation of revelation are inadequate and that theology is necessary for the interpretation of revelation. Now we see how and why. Revealed texts by themselves offer no guidance as to how they are to be interpreted. Indeed, the very notions of revealed text and revelation are theological, and so are the notions of the revealing divinities, instrumental authors, and believers. Theology also determines the canon of revelation, the actual interpretation of certain texts, the relative value of these texts and their interpretations, and even the very hermeneutical principles used in interpreting. Theology governs, both epistemically and ontologically, the interpretation of revealed texts, and only through it can the Hermeneutic Circle be broken in the interpretation of revelation. It is only through theology, moreover, that divine intentions can be gleaned and interpreters can effectively respond to the problem of textual errors. In short, only in the theological approach to the interpretation of revelation can one find solutions to the difficulties faced by other kinds of interpretations.

The relational nature of theological interpretations and the fact that they are theology specific raise further questions, three of which are particularly significant. First, is it possible for there to be definitive interpretations of revealed texts? Second, are all interpretations of revealed texts relativistic? And third, does my thesis concerning the need for the interpretation of revelation to be theological and the inadequacy of sociological and literary interpretations assume, contrary to my explicit claim, the authenticity of revelation? The first question is answered in chapter 7, and the second and third in chapter 8.

Chapter 7 ⊷

Definitive Interpretations

One of the most fundamental questions for religions that accept revealed scriptures as a source of doctrine and belief is whether believers can understand them correctly, or, to put it in another way, whether there can be definitive interpretations of revealed texts.[1] Indeed, this is essential for the justification of some of the actions taken by religious communities with respect both to their members and to those outside the communities. What else but the possession of a definitive understanding of what the divinity means can justify religious wars, religious confessions of faith, and much religious practice? The possibility or impossibility of definitive interpretations, in principle or in fact, is then an essential issue for communities of believers.

Generally, three answers have been given to the question of definitive interpretations of revelation: (1) There can be because in fact there are definitive interpretations of revealed texts, at least in some cases; (2) in principle there can be definitive interpretations of revealed texts, but in fact there are none; and (3) there can be no definitive interpretations of revealed texts.[2]

All three positions are well represented in the history of religious hermeneutics, but the popularity of each has varied from age to age. Today, the third position is truly in vogue in the West, although a few dissenting voices in favor of the other two can be heard occasionally. The impact of contemporary interpretation theory, particularly postmodernist approaches, is evident in religious hermeneutics.[3]

Often, these positions are adopted for reasons that are foreign to hermeneutical considerations. Indeed, it is common to see moral and pragmatic justifications for the view that there can be no definitive interpretations of revealed texts. The argument goes something like this: There cannot be definitive interpretations of revelation because if there were, they could be used to suppress dissent and to oppress those who claim to have different interpretations from those claimed to be definitive.[4]

This kind of justification may appeal to some who dwell on the long history of religious persecution and dogmatism, but it should be obvious that strictly speaking it is not only invalid but also has little to do with the hermeneutical issue itself. Part of the problem is a certain lack of clarity in the formulation of the issue. Indeed, it is one of the theses of this chapter that often the way in which the issue is framed rests on ambiguity. To make any headway, then, requires that we next introduce certain clarifications. I begin by pinning down the meaning of 'definitive interpretation,' although rather than a full defense of my understanding of this expression, I merely establish how I use it here.

Apart from the general aim of clarification, I argue that definitive interpretations of revelation are in principle possible, although quite difficult in practical terms. Moreover, as should be expected from what was said in the preceding chapter, I claim that theological definitive interpretations are relative to theological frameworks, and thus depend on particular religious traditions. For these reasons, one must be wary of unqualified claims about the definitive interpretations of revelation in general, and as a consequence, of the validity of any actions based on them. There is, then, no justification for intolerant attitudes and oppressive actions based on claims of possession of definitive interpretations.

Definitive Interpretations

I propose that an interpretation is *definitive* when it fulfills its function in such a way that no other interpretation can fulfill it in a better way, and I take 'better' to mean more effectively and accurately. A definitive interpretation is canonical in the sense that it is a model or standard for all other interpretations aimed to fulfill the same function and that can, accordingly, be judged by comparison with it. Any departure from the standard potentially puts the kind of understanding of the text that is being sought in jeopardy.

Now we must go back to the distinction between interpretations$_1$ and interpretations$_2$. The first are acts of understanding, the second are texts. The main purpose of the second kind of interpretation is to cause the first kind in an audience. And we must be careful to understand correctly the claim that there can be only one definitive interpretation of the first kind. As an act or set of acts of understanding, an interpretation$_1$ can be one in two senses. In one sense, it can be numerically one insofar as there is only one act, or set of acts, of understanding—for example, if there is only one person who understands the text at one time. If there is more than one person who understands the text, or if the same person understands the text at more than one time, we cannot speak of one interpretation$_1$ in this sense. This might be called an *extensional* conception of interpretations$_1$.

Interpretations$_1$ may also be taken to be one in a different sense, that is, because the same thing is grasped, even if in grasping it more than one act of understanding is involved. This is the case, for example, when you, I, or someone else understands Genesis in the same way. Clearly, here we have several individual acts of understanding by different persons, but if what these persons understand is the same, one can speak of one understanding or interpretation$_1$. If different things are grasped, however, then we do not have one interpretation$_1$, but rather as many interpretations$_1$ as things grasped. If, for example, by the text 'God created the world in six days' you understand that God created the world in six periods of 24 hours each and I understand that he created it in several periods of several million years each, we have two understandings or interpretations$_1$ of the text. This might be called an *intensional* conception of interpretations$_1$.

It makes sense to say that a definitive interpretation$_1$ is one only in an intensional sense, for extensionally there is no reason why it would not be possible for there to be more than one definitive interpretation$_1$. That is, there is no reason why several people, or even the same person, may not understand the same thing at different times. On the other hand, it makes no sense to speak of a definitive interpretation$_1$ that is not one intensionally.

The situation with interpretations$_2$, however, is quite different. In this case, we are speaking of texts whose function is to produce understandings (i.e., interpretations$_1$) of an *interpretandum* in an audience, and there is no compelling reason why several of these texts cannot fulfill the same function in such a way that no other interpretation does it better.[5] The key here is the effect of the interpretation$_2$. Many interpretations$_2$ can be definitive as long as no other interpretation$_2$ fulfills its function better than they do. What counts here are the acts of understanding produced in a particular audience in a particular context. The character of the language used, that is, the *interpretans*, may vary as long as the acts of understanding produced in the audience are the same. Factors such as elegance, polish, grammar, and so on are important only to the extent that they affect the audience's understanding.

From this it follows that, unlike a definitive interpretation$_1$, a definitive interpretation$_2$ does not rule out other interpretations$_2$ that accomplish a similar effect, but it does rule out those that do not. For example, if an interpretation$_2$ causes a certain understanding that is deemed to be the one sought, and another causes an understanding that contradicts it, then the first interpretation$_2$ rules out the second, for the simple reason that the second does not accomplish what is intended for it.

The conception of definitive interpretations I have given is somewhat narrow. Some may want to object that a definitive interpretation, whether interpretation$_1$ or interpretation$_2$, need not be canonical or final in any way.

The rationale behind this objection is that a narrow conception of definitive interpretations precludes the possibility that there be any—so the argument goes—for no interpretation can ever be final. It is always possible that there be better ones. Hence, we would do better by conceiving definitive interpretations as interpretations that are effective as far as they go, or up to a certain point in time, but that can be subsequently superseded by other, more complete interpretations. A definitive interpretation does not necessarily set a standard that must be followed, nor does it preclude the development of other and better interpretations.

Conceiving definitive interpretations in this broader way naturally increases the possibility of an affirmative answer to the question explored in this chapter. Still, I would rather first attempt an answer to the question based on a narrower conception of definitive interpretations for two reasons. First, once this is done, if the answer is negative, we can always explore answers in terms of broader conceptions. But if the answer is affirmative, then exploring broader conceptions would be unnecessary insofar as surely there could be definitive interpretations of that sort as well. Second, religious oppression has been usually based on a narrow conception of interpretation, by which the religious community claims it has the proper understanding of what the divinity wishes to be understood through revelation.

Definitive Meaning Interpretations of Revealed Texts

The question raised at the beginning of this chapter was the following: Can there be definitive interpretations of revealed texts? Using 'interpretation' in the two senses we have indicated, we can reformulate the question into two others: (1) Can there be acts of understanding with respect to a text regarded as revealed that fulfill the particular interpretive function being sought in such a way that no other understanding fulfills it in a better way? And (2) can there be texts that cause acts of understanding in audiences with respect to the *interpretandum* that fulfill the particular interpretive function being sought to a degree that no other interpretation fulfills it in a better way? Let us examine the various functions in question, first the meaning functions discussed in chapter 2, and then some examples of relational functions.

Definitive Meaning Interpretations$_1$

Meaning interpretations$_1$ come in four varieties: authorial, audiencial, independent-meaning, and implicative. Let us take each of these in turn.

Authorial Interpretations$_1$.   A definitive authorial interpretation$_1$ seeks to be an understanding of a text that is similar to the understanding the author had of it, or that the author intended, in such a way that no other under-standing could be better. By better it is meant that the interpretive under-standing is as close to the understanding, or intended understanding, of the author as the interpreter could have. Indeed, ideally the understanding, or intended understanding, of the author and that of the interpreter would be intensionally the same, that is, what is understood through the numerically distinct acts of understanding of both the author and the interpreter would be the same thing. Thus, when St. Paul writes in I Corinthians 13:4 Ἡ ἀγάπη μακορθνμεῖ, χρηστεύεται (Love is patient and kind), a definitive interpretation of this would ideally yield an act of understanding in the in-terpreter that would have as object the same proposition St. Paul under-stood, or intended to be understood. But is this possible?

In principle, there is no reason why it cannot be possible in the case of an instrumental human author. There is no logical contradiction in holding that two human beings have the same intensional understanding, that is, that they understand the same thing. Indeed, our lives are built on this as-sumption. When I say, "Good morning," I assume the person to whom I say it understands me to mean exactly what I mean. Conversation, discourse, and communication are predicated on the notion that this is possible, even if some philosophers have questioned it.[6] Moreover, differences—whether major or minor—between the historical location of the author and that of the interpreter should not in principle make any difference. When I under-stand that two and two make four, I understand the same thing that Pythagoras understood, even though there are major differences in historical location, including cultural differences, between the two of us.

Matters are not so simple, however, when we are considering cases in which the historical and cultural differences are great and in which the lan-guage used in the text in question is not technical. It is one thing to say that Pythagoras and I have the same understanding, namely, that 2 + 2 = 4, and another to say that St. Paul and I have the same understanding of what he said, namely, Ἡ ἀγάπη μακορθνμεῖ, χρηστεύεται. Even if both are logi-cally possible, as I have claimed, the factual possibility of the second di-minishes in proportion to the distance—temporal and cultural—between St. Paul and me. The reason is that these distances decrease the likelihood that the denotation and connotations of the terms used by St. Paul and those I use coincide. The meaning of ἀγάπη in Hellenistic Greek is cer-tainly not equivalent to the meaning of 'love' in contemporary English. In-deed, much work may be necessary to arrive at a text in contemporary English—we might need not just a translation, but also a gloss, or even a commentary, that is, an elaborate interpretation$_2$—that will convey the meaning St. Paul had in mind and thus produce in me a similar under-standing to the one he had or intended me to have. Naturally, the more elaborate this process becomes, the more difficult it is to claim that I can understand exactly what St. Paul understood or intended to be understood when he wrote the text in question. Moreover, it is also obvious that authorial interpretations$_1$ depend on authorial interpretations$_2$ when there is a substantial cultural and historical distance between the author and the interpreter. I do not need an interpretation$_2$ to understand what my wife means when she says 'The cat just went outside.' But I need an elaborate interpretation$_2$ to grasp what St. Paul meant when he wrote the mentioned text in Greek.

In short, in principle authorial interpretations$_1$ of revealed texts are possible when the understandings in question are those of human authors. In practice, however, these interpretations are very difficult in most cases, because there is a significant historical and cultural distance between authors and interpreters. Moreover, in this case, interpretations$_1$ depend on interpretations$_2$, a fact that, as we shall see, increases the difficulty of their being definitive.

The case of interpretations that aim to be, or to cause, understandings of what a divine author understands or wishes believers to understand is different. Of course, as we already saw in chapter 3, it is not possible for a human being to have an understanding of any text that is similar to the understanding a divinity has of it if the divinity is conceived in the terms in which the Judeo-Christian God is conceived. What the divinity understands and what a human being can understand do not match insofar as understanding is proportional to the knower, and God's nature is supposed to be infinitely greater than human nature. Indeed, even in cases in which the divinity is not conceived in infinite terms but merely as a superhuman being, as the Greeks conceived their gods, the divinity's understanding would be much greater than human understanding. On the other hand, the case is different if, instead of sameness between the divine author's understanding and human understanding, we spoke of the understanding the divinity wishes or intends humans to have. In principle, it appears possible to have a definitive understanding of what the divinity wishes us to understand. But we saw already that even if this is so, the notion of definitive authorial interpretation$_1$ of revealed texts makes no sense apart from a specific theological context. So, it is that context that provides the answer to this question.

Audiencial Interpretations$_1$.   The answer to the question of whether audiencial interpretations$_1$ of revealed texts can be definitive is similar to the answer to the question of whether authorial interpretations$_1$ can be definitive in the case of human authors. In principle, there is no reason why they cannot be such, but in practice the difficulties mount in proportion to the historical and cultural distance between the audience and the interpreter. Indeed, the obstacles here are even greater than the ones we encountered in the case of the instrumental author, for audiences are seldom a single person, and therefore, the likelihood that all members of an audience of a revealed text had the same understanding of it, which an interpreter from another age could produce, is very small. Frequently, the members of a particular audience of a revealed text are quite divided as to what the text means. Consider, for example, how some of St. Paul's Epistles appear to have been written precisely to dispel what he considered misunderstandings of his own writings among different Christian communities.[7]

It is logically possible, then, as in the case of the instrumental author, to have definitive audiencial interpretations$_1$ of revealed texts provided the audience consists of one person only or, if the audience consists of more than one person, all members of the audience have the same intensional understanding of the text. In fact, however, the obstacles to such an interpretation, even under these conditions, are quite formidable and, as in the case of authorial interpretations$_1$, make these interpretations dependent on audiencial interpretations$_2$.

Independent-Meaning Interpretations$_1$. Independent-meaning interpretations$_1$ are as practically difficult as, if not more difficult than, authorial and audiencial ones, even if in principle, like these, they are possible. The reason is that the meaning of a text can be taken in various ways, as we saw in chapter 2. We can speak of authorial or audiencial meaning, in which case the issue amounts to the ones discussed in the previous two sections. But meaning can also be understood in other ways. Some of these ways facilitate matters, of course. If the meaning of a text is determined by an interpreter or a contemporary audience, as some practitioners of hermeneutics seem to claim, then any interpretation$_1$ of a revealed text turns out to be definitive:[8] The definitive understanding of a text is whatever anyone understands by it. This position is based on very old views, well expressed already in the Platonic Dialogues by characters such as Protagoras. To adopt it, however, amounts to a trivialization of the claim of definitiveness. For any understanding of a revealed text turns out to be definitive by the very fact that it is an understanding of a text, and this means that there are no non-definitive understandings of texts. Under these conditions, the notion of definitive interpretation loses its force.

Implicative Interpretations$_1$. The notion of implicative interpretations$_1$ is dependent on the notion of meaning, because it is concerned with the understanding of the meaning of a text and its implications. As such, definitive interpretations$_1$ of this kind encounter the same difficulties at the outset as those encountered by the ones already discussed. In short, implicative interpretations carry all the burdens of other types of interpretations, plus the additional burden of figuring out what the implications are. So we need not add further details about them here.

Definitive Meaning Interpretations₂

Definitive interpretations$_2$ are texts intended to fulfill their function in a way that no other interpretation$_2$ can fulfill in a better way. We must turn to their functions, then, to determine their viability.

Authorial Interpretations$_2$.   The function of authorial interpretations$_2$ is to cause in an audience acts of understanding that are intensionally similar to those of the author of the text or to those intended by the author of the text. In principle, this should be possible. There is no reason why it should not be possible for me to cause in my students an understanding of what the author of a text understood or intended to be understood when he produced the text. We know already that the first is not possible in principle when the act or acts in question belong to a divinity such as the Judeo-Christian God, but it is certainly possible if we are speaking of the human author of the revealed text. There is no reason why I should not be able to make my students understand what St. Paul understood when he wrote the Greek text that is translated in English as "Love is patient and kind," let alone what he intended for us to understand by it.

Yet, we saw already that in practice the difficulties of understanding a text increase proportionally with the historical and cultural differences that stand between the author and anyone else who wishes to understand it, so that definitive understandings (i.e., definitive interpretations$_1$) are difficult in practice. Indeed, they seem to depend on interpretations$_2$. That is, an interpreter of a text needs to produce interpretations$_2$ of the text in order to understand what its human author understood; she needs to "translate" the text into her own language in order to get at its meaning.

This in itself poses a serious difficulty, a kind of vicious circle: In order to understand a text, an interpreter needs to translate it, but in order to translate it, she must understand it. This is a version of what has come to be understood as the Hermeneutic Circle. The topic is too complex to be dealt with in passing, but I have partly discussed it earlier and in more detail elsewhere.[9] Here, then, I shall merely state that the circle can be broken by introducing the notion of expectation. We know that we have understood a text in a certain context, even though we do not have access to its author, user, or their behavior, when other parts of the text fit our expectations. If we can anticipate correctly parts of a text we have not yet considered, on the basis of parts we have already considered, this indicates that we have correctly understood the latter. If, on the basis of reading the first three articles of the first question of Aquinas's *Summa theologiae*, I can anticipate his answer to the issue raised in the fourth article, this constitutes strong evidence that I have understood the first three correctly.

Even supposing the Hermeneutic Circle can be broken and the interpreter has a definitive understanding of the text (i.e., a definitive interpretation$_1$), she still faces the challenge of "translating" the text to her audience in a way that cannot be improved upon by any other interpretation in order to have that audience have a definitive interpretation$_1$ of the text. This, again, should be possible in principle. There is no reason why, if I have a definitive understanding of what St. Paul means when he says that love is patient and kind, I cannot produce a text that will make my students have a definitive understanding of what St. Paul means. In practice, this seems to be easier than producing my own definitive understanding of the text of St. Paul, for once I know what it means it should be relatively easy for me to communicate this meaning to an audience contemporaneous with me and with which I share a language and culture. The problem with the production of definitive authorial interpretations$_2$ arises from another quarter, namely, the identity of the audience. This audience changes with time and circumstances, so that, even if I am able to produce a definitive interpretation$_2$ of St. Paul's text for a particular set of students at a particular historical juncture—leaving aside the difficulties already raised with respect to the composition of the audience—this interpretation may not be as effective with later audiences or audiences of other sorts. This means that the definitive character of interpretations$_2$ are audience specific.

Historicists, of course, rule out the possibility of any definitive authorial interpretation$_2$, whether of revealed or non-revealed texts. They believe that the differences between historical locations override any similarity, so that no event can ever be the same, in any fundamental way, as another event.[10] If this is so, no two fundamentally similar understandings are possible, let alone any two fundamentally similar understandings of the same text.[11] But I am going to lay aside the historicist claim for present purposes, both because it is not an objection particularly directed to the interpretation$_2$ of revelation and because I have argued against it elsewhere.[12]

As for interpretations$_2$ that aim to cause in audiences understanding of what the divinity wishes believers to understand, it is in principle possible to have definitive meaning interpretations$_2$ of revealed texts, for presumably, the understandings the interpretations$_2$ are supposed to cause are within the capacity of the human audiences for whom the interpretations$_2$ are provided. There is nothing wrong in principle with holding that there can be a definitive meaning interpretation$_2$ of a complex text like Genesis, or of a simple text like 'Abraham begat Isaac.'

Audiencial Interpretations$_2$.   The case with interpretations$_2$ that cause definitive interpretations$_1$ in a contemporary audience of what a particular audience understood is similar to that of definitive authorial interpretations$_2$. They are, in principle, possible but in practice very difficult. Moreover, they are audience specific and, therefore, their definitive character is rather limited. They appear not to have idiosyncratic features relevant to our discussion, so we need not dwell on them any further.

Independent-Meaning Interpretations$_2$.   The third kind of meaning interpretation$_2$ is the independent-meaning interpretation. Can revealed texts have definitive interpretations$_2$ of this sort? The meaning in this case is supposed to be independent of what the author (whether human or divine) understood or intended, or any particular audience understood, it to be. But we saw in chapter 3 that for revealed texts it makes no sense, *qua* revealed, to ignore the wishes of the divinity. So there is no need to raise the question of definitive interpretations$_2$ here.

Implicative Interpretations$_2$.   The case with the fourth kind of meaning interpretation$_2$, the implicative, is parasitic on the case of meaning interpretations$_2$, for the function of an implicative interpretation$_2$ presupposes a meaning and the implications of that meaning. In principle, then, the possibility and viability of definitive implicative interpretations$_2$ of revealed texts follow from the possibility and viability of the other definitive meaning interpretations$_2$, and therefore we need not give this case separate attention. It should suffice to say that definitive implicative interpretations$_2$, just as other definitive meaning interpretations$_2$, are possible in principle but difficult in practice.

Definitive Relational Interpretations of Revealed Texts

Can there be definitive relational interpretations of revealed texts? The answer to this will depend on the function of the interpretation in question. Recall that this kind of interpretation seeks to have (interpretation$_1$) or to cause (interpretation$_2$) an understanding based on the relation of a text, or its meaning, to something brought into play by an interpreter. And recall also that there are many kinds of these interpretations.

Definitive Relational Interpretations$_1$

A definitive relational interpretation$_1$ is an understanding of a revealed text, based on the relation of the text, or its meaning, to something brought into the interpretive process by the interpreter, such that no other understanding can be better than it on those bases. For example, in a Freudian interpretation of this sort, the Song of Songs is understood in terms of Freudian principles and in such a way that no other Freudian understanding can be better. And the same can be said about other definitive relational interpretations$_1$, whether they be feminist, sociological, philosophical, or so on. Now, the question for us is whether there can be such definitive relational interpretations$_1$.

In principle, it appears possible; there is no logical contradiction in the idea of a Freudian understanding of a revealed text that can have no better. Of course, in order for this to be so, there must be criteria for what makes a particular kind of relational interpretation$_1$ better than others. If there are no such criteria, then no relational interpretation$_1$ can be definitive, or what amounts to the same thing, all are definitive insofar as there is no way of measuring that one is better than another. Moreover, these criteria must be specific. Earlier I said that 'better' was to be understood as more effectively and accurately, but this is not enough. We need to know in respect to what they are to be judged more or less effective or accurate. And even under these conditions, matters may not be clear insofar as it might not be possible to have a definitive relational interpretation$_1$ because the criteria involved either allow for some flexibility or are such that no clear determination is possible.

For our purposes, the most important kind of relational interpretation$_1$ is the theological, so that the pertinent question here is whether theological interpretations$_1$ can be definitive. In principle this appears possible. There is no logical reason why we cannot have a definitive, say, Lutheran or Roman Catholic interpretation$_1$ of the Gospel According to St. Matthew. But, of course, whether it is possible depends on the theological principles in terms of which the revealed text is to be understood. Some of these principles might allow for such a definitive understanding, but others might not. In some cases, the principles in question might be such that more than one understanding of the text in relation to the principles is possible, and therefore there might be more than one interpretation$_1$. Thus, there might be two or more definitive interpretations$_1$ of the Song of Songs. On the other hand, there might be some theological principles that allow no such latitude.

For some theological traditions, there is a further complication, however. If doctrine is not taken to be fixed, but develops in time, then clearly theological interpretive principles may also change.[13] If this is so, it makes no sense to speak of definitive interpretations$_1$ for all times (panchronic), although it might still be possible to speak of them at particular times (synchronic or diachronic) and places.

In practice, the possibility of having definitive theological interpretations$_1$ of revealed texts, or for that matter other relational interpretations$_1$, is not promising. Theological systems are often too complicated to yield the kind of understanding we are talking about. Most of what we have, rather, are degrees of approximations to definitive interpretations$_1$. Aquinas's Roman Catholic understanding of the Song of Songs may be better than that of Peter Lombard, but that does not mean that it cannot be improved upon. Moreover, one must also keep in mind the very complexity of revealed texts. Most of these, like the Song of Songs—let alone the Pentateuch, the Torah, or the Protestant Bible—are long and complicated. If instead we were dealing with a short and simple verse, perhaps it would be easier to come up with a definitive interpretation of it (although, as we saw earlier, simplicity often results in greater polysemy). But the likelihood of achieving definitive interpretations of complex texts is small. So, again, the most that can be reasonably expected are degrees of approximation to definitiveness, rather than definitiveness itself.

Definitive Relational Interpretations$_2$

The case for definitive relational interpretations$_2$ depends, as in the case for interpretations$_1$, on the criteria proper to the particular kind of interpretation. For those in which the criteria are strict and clear, such interpretations are possible. But for those that have vague and unclear criteria, they might not be.

Consider, for example, a case of a Freudian interpretation$_2$. Whether a definitive interpretation$_2$ of this sort is possible will depend on the conditions under which Freudian interpretations$_2$ are effective in causing the kind of understanding they are intended to cause, and whether it is possible, according to the rules that govern such interpretations, that there be one or many that can produce the same effect and to what degree. If there are Freudian interpretations$_2$ of the Gospels, their function is to cause in audiences understandings of the Gospels in Freudian terms. These interpretations do not seek to cause in audiences understandings of the Gospels similar to those of historical authors or particular audiences, of the meanings of the texts and their implications, or of what God understands or wishes us to understand through them. Rather, they try to look at the characters and events described in the Gospels in terms of Freudian principles and categories.

I do not know enough about Freud and psychoanalysis to judge whether in fact there are, or even whether there can be, definitive Freudian interpretations$_2$ of the Gospels, or of any other revealed text, or of any text for that matter, although current practices of Freudians seem to go contrary to these possibilities. This is a question that only Freudian psychoanalysts can answer. Now, what has been said concerning the psychoanalytic interpretation of the Gospels applies also to other kinds of relational interpretations, such as philosophical and particularly theological.

How Do I Know I Have
a Definitive Interpretation?

Apart from whether there are definitive interpretations of revealed texts, there is, further, the question of how in fact believers know when an interpretation of a revealed text is definitive. How does an English-speaking Christian know that 'Abraham begat Isaac' is a definitive translation of the Hebrew text for English audiences? This is an important question because we are not easily contented with just having definitive interpretations; we want to know that we have them.

Religions have developed many criteria for this.[14] Some favor personal intuition: Believers know that an interpretation is definitive when individual believers have the right intuition about it. Others favor consensus: Believers know an interpretation is definitive when all (or most) believers accept it as such. Others point to an authoritative person or group of persons, such as a prophet, leader, council, group of elders, and the like: Believers know an interpretation is definitive when it is endorsed by, say, a council. Still others point to a living tradition as criterion, although the notion of tradition may be understood in many ways.[15] There are some religions that have accepted combinations of these criteria, for example accepting a living tradition and an authoritative body or leader. And, finally, there are some that reject the possibility of achieving certainty in this regard: No one can ever know whether an interpretation is definitive, even if it turns out to be so.[16]

The issue of how believers can know when an interpretation of a revealed text is definitive involves too many questions for present consideration, so I leave it for another occasion. What matters here is that, in principle, it is possible to have definitive interpretations of revealed texts without knowing that one has them, and that the certainty in knowing depends on the criteria adopted. Moreover, insofar as the criteria vary according to theological tradition, one cannot easily generalize as to the certainty of this knowledge. To underscore one conclusion of the previous chapter, disagreements concerning interpretation often have to do with hermeneutical method and interpretive criteria rather than doctrinal understanding. One should not anticipate interpretational agreement of biblical texts between Roman Catholics and Lutherans, for example, until these groups agree on interpretive ground rules.

Conclusion

In sum, the answer to the question posed at the beginning of this chapter is that, indeed, there can be definitive interpretations of revealed texts, although this is a matter of principle, not of fact, and may not apply to all kinds of interpretations. There is nothing contradictory in the view that certain kinds of interpretation of revealed texts fulfill their function in such a way that they cannot be improved upon by any other.

This does not mean, however, that we are always able to know if an interpretation of a revealed text is definitive. Whether this knowledge is possible will depend to a great extent on the kind of interpretation in question and on the criteria a particular theological tradition adopts with respect to this issue. Nor does it mean that in fact there are many, or even any, definitive interpretations of revealed texts in existence.

In the case of interpretations$_2$ in particular, we must keep in mind that they are texts, and hence the effective fulfillment of their function depends on the audiences and the contexts in which they are given. This also entails that an interpretation$_2$ of a revealed text may be definitive for an audience at a particular time and in a certain context because it carries out its function so effectively that no other interpretation$_2$ of the revealed text can do so better than it at that time, for that audience, and in the mentioned context. All the same, the interpretation$_2$ may not be definitive for another audience, at another time, and in a different context. The translation of a revealed text into a particular language will be effective only with persons who know the language in question.

The definitive character of an interpretation$_2$ always depends on the audience and the context, and thus is contingent on the similarities of the audiences and the contexts in question. Of course, not all contexts and features of audiences are pertinent for the way in which an interpretation$_2$ fulfills its function. For this reason, it can happen that a definitive interpretation$_2$ for an audience in a certain context may also be definitive for another audience in a different context.

I must clarify one further point. If one accepts the view that different causes can produce the same effect, then it is always possible to have more than one definitive interpretation$_2$ of a text, regardless of the kind of interpretation$_2$ and text in question—be it revealed or not—as long as the understanding produced in the audience for which the interpretation$_2$ is provided is the same. Remember that we have conceived an interpretation$_2$ as a text whose aim is to cause acts of understanding in an audience in relation to an *interpretandum*. For example, for English audiences that know Italian, the following two interpretations$_2$ may cause the same understanding and, therefore, may be considered equally effective in appropriate contexts: "'Buenos días' means 'Good morning'" and "'Buenos días' means 'Buongiorno.'" And for English audiences familiar with arithmetical symbols, again the following two interpretations$_2$ appear to be equally effective:

"'Dos y dos son cuatro' means that 2 + 2 = 4" and "'Dos y dos son cuatro' means that two plus two make four."

For all intents and purposes, then, there can be several definitive interpretations$_2$ of a revealed text. It would make no sense to speak of one of them as definitive and not the others as long as they fulfill the same function with the same degree of effectiveness and accuracy. Of course, if they do not fulfill the same function, or they fulfill it with different degrees of effectiveness, because, perhaps, the contexts are different, or the audiences are different, then only one or perhaps neither can be considered definitive.

So far in this conclusion, I have been speaking of interpretations conceived as texts, i.e., as interpretations$_2$. I must now say something about the first kind of interpretation, namely, interpretations conceived as understandings (i.e., interpretations$_1$). The question concerning these may be rephrased as follows: Can there be definitive understandings of revealed texts? But the answer is not very different in this case from the one we got concerning interpretations$_2$. In principle, we can have understandings similar to those had by the historical authors and audiences or intended by the historical authors, even though our understandings cannot be similar to those of God. Moreover, with the provisos made earlier, we can have definitive understandings of the meaning of a text God wishes us to have, and the same applies to the understandings of the implications of that meaning. Finally, we can in principle have definitive understandings of revealed texts in relation to certain perspectives or principles, be they Marxist, feminist, or what have you, provided these perspectives allow for such definitive understandings.

However, even though it is in principle possible to have some definitive understandings of revealed texts, in fact the possibility of having such, let alone knowing that we have been successful, is fraught with difficulties. It is not just that we cannot duplicate God's own understandings, but that it is difficult to duplicate even the understandings of past human authors (or those intended by them) and audiences. And something similar may be said about the meaning God wishes us to understand, or the implications of that meaning, short of direct divine intervention. Indeed, even in the case of relational understandings, the possibility of arriving at anything definitive here is very difficult, a fact amply illustrated by the contested validity of the interpretations of revelation. We must, then, do the best we can. We should use the notion of definitive interpretation merely as a regulative ideal, a goal to be pursued even though seldom achieved.

Of course, as mentioned earlier, we could always weaken the notion of definitive interpretation in order to increase the possibility of arriving at such interpretations. But this would not change the conclusion we have reached, although it would perhaps make us feel better. Indeed, in some ways it might be dangerous, for, trading on a confusion between more and less strict senses of 'definitive,' it might lend itself to the kind of dogmatism that has justified much oppression and religious persecution.

This conclusion leads naturally to the question of the relativity of interpretations. Does what has been said entail that interpretations are not just relative, but also relativistic? This is the question addressed in the next, and final, chapter.

Chapter 8 ⟶

Relativism in Interpretation

One frequently hears that interpretations are matters of opinion and that one interpretation is as good as any other. Indeed, sometimes the very use of the term 'interpretation' signals the idea that we are speaking about something about which different and conflicting views are not just possible but legitimate. To say that something is a matter of interpretation is often taken to mean that it is a matter in which disagreement is possible because no single view may be regarded as the correct one. This is the way the term is frequently used in literary and aesthetic contexts. Good taste, aesthetic value, literary significance, and so on, are often taken as matters in which reasonable persons may legitimately disagree. We may have different opinions as to the aesthetic value of a Rauschenberg Combine, the literary significance of *El Cid,* or whether it is good taste to cut vegetables with a knife or a fork. But there are areas in which such disagreement is not regarded as legitimate. For example, we do not tolerate disagreement concerning such things as the shape of the Earth (it is not flat), the sum of two plus two (it is four and not five), or Napoleon's marriage to Josephine (it took place).

When it comes to the interpretation of revelation, often those who express themselves in these ways, saying that the interpretation of a revealed text is a matter of opinion or that one interpretation of a text is as good as any other, are accused of being relativists.[1] Yet, the views of those who are accused of this hermeneutical sin and of those who are the accusers are rarely clear. In this chapter, I try to clarify the issue at stake between the accused and the accusers. I also try to explain the sense in which the interpretation of revelation can be relative and at the same time not be relativistic, even though these interpretations should always be developed from a specific theological point of view. I begin with the general issue of relativism in interpretation in general.

Relativism in Interpretations

Are the interpretations of texts a matter of opinion? Is one interpretation as good as another? Can there be contradictory legitimate interpretations? Or, put in a more ambiguous, even if more frequently found, form: Are all interpretations relativistic?

It is clear that all interpretations, including both meaning and relational interpretations, are relative. That they are so means that they depend on something other than themselves; they do not stand alone for their meaning, value, or legitimacy. And this is the case whether we take interpretations to be understandings (interpretations$_1$) or texts aimed to cause the understanding of other texts (interpretations$_2$). As understandings, they necessarily depend on those who have them as well as on that of which they are the understandings. Understandings do not stand by themselves, separate from subjects who have them, and they are always understandings of something. Understandings are acts located on subjects and directed to whatever it is that the ones who have them understand.

As texts aimed to cause the understanding of other texts, interpretations depend on all the factors that constitute the necessary and sufficient conditions of a text. Moreover, sentences of any kind, whether analytic or synthetic, depend for their truth value on something else. Consider the case of analytic sentences. One would think that these are not relative, insofar as their truth value depends only on the meaning of the terms that are part of the sentence. But this very fact indicates that their truth value depends also on the conditions that establish the meanings in question. The truth value of 'Two plus two makes four' depends on 'Two' meaning two, 'plus' meaning plus, and so on. And the connection of these meanings to the signs in question is a matter of convention, established by language users. The case of sentences that are synthetic is even more clear, for their truth value depends not just on the meanings of certain terms, but on states of affairs, or facts, that render them true or false. The truth value of the sentence 'This page contains 700 words' depends not only on 'This' meaning this, and 'page' meaning page, but also on this page containing 700 words.

But now let us take up the more serious claims, namely that all interpretations are a matter of opinion and that one is as good as another, so that it is legitimate to have different and conflicting interpretations of the same text. Even put in this way, the issues are too complex to be resolved with any degree of clarity, for we must first distinguish whether the issues have to do with different interpretations within the same kind—whether meaning or relational—or with different interpretations of different kinds. Do we mean to ask, for instance, whether all Marxist interpretations of a text, assuming there are more than one, are equally legitimate, or whether Marxist and

Freudian interpretations of the same text are equally legitimate? In order to make sure that these questions are not confused, I divide the subsequent discussion into three parts, two dealing with relativism within the same particular kind of interpretation—meaning and relational—and the third dealing with relativism across different kinds of interpretations.

Relativism within Meaning Interpretations

To determine whether relativism applies within meaning interpretations of particular kinds, we must pose the question in terms of the several kinds of these interpretations distinguished before: authorial, audiencial, independent-meaning, and implicative. Let us begin, then, by testing the claim, against these, that all meaning interpretations are relativistic.

Authorial Interpretations.   Even cursory attention shows that authorial interpretations are not a matter of opinion, that they can have unequal value, and that some of them may be more legitimate than others. Recall that an authorial interpretation is an understanding (interpretation$_1$), or a text that seeks to produce an understanding (interpretation$_2$), of what the author of the text understood, or intended to be understood, by it. The opinion of the interpreter, then, has little relevance for the value and legitimacy of the interpretation. What counts is the author's understanding, or intended understanding, and how far the interpretation reflects it or causes an understanding similar to it in an audience. Indeed, in this particular case, even if the author misunderstands what she says or writes, as judged by the rules that apply to the text within the community to which the author belongs, the interpretation is concerned with the author's understanding or intended understanding. Consider the case of slips of the tongue and similar phenomena. In these situations the interpreter seeks to understand, or produce an understanding of, what the author means or intends to say, even if what she means or intends to say is something quite different from what she actually says. This entails that there is no room for the interpreter's opinion when it comes to this interpretation. An interpretation of this sort is judged more or less adequate and more or less legitimate in the degree that it reflects the understanding, or intended understanding, of the author, or causes in an audience an understanding that reflects with more or less accuracy such an understanding.

Suppose, for example, that by the sentence 'The existence of God cannot be demonstrated *propter quid*,' Thomas Aquinas understood, or intended to be understood, that the existence of God cannot be demonstrated on the basis of the nature of God, and an interpreter (e.g., one of my students) understands it to mean that the existence of God cannot be demonstrated from

God's effects. In this case, clearly the interpreter's understanding is at fault, regardless of what he or anyone else may think about it.

Does this assume that the author always has a clear understanding, or intended understanding, of the text he produces? No. An author may have a very unclear understanding of the text he produces, and still the rules of authorial interpretation apply insofar as the aim of an interpretation in this case is to reflect the very confusion that characterizes the author's understanding or intended understanding.

Consider the case in which an interpretation is supposed to be the understanding of what an instrumental author understands by a revealed text. In this instance, it is obvious that what the author understands functions as the criterion that establishes when the interpretation is correct, even if that understanding is only a confused reflection of what the divine author intends to be understood.[2] An interpretation that aims to be an understanding of what an instrumental author understands and is not, or is so only to some degree, clearly is not as good as another that is closer to what the author understands. Nor does this depend on the opinion of anyone. The relation between the understanding sought by the interpreter and the understanding of the instrumental author is independent of anyone's opinion, including that of the interpreter. The interpreter may think she has a good interpretation when in fact she has a bad one.

Of course, someone might want to argue that no authorial interpretation is ever possible, that to produce understandings in someone similar to the understandings or intended understandings an author of a text had is impossible, because all understandings and intentions are historical and as such cannot be reproduced, not just numerically, but even in content. According to this view, it is necessarily the case that the sentence '2 + 2 = 4' mean something different when Russell understood it and when I understand it, or for that matter when I understand it and you understand it, because the circumstances that accompany Russell, you, and me, when each of us considers it, are different.

This view is based on a misunderstanding between the historical context of a sentence and the historical content of the sentence. I have referred to this before by calling the first the intensional historicity of sentences. Every sentence—and I am speaking of individual or token sentences—by virtue of what it is, is historically located, for sentences of this sort exist only when they are said, written, or imagined by someone at some time. But this does not mean that the content, namely, what the sentence says, is always historical. Many sentences make claims that are not historical, so that their intensional import has nothing to do with historical facts, whereas there are others that make historical claims and thus have a historical import. 'I drank a glass of wine last night' is both extensionally and intensionally historical, but '2 + 2 = 4' is only extensionally historical, not intensionally historical.

If there are sentences whose content is not historical, then the understanding of that content need not be subject to historical circumstances in the sense that such circumstances affect the content or its understanding. The fact that I, or someone else, understands the sentence depends on all sorts of historical circumstances. In order to understand the sentence, I have to be alive; I have to perceive the sentence; I have to know the language in which it is written or said; and so on. But none of this modifies what I understand when, and if, I understand the sentence, which in the case of '2 + 2 = 4' is that two plus two equal four. Indeed, there are even some sentences that are intensionally historical and do not depend on particular observers or points of view. There is a difference between saying 'I drank a glass of wine last night' and 'I drank too much wine last night.' In the first case, we have a sentence that is both extensionally and intensionally historical, but whose truth value does not depend on anything but the fact of whether I drank a glass of wine last night or not. The second sentence is different, for it is not only extensionally and intensionally historical, but what the sentence says depends on a certain view of what constitutes too much wine drinking. Perhaps it makes sense to say that the understanding of sentences that are intensionally historical depends to a certain extent on someone's opinion or perspective, but it does not make sense to say that the understanding of all sentences does.

Against this, someone might object that even sentences that are not intensionally historical use historical terms, belonging to a language, and express concepts that are the products of historical forces. To this extent, so the argument goes, the understanding of all sentences depends on historical circumstances. And this is right, but it does not entail that understanding a sentence requires a particular perspective, or that understandings are irreproducible, as long as what the sentences in question say are not matters of perspective or history. In principle, even if difficult, we can grasp with precision what someone else understands or understood with a word, and we can entertain a concept that someone else entertains or entertained. That it is difficult to do so, or perhaps even practically impossible in many cases, does not justify saying that it is so in all cases, or that it is necessarily so.

Audiencial Interpretations..   The situation with audiencial interpretations is very similar, *mutatis mutandis,* to that of authorial interpretations. These interpretations are not a matter of opinion, and their value and legitimacy are not necessarily the same. In this case, however, the criterion for value and legitimacy is not the author's understanding or intended understanding, but the audience's understanding. Of course, an audience, unlike an author, is usually composed of many persons who find themselves in different circumstances. This means that there may not be a single understanding that one can point to and call audiencial understanding. There may in fact be many understandings of the same text in an audience, some even contradictory. But this should not undermine the point I am making, namely: Whatever understanding or understandings an audience has determines the value or legitimacy of audiencial interpretations, and therefore they cannot be considered relativistic. One might legitimately argue that given the variety of understandings in an audience, there cannot be one audiencial interpretation of a text, but this is not to say that one interpretation is as good as any other, or that there are no bases on which to judge the legitimacy of different interpretations.

Independent-Meaning Interpretations.   The argument for relativism in the case in which the meaning is taken as independent of what authors and audiences understand is based on the fact that the meaning may change from time to time, depending on various circumstances. A text may mean something at the time it was composed, but it may mean something different at some other time. This entails that what a text means may be a matter of opinion and that one meaning may be as good or as legitimate as any other. But this is not quite right, for even if we assume that the meaning of a text changes, in most situations there will be one meaning that is appropriate or better under the circumstances and others that are not. The situation here depends very much on the view one holds concerning what determines the meaning of a text. There are several possibilities. It could be the author, a particular audience (an individual person, a group of persons, a society), the context, the language, the text itself, or the cultural function of the text in a particular society.[3] If we adopt the last of these, then we do not have a case of interpretive relativism of the sort we have been speaking of, for the cultural function of a text in a society establishes the parameters of meaning and, therefore, of what enters into making an interpretation good or bad, legitimate or illegitimate.

In short, independent-meaning interpretations are not a matter of opinion, and not every interpretation is always as good, or as legitimate, as any other. In principle, there are criteria of the value of these interpretations, whether conceived as understandings or as texts that aim to produce understanding in audiences. That producing such understandings may be difficult or factually impossible for a variety of reasons in particular circumstances does not change this.

Implicative Interpretations.   Implicative interpretations are understandings of a text's meaning taken together with its implications (interpretations$_1$), or texts that aim to produce understandings of that meaning and its implications (interpretations$_2$). In either case, they depend on interpretations of the kind just discussed, and all that applies to the latter apply to them as well. There is no need, then, for us to devote any space to them beyond which we have already done.

Relativism and Meaning Interpretations of Revealed Texts

So far we have been discussing meaning interpretations in general, but all we have concluded about them should apply to meaning interpretations of revealed texts as well. The meaning interpretations of revealed texts are relative to various factors, but they cannot be considered to be relativistic in the senses discussed earlier. Their value and legitimacy are not matters of opinion and they do not always have equal value or legitimacy. However, we saw earlier that meaning interpretations do not make sense in the case of revealed texts, so the very question of relativism for them is moot.

On the other hand, the situation is quite different when we come to relational interpretations, for I have argued that theological interpretations are essential for revealed texts, and theological interpretations are relational. Before we take up this question, however, let us consider relativism within relational interpretations in general.

Relativism within Relational Interpretations in General

If the claim that interpretations are relativistic is going to make sense at all, it certainly has to make sense in the case of relational interpretations. After all, the aim of these interpretations is to establish understandings based on the relations between a text, or its meaning, and something else that the interpreter brings into play. This seems to suggest that, indeed, an interpretation depends on what the interpreter brings with her, and the validity of the interpretation depends on the opinion of the interpreter. A Marxist interpreter will try to relate a text, or its meaning, to Marxist principles, and a feminist will do likewise but with feminist principles, and so on.

Three comments are in order. First, many of those who put forth relational interpretations claim that their interpretations are correct, objective, and even true. Indeed, sometimes they claim that they have the only correct interpretation, or at least the best of all those that had been given. This, of course, does not mean that these interpretations are what their proponents claim them to be, or even that there are interpretations that can have these characteristics. It is altogether possible that the proponents of these claims are wrong not only about the value of their interpretations, but also about the possibility that some kinds of relational interpretations can be correct, objective, true, or even better than others, let alone the best. But it does tell us that those engaged in producing these interpretations think, or at least act—and I say this because often one finds contradictions between what interpreters say they do and what they actually do—as if their aim is to produce interpretations that are better than others. This in turn would seem to suggest that they have in mind criteria of validity, correctness, and so on that are more than just matters of opinion.

Second, those who produce relational interpretations also frequently act as if these interpretations could be subjected to careful scrutiny on the basis of established criteria that can be considered and applied independently of the particular interpreter's point of view. Indeed, frequently interpreters engaged in this procedure will also engage in careful and detailed discussions to show how they meet these criteria and how other interpreters who are trying, or have tried, to produce interpretations of the same sort have failed where they themselves have succeeded. Marxists will fight among themselves about the understanding of a particular text, and so do feminists, historians, and other interpreters of texts engaged in relational interpretations. If these interpreters did not think that their kinds of interpretations were subject to established criteria, independent of the opinion of particular interpreters, their actions would make very little sense. They would not amount to more than a power struggle among parties who are engaged in the deception of others but who know that in fact the only thing that counts when it comes to the judgment of the value of their interpretations is to establish their own over those that differ from them. If they are aware of this, then their behavior may be described as hypocritical.

Finally, we come to the most important point. Although it is no doubt true that in the case of many kinds of relational interpretations there are no established criteria to judge their value, and in many cases the criteria available and used vary from group to group, or even from interpreter to interpreter, and as a result these interpretations are subject to bitter disputes, this is certainly not the case in many others. It would not sit well with Marxists to tell them that there are no Marxist criteria of interpretation when it comes to texts, that what Marxists do when they try to give an interpretation of Aquinas's *Summa theologiae* is a matter of personal opinion and based on personal preferences, and that the result is not something objective, based on the proper understanding of history and the location of the text in question within the whole historical scheme as understood in Marxism. They will point to the fact that history moves along certain dialectical patterns according to economic forces and that, when Marxist theory is applied to a medieval text like that of Aquinas, it yields a certain understanding of the text; this is what their commentary aims to cause in the audience for which the interpretation is being provided.

Marxists are not alone in this. Freudians will tell you something similar. Yes, they might tell you also that, unlike mathematics, the science of interpretation is not exact, but they will insist that it is not a matter of opinion or that one Freudian interpretation is as good and legitimate as another. Freudians spend years of their lives learning the interpretive principles that they then apply, something that would not be necessary if they believed interpretations to be matters of personal perspective or whim. Indeed, according to their scheme, certain words have certain meanings they do not ordinarily have and, therefore, can be used as evidence of the psychological significance of a text.

The historian will not be far behind. Historians generally develop a strict methodology, and those devoted to the study of particular historical periods spend much time acquiring specialized skills, knowledge of certain languages, cultures, events, and so on. They learn to make assertions on the basis of certain evidence, to question evidence of certain kinds, and to see texts in a certain way. This means that the conclusions of a historian are contestable, but only because there are reasons for it, perhaps because the historian in question did not follow proper procedures, the conclusions are not supported by the evidence, and so on. All these are used as criteria to judge historical interpretations. Naturally, historians are allowed to, and indeed must, bring to interpretations their own particular take and point of view. But this take and point of view must be consistent with much that is based on established procedures and criteria. This is why a particular historical interpretation can be judged to be more valuable than another or more objective than another, or even more correct than another. If, for example, a historian claims that Aquinas borrowed a certain doctrine from another author, she must provide evidence to this effect. There must first be found similar statements of the doctrine in both authors, and then there must be some evidence that indicates that Aquinas had access to the other author's view. A historical interpretation that makes a claim like this, and does not provide evidence for it, is quickly dismissed by other historians.

This brings us to an important point. Relational interpretations generally take place within established communities, and it is within these communities that the procedures for developing, and the criteria for judging, them are established.[4] This is why interpretations cannot be said to be matters of opinion. Indeed, the supervision that these communities exercise over interpretations is often so strict that sometimes it discourages innovation and change. The latter are often brought in at a great cost to those engaged in the development of interpretations based on novel interpretive procedures. These communities tend to be conservative and set in their ways, and development is usually tolerated only within narrow parameters and at a slow pace. This is obviously good and bad, but its value is not the topic of our discussion. Our topic here is whether relational interpretations of the same kind are relativistic in the senses mentioned, and the answer is that they are not, even in cases of interpretations that appear on the surface to fit this description.

Of course, it is altogether possible that there be communities whose rules of interpretation are very liberal or that even prescribe that it is up to the individual person to interpret a text as he or she wishes. Under these conditions, it is obviously the case that interpretations are a matter of opinion, namely, that of the individual person, and that all interpretations are legitimate, regardless of whether they contradict each other or not. But this, surely, is a very special case, and again, is so because the community accepts it to be so.

Relativism within Relational
Interpretations of Revealed Texts

Relational interpretations are relative insofar as they depend directly on the elements that the interpreter wishes to relate to the *interpretandum*. If the interpretation is Freudian, then the interpretation depends on the Freudian principles in terms of which the text is understood. But relational interpretations need not be relativistic in the sense we have mentioned, insofar as the interpretive scheme used by the interpreter may include strict rules for validity and legitimacy. Accordingly, a Freudian interpretation, for example, need not be a matter of opinion, and its value and legitimacy need not be equally acceptable, provided Freudians accept strict criteria of value and legitimacy for their interpretations. And, indeed, most relational interpretations do so to a certain extent. Not every Freudian interpretation of a text is considered, by Freudians, to be of equal value and legitimacy, and its value and legitimacy is not generally taken to be a matter of opinion, but rather to depend on well-established principles. This applies to all texts regardless of whether they are considered to be revealed or not. A Freudian interpretation of I Corinthians 13 is not relativistic as long as the community of Freudians have developed pertinent criteria for judging it.

Relativism within Particular Theological
Interpretations of Revealed Texts

Something similar can be said about relativism within particular theological interpretations of revealed texts. In certain religious traditions, the interpretation of revealed texts is not relativistic because these religions accept strict criteria for the value and legitimacy of interpretations. But there are religious traditions that have developed no criteria or have developed very flexible criteria. In Roman Catholicism, criteria for biblical interpretations tend to be strict. No interpretation that contradicts established Church doctrine is acceptable. Moreover, interpretations are not a matter of individual opinion but must be sanctioned by the Church, and this means by Church councils, tradition, and ultimately the authority of the pope. This is the reason for the well-known *Nihil obstat*. For some other Christian denominations, the criteria appear to be centered on personal experience, and therefore there is considerably more latitude. In short, the relativity of the interpretation of revealed texts depends very much on the theology of the particular religion or sect within a religion in question.

Relativism across Different Kinds of Interpretation in General

Now let us turn to the question of relativism across different kinds of interpretations. Can we say, for example, that a meaning interpretation of a revealed text, in which the meaning is identified with the instrumental author's understanding of the meaning, is better than a historical interpretation of the text? In the first case, the interpretation has for its aim the understanding of what the instrumental author understood through the text, whereas in the second the aim is to understand the text in its historical context. Or, in another example, can we say that an interpretation in which the aim is to understand what the historical audience understood through a text is better than a Freudian interpretation in which the aim is to understand the text in relation to a Freudian psychoanalytic scheme? Finally, is a Freudian interpretation better or more legitimate than a feminist one? Or are all these matters of opinion?

These questions have to do with how to measure the value and legitimacy of the interpretations. Understood in this sense, there are at least four factors on which the answers to the questions depend. Two of these point to particular individual or social contexts. The first is the purpose of the interpretation as determined by the interpreter or the interpretive community to which the interpreter belongs; the second is the social function of the text under interpretation. The other two factors point to more general or universal contexts. The first of these latter two is the validity of the interpretational scheme being used; the second is the contribution of the interpretation to an overall, encompassing understanding of the world.

Does it make sense to ask the question of the value and legitimacy of different kinds of interpretation in terms of the first factor? Can we say that a certain kind of interpretation is more legitimate than another when in fact the interpreter, or the interpretive community to which the interpreter belongs, aims only to produce one of those interpretations? Yes and no. It makes no sense to say that a kind of interpretation, say kind A, is better or worse than another kind of interpretation, say kind B, when in fact the interpreter seeks kind A, although it makes sense to say that kind A is legitimate and kind B is not. If an interpreter is seeking to have, or to cause, an understanding of what an author meant by a text, then it makes no sense to compare this kind of interpretation with a Freudian one, which does not have as its purpose to produce such an understanding, although it does make sense to say that the Freudian interpretation is not legitimate under the circumstances.

Likewise, if the value and legitimacy of an interpretation are measured in terms of the social function that a text has, then it makes very little sense to say that a particular kind of interpretation is better or more legitimate than another, provided that the interpretations in question are all allowed in terms of the social function of the text. I assume that in this case there are only certain kinds of interpretations that are allowed, and their value and legitimacy are not a matter of their kind, but a matter of the criteria used within the kind. Consider the case of a will. Wills are legal documents that have a certain definite function, namely, to make known the deceased's views as to how his or her property is to be distributed. But society also treats wills as social documents that give information about the customs of particular social groups (social history, sociology) and even about the character of the author of the will (psychology, biography). This means that there are several legitimate kinds of interpretations that may be given of a will. But these, again, will not be competing for legitimacy and value, since their purposes are different. Their value and legitimacy are judged only within the parameters of the kind of interpretation in question, not across kinds of interpretation. In this case, as in the case of the first factors, interpretations may be judged to be better or worse within kinds but not across kinds; across kinds, they may be judged only to be legitimate or illegitimate.

The other two factors we saw earlier, however, cut across interpretation kinds. The first asks the question of the legitimacy of certain kinds of interpretations, not in the context of what a particular interpreter wants, or in terms of the function a text may have within a particular society. Rather, it asks the question of legitimacy independently of these considerations. It asks simply, for instance: Are Freudian or feminist interpretations legitimate?

This brings us to an even broader context, in which a judgment is sought concerning a particular kind of interpretation in terms of what it contributes to our overall understanding, not just to the understanding of a particular text in certain circumstances. Thus, for example: Does a Freudian interpretation of texts contribute to our overall understanding of the world? This question points to more fundamental issues, for it does not have to do with interpretation as such, but rather with the right kind of knowledge. It concerns the value and legitimacy of certain theoretical schemes and their usefulness in understanding the world. If one holds that there is no answer to this question, then one must accept that ultimately there are no kinds of interpretations that are better than others, or more legitimate than others, and therefore that one kind of interpretation is as good as another and the value and legitimacy of an interpretation depend ultimately on the aims of an individual person or the customs of a particular society. If, on the other hand, one accepts that there are criteria whereby theoretical schemes can be judged to be better and more legitimate than others in understanding the world, then one must also grant that there must be certain kinds of interpretations that are better and more legitimate than others.

This poses a very important but controversial issue about which much has been written not just in recent years, but throughout the history of human thought. To attempt a resolution of it here that claims to be more than an opinion would certainly be irresponsible. On the other hand, not to say where I stand on the issue would be misleading. So I shall merely offer an opinion and indicate a line of possible argumentation to support it.

The opinion is that there are at least three fundamental criteria to help us judge among interpretations of different kinds. This is to say in fact that these criteria help us directly to judge the value and legitimacy of different theories about how to understand the world, and only indirectly to judge the value and legitimacy of particular interpretations. The criteria are not intended to be used to judge the value and legitimacy of interpretations themselves, but rather the conceptual frameworks on which they rest. As noted earlier, it makes sense to engage in judgments of the former sort only in terms of criteria stipulated within particular kinds of interpretations, not across them. But I believe it is also possible to judge the value and legitimacy of the theoretical schemes in terms of these three criteria: logical consistency, experiential adequacy, and parsimony.[5]

According to the first criterion, if a theoretical scheme is self-contradictory, then it must be rejected as illegitimate, even if parts of it may be useful in the development of an overall understanding of the world and can, therefore, be integrated into that understanding. The violation of the laws of thought is unacceptable because a contradiction entails anything, and this would not help us in the understanding of the world. From P and ~P follows both that I am Jorge Gracia and that I am not Jorge Gracia. Thus, a view of this sort does not advance understanding, but leaves us where we were before we entertained it; it is not informative. We do not know anything that we did not already know. Moreover, if two theoretical schemes contradict each other, this is an indication that one of them is unacceptable and must be rejected (or modified).

Of course, it is essential to make sure that a theoretical scheme is really inconsistent rather than only apparently inconsistent. An interpretation based on it may appear inconsistent to those who do not appreciate its complexity. Or it may appear inconsistent to a particular audience because the audience does not supply elements that are presupposed by it. The interpretations that different theoretical schemes yield are always contextual and audience directed. A change of context or audience might lead to misunderstanding. Someone, for example, might describe what someone else said as an insult when in fact, in context, it was a compliment. When American athletes were visiting Korea for the Olympic Games, they wore T-shirts that read "Koreans are bad!" This was taken by Koreans as an insult, when in fact Americans meant it as a compliment. In slang, to say you are bad has come to mean that you are good. The problem was that Koreans lacked a key piece of information about the use of 'bad.' Their knowledge of English was dated. For them, it was unthinkable that 'Koreans are bad' should mean "Koreans are good." This interpretation was inconsistent with their knowledge.

One must also keep in mind that theoretical schemes are often very complex and extensive. That there may be some inconsistency in part of one, or in some of the interpretations it yields, does not entail that the whole theoretical scheme must be rejected. We do not throw out a whole apple because it has a bad spot. A theoretical scheme with some inconsistencies might turn out to be much better than one that is completely consistent, insofar as consistency is not the only criterion to measure the value of a theoretical scheme.

Even more important, perhaps, is that the criterion of consistency does not entail the rejection of theoretical schemes that we do not fully understand or that appear puzzling or mysterious. Theoretical schemes such as these do not imply that there is anything contradictory in them. There may be, but obscurity and mystery are not the same as contradiction.[6] Our understanding of the world is very limited, and often it is not clear how different parts of it fit together. Yet, this does not require that we reject it. Mystery and ignorance are not the same as contradiction. A theoretical scheme that holds both that P and that ~P is unacceptable. But a theoretical scheme that holds both that P and that Q, even though we do not grasp how P and Q fit together, need not be rejected. Most religions hold doctrines that are puzzling and mysterious and that defy our understanding, but this does not necessarily mean that they are contradictory.

The Christian doctrine of the Trinity, for example, holds that God is both one and three. But this does not clearly entail a contradiction insofar as the way Christians believe God is one is not the way in which they hold he is three—he is one in substance and three in persons. Nor does the fact that no one has been able to explain satisfactorily how this is so entail that the doctrine is contradictory and must be rejected. Many philosophers have spent considerable effort trying to prove that the notion of God as benevolent, omniscient, and omnipotent is incompatible with the reality of evil, but so far no one has been able to do so to the satisfaction of a significant number of other philosophers. God's nature and his exact relation to the world remains a mystery, but this is not to say that the notions of a Trinitarian God and one who is benevolent, omniscient, and omnipotent are contradictory and must be rejected.

But it is not religions alone that hold mysteries. If by mystery one means a situation in which persons hold two views whose relation and explanation are unknown to them, then all of us live in a world of mystery. Consider the notorious relation of the mind to the body. We speak as if there were both minds and bodies, and as if their properties were not of the same sort. We speak of minds as not being material and of bodies as being material; of minds as being unextended and of bodies as being extended; and so on. Moreover, we speak of minds and bodies as somehow having causal relations between them. But so far no philosopher or scientist has articulated a satisfactory explanation of how they interact. The solutions have hovered around four basic strategies: there is only mind and no body (idealism); there is only body and no mind (materialism); there is both body and mind (dualism); and there is a body and its functions (functionalism). All views appear highly inadequate, yet we keep talking as if there were bodies and minds affecting each other in significant ways without knowing exactly how they do. Isn't this a mystery?

If this is not a satisfactory example, consider something even closer to home: the effectiveness in communicating ideas. Here you are, reading these marks on the page and thinking thoughts of a highly abstract nature, and presumably thoughts that are similar to the ones I thought while I was making the marks. So far no one has articulated a theory that explains satisfactorily how this happens. Indeed, some philosophers have gone so far as to say that there is no way of knowing that you and I in fact think the same kinds of thoughts in relation to these marks.[7] Is not this as puzzling a mystery as that of the Christian doctrine of the Trinity?

Situations like this should lead to the evaluation of these theoretical schemes on the basis of a second criterion: experiential adequacy. The measure here has to do with the explanation that best fits our individual and collective experience. Adequacy in this sense is to be broadly understood so as to include everything in our experience that we use to live by. At stake here are beliefs that help us make sense of our lives even though we do not fully understand them or their implications, and we have no demonstrable proof they are justified. Naturally, most religious beliefs fall into this category, but they are not the only ones that do so. We live in a world about which most of us understand very little, and we rely on others for our views of it. I believe what my physician tells me about certain medications I should take when I am sick; I trusted my mother about how to do many things; and so on. And I have proof for none of these, and for some of them there is no proof, but just a kind of collective or individual experience. Our individual and collective experience, then, must be used to judge theoretical schemes insofar as, apart from it, we have nothing substantial (logic is merely a formal requirement) to judge their value, or the value of anything else for that matter.

It is important to stress the breadth of experience to which we appeal under this criterion. Experience should include as much as possible in terms of those who have it, the kinds of experience involved, and the different cultures in the context of which it arises. We must bring to bear as much of the cumulative experience of humankind as possible. Otherwise, we could easily make narrow and idiosyncratic judgments. The experience of others should be an effective check to this as long as our judgment is also guided by the criterion of consistency.

The third fundamental criterion has to do with parsimony. Any theoretical scheme that, being simpler, accounts for the same facts is to be preferred to any other. And the more facts for which a theory accounts, the better the theory. The importance and validity of this principle derives from the very nature of an explanation. The notion of explanation is based on a metaphor: to ex-plain is to look at something from a flat surface; it is in a sense to make something flat by reducing an irregular surface to a single plane.[8] It has to do with reducing multiplicity, connecting, and unifying. From this it follows that, in general, explanations that can gather more phenomena under one principle fit the nature of explanation better, other things being equal. An explanation that does not reduce the number of phenomena it aims to explain, or does not reduce that number significantly, is not much better than a description of the phenomena. This is the reason science and philosophy favor the principle of parsimony, and why we should also seek to apply it to determine the relative value of theoretical schemes.

Naturally, there will be cases in which no decision as to the ultimate value and legitimacy of a theoretical scheme is possible for one or more of a variety of reasons, such as that our experience is limited, the evidence appears conflicting, we do not completely understand the theoretical scheme in question, or our knowledge is insufficient. And there will be cases in which the nature of the theoretical scheme will be such that it is difficult, or practically impossible, to reach a decision. Moreover, there is also the possibility of cases in which the decision reached must be regarded as provisional. But this does not mean that decisions are impossible. Finally, we may not be able to achieve certainty concerning the positive ultimate value and legitimacy of all theoretical schemes, but it is often possible to reach decisions concerning the inadequacy of many of them.

Decisions concerning the value and legitimacy of theoretical schemes are frequently possible, but there are cases in which matters are not easy or even practically possible. Sometimes a decision may not be reachable under certain conditions. And this is the point of contention. Some hold that decisions of this sort must in principle be reachable, even if in practice they may not be, whereas others hold that there are some situations in which decisions are not reachable even in principle. I cast my lot with the first group, for the second position undermines the foundations of all knowledge and contradicts my own experience.

Against what I have suggested, someone could trot out the objection that the three criteria I have proposed are themselves relative to a point of view and, therefore, cannot liberate us from relativism. Logic, experience, and parsimony are, like the theoretical schemes they purport to judge, part of theoretical schemes themselves.

The detailed answer to this objection would take us too far from our topic, but let me say a few words as to a direction the answer could follow. First a general point that applies to all three criteria: If the aim of a theoretical scheme is to produce a cognitive and rational understanding of the world, then it must necessarily use the three criteria suggested for reasons already stated. Understanding requires consistency, experiential adequacy, and parsimony. An inconsistent understanding is no understanding insofar as it does not tell us which of two contradictory options is acceptable and which is not. An understanding unrelated to our experience is no understanding insofar as it does not enlighten us about the very things we seek to understand. And an understanding that is not parsimonious is no understanding insofar as it does not bring unity to a multiplicity. Of course, the aim of a theoretical scheme may not be to produce understanding. It may, for example, aim to confuse, persuade, make one have certain feelings, earn fame or money, make someone happy, produce certain actions, dominate or exploit certain persons, and so on. These are all perfectly legitimate aims (although some of them may be abhorrent or immoral). Who is to say they are not? But they are not the same aims as understanding in cognitive and rational terms. This is not what a scientist tries to do, and hopefully it is not what a philosopher or a theologian aims to do.

Second, and more specifically, one could respond that logic is indispensable insofar as it is presupposed even by the objection; experiential adequacy is indispensable insofar as there would be no use for a theoretical scheme unrelated to it; and parsimony is indispensable insofar as its absence would lead nowhere.

Relativism across Different Kinds of Interpretations of Revealed Texts

What has been said applies also to the interpretation of revealed texts. In order to judge the value and legitimacy of different kinds of interpretations of revealed texts, we must accept criteria that are not specific to a particular kind of interpretation unless those criteria are held to be universally valid and applicable. Is a historical interpretation of revelation better, or more legitimate, than a theological one? Is a Freudian interpretation of I Corinthians 13 better, or more legitimate, than a feminist interpretation of it? These questions make sense only if there is a set of interpretive criteria that apply to all interpretations and according to which we can judge the value and legitimacy of the very schemes—Freudian, feminist, and theological in this case—used to judge the value and legitimacy of specific interpretations of it.

Now, part of my argument in this book has been that a theological perspective is essential for the interpretation of revelation, and in this sense I have made a judgment in favor of non-relativity. However, the essential character of theological interpretations does not entail that all theological interpretations are good, or even better, than non-theological ones. Moreover, neither does saying this entail that non-theological interpretations are useless or illegitimate. The judgment varies, depending on the case.

Finally, as noted before, I do believe there are conditions that all interpretations must satisfy, and insofar as this is so, decisions of value and legitimacy across interpretations of different kinds should be possible.

Relativism across Different Theological Interpretations of Revealed Texts

The case across different theological interpretations of revealed texts is similar to the one just mentioned. Consider the case of Lutheran and Roman Catholic interpretations of the verses of the Gospel According to St. Matthew 12:46–7 and 13:55, in which Christ's brothers are mentioned.[9] Lutherans understand these texts to mean that Christ had maternal brothers, children of Mary and Joseph, and this implies that Mary was not always a virgin. Most Roman Catholics, on the other hand, understand these texts to mean that Christ had cousins rather than maternal brothers and, therefore, do not see these verses as a counterexample to the view that Mary was always a virgin.[10] The dispute over the meaning of these verses is heated, for much is at stake, and considerable scholarship has been brought to bear on them. In spite of all these efforts, however, no consensus has been reached. The reason is that the verses in question are interpreted in terms of different hermeneutical principles. For Roman Catholics, they must be interpreted in terms of the doctrinal tradition of the Roman Catholic Church, that is, of beliefs passed down from age to age beginning with Christ's Apostles and Disciples.[11] According to this tradition, 'brother' means cousin in these texts. Lutherans, on the other hand, reject this criterion and accept only the Scriptures. If the Scriptures say 'brother,' it must be brother.

Clearly, this is a case of relativism across theological interpretations, for the value and legitimacy of the interpretation is judged in relation to criteria specific to a theological tradition. The question is, Can we judge the value and legitimacy of an interpretation of a revealed text outside particular theological traditions? The answer is no, although we can determine the relative value and legitimacy of different theological traditions themselves. But how can this be done?

The answer to this question has been hotly debated within Judaism, Christianity, and Islam from the very beginning of these religious traditions. Generally, the many views adopted in the long history of this controversy can be gathered under three basic positions. The first, which might be called *fideist,* argues that only faith can be the judge of religious doctrine. Outside faith, religious beliefs make no sense and cannot be judged.

Within Christianity, this position had early defenders and has always had a prominent place. Those who argue for it often refer to St. Paul's suggestive verse in I Corinthians 1:18, in which he says that the wisdom of Christ is foolishness to those who are not believers. Among its first and strongest defenders is Tertullian, the author of the well-known formula *Credo quia ineptum.* Echoes of Tertullian are present throughout the history of Christian theology and are clearly discernible in Kierkegaard, for example. In the thirteenth century, Bonaventure launched a well-structured defense of it. According to him, there is a hierarchy of authority, with revealed scriptures at the top and secular learning (which he gathered under the term 'philosophy') at the bottom. Anything other than revelation is suspect, and this includes the work of the Fathers of the Church and the Masters of medieval universities. Secular learning is the most dangerous. As he puts it: " . . . the greatest danger is in . . . philosophy. . . . [T]he masters and doctors of Scripture ought not prize the writings of philosophers, making themselves disciples in the example of those who cast away the waters of Siloe, in which there is the highest perfection, and go to philosophy, in which there is dangerous deception."[12] Bonaventure's view is less extreme than Tertullian's, for the latter rejected any learning other than revealed truth, whereas Bonaventure at least gave secular learning a place in the hierarchy of knowledge and accepted the possibility that some of it may be of value.

If we take this position seriously, the value of a theological scheme can be judged only from within that scheme. Of course, Tertullian and Bonaventure would argue that since they know their scheme to be the true one because it is based on divine revelation, they can also judge other schemes from their own perspective. This is a partisan point of view common to most believers who accept an internal mechanism of judgment. Interpretation of theological traditions can be judged only from within, and no judgment can be made across traditions. But clearly this is unacceptable to an objective, independent observer, and certainly to a philosopher. It amounts to giving up on rationality and precludes agreement.

A second position goes to the other extreme: Faith is either illegitimate or a lower kind of knowledge. For nineteenth-century positivists, religious doctrines are, like metaphysical doctrines, unproven hypotheses, guesses as it were about what we do not know and have yet no way of finding out.[13] For twentieth-century logical positivists, they are, again like metaphysical views, a kind of nonsense.[14] And for Averroes, the greatest rationalist of the Middle Ages, they constitute a lower form of knowledge, appropriate for those who are incapable of understanding true science (which he identified with philosophy).[15] The conclusions reached by theologians, according to Averroes, differ from those reached in science in that they are based on opinion (that is, undemonstrated beliefs). Because of this, science is superior and is the ultimate arbiter of its value. The most important implication of this position, for our issue, is that the value and legitimacy of theological traditions are to be judged in terms of the non-theological, scientific knowledge we have.

Clearly, this position is unacceptable to the members of religious faiths insofar as it does not take seriously religious claims, dismissing them as somehow pre-scientific or anti-scientific. Since one of the assumptions under which I have been working is that philosophers who investigate the issues discussed in this book need to accept the *prima facie* value of religious belief, we cannot very well accept this point of view unless it becomes clear that no other avenue is open.

But there is a third avenue. This middle ground was well articulated first by Aquinas, although his view is only partly satisfactory. For Aquinas, there are two legitimate ways in which knowledge is acquired. One way is through faith and another is through reason, and not all knowledge is acquired in the same way. Some truths, such as "Christ is God," can be known only through faith, because our reason is insufficient to reach them. Some truths, such as "The Earth moves around the Sun," can be known through reason alone, because they are not part of God's revelation and we are equipped with reason, which is sufficient to know them. And some truths, such as "God exists," can be known through either reason or faith. This means, for Aquinas, that we cannot reject faith or reason, or the knowledge we acquire through them, for to do so would be to limit the truths we can know, and we need the truths of faith for salvation and the truths of reason to satisfy our natural curiosity and carry out our lives on Earth.

So, what do we do when there are irreconcilable conflicts between what theology tells us and what science tells us? Ultimately, for Aquinas, faith has the last word, because the truths of faith are directly given to humankind by God, whereas the truths of reason are only the result of human investigation, and whereas God cannot err, humans can. This is not very different in some ways from what Bonaventure says, except that for Bonaventure it applies to all truth and for Aquinas reason both has an independent domain, even if a part of this domain overlaps with faith, and when correctly employed does not fall into error. Moreover, this needs to be qualified with what was said in chapter 5 concerning the metaphorical interpretation of revelation. Obviously, if a metaphorical interpretation of the Scriptures is possible and eliminates the conflict, then no choice between faith and reason need be made.

Aquinas can assume the ultimate superiority of faith over reason in the *Summa theologiae* because there he is acting as a theologian. Philosophers, on the other hand, cannot do this. They cannot, like Aquinas, say that a particular theology can correct reason because, *qua* philosophers, they cannot accept the dictates of faith—even though they can accept that faith may be right—particularly when they know that different theologies within and without different theological traditions conflict. Philosophers, *qua* philosophers, can never surrender reason. To put it in Dante's terms: They can never enter Paradise. Now, it is perfectly possible for philosophers to come to the threshold of faith, and even to conclude that faith may have answers to questions for which philosophy has no answers. And certainly they can understand that some faiths make more sense than others, and that some make no sense at all. But, *qua* philosophers, they can never surrender reason to faith. To think otherwise is to confuse philosophy with theology, or vice versa. In short, from a philosophical perspective, Aquinas's position is still too internal, for it is indeed a theological position.

The philosopher, *qua* philosopher, can accept only that (1) there are some claims based on reason alone; (2) there are some claims based on faith alone; (3) there are some claims based on reason that coincide with claims based on faith; and (4) there are some claims based on reason that contradict claims based on faith. The last category of claims may in turn contain claims of two sorts: (A) claims well established and proven by reason, such as "2 + 2 = 4" (analytic) and "The Earth moves around the Sun" (synthetic, but based on overwhelming evidence); and (B) hypothetical claims based either on considerable evidence (a) or on limited evidence (b). An example of (a) is "Human beings evolved from lower forms of life"; an example of (b) is "Human actions are exclusively determined by physical processes."

Now, when conflicts between faith and reason arise, the philosopher needs to consider the nature of the claim and the rational support available for it. If a theology supports a claim that contradicts well-established and proven claims of reason, the theological claim must be rejected. To accept a theological claim that "(P.~P) is true" is impossible, *malgré* Tertullian and Kierkegaard. Only a fool, or someone completely mad, could do it. Likewise, to accept a theological claim that says "The Sun moves around the Earth" is impossible for a reasonable and rational person. If, on the other hand, a theological claim goes against a claim of reason that has considerable, but not overwhelming, evidence behind it, then the theological claim should not be rejected summarily, although it must be suspected and therefore subjected to serious scrutiny. One should not rule out the theological doctrine of creation in six 24-hour days just because it contradicts the theory of evolution unless the evidence for the theory of evolution is overwhelming. But it makes sense, to a reasonable and rational person, to suspect that such an understanding of creation is untenable and should be subjected to careful scrutiny, precisely because the theory of evolution has so much evidence in its favor, even though it has not reached the status of the view that the Earth moves around the Sun. In the case of a claim of reason that has only weak evidence in its support, then both the theological claim and the claim of reason should be subjected to careful scrutiny, but neither can be rejected out of hand.[16] Considering the conflicting rational evidence available for and against the physical determination of human actions, it would not be reasonable or rational to reject summarily either the view that human actions are not exclusively determined by physical processes or the view that they are. In this case, both the scientific physicalist theory and the non-physicalist theological doctrine should be subjected to scrutiny.

In a case in which a theological doctrine conflicts with a proven truth of reason or one for which there is substantial evidence, and the theological doctrine in question is not fundamental, one must try to establish how the doctrine became part of the theology. This is important, for it may undermine or strengthen, depending on what is discovered, the authoritative body of the faith, and this in turn may affect the status of the theology.

So far I have been speaking largely of particular claims within theological traditions, not about the set of all claims that constitute a theology. But we may ask how the status of particular claims affect the status of a whole theology. If some claims of a theology must be rejected or put into question because of how they stack up when put next to the claims of reason, what should we make of the theology considered as a whole?

Two considerations are important for answering this question: first, the status with which the religious community regards the claims in question; second, the logical relation of other theological claims to the ones in question. A theology is a view of the world that seeks to be accurate and consistent as well as founded on revelation. As such, a theology is a conceptual edifice built on the beliefs accepted by a religious community.[17] But as an edifice, there will be parts of it that are regarded as more fundamental than others by the religious community. It is, for example, more fundamental to the Christian Faith that Christ is God than that Joseph played the role of father to him when he was a child. Moreover, regardless of what the religious community believes, as a conceptual and doctrinal edifice, there will be parts of it that are more fundamental than others. Independently of what the Christian community holds, the Christian doctrine of the Trinity is more fundamental to Christianity than the number of commandments God gave Moses.

Both of these factors play important roles in determining how the status of particular doctrines affect the status of a whole theology. If some doctrines need to be rejected or put into question, but they are neither fundamental nor believed to be fundamental by the religious community, then their rejection does not much affect the status of the theology as a whole. However, if they are either fundamental or believed to be fundamental, then the whole theological edifice acquires the status of the doctrines. A reasonable and rational person, acting reasonably and rationally, must reject voodoo and animistic beliefs precisely because their fundamental doctrines go contrary to much that we know is not true as determined by science.

Now, let us go back to theologians, since I have been speaking as a philosopher. I part company with those who hold that theology has to answer to no one. Theology, as the understanding of faith, must answer both to reason and to faith. Believers cannot understand their faith without faith, that is, without accepting as true the doctrines of the religion to which they belong, including those revealed. But they cannot understand faith without reason, that is, without using the natural tools they have as human beings, and the knowledge they have derived from them. Indeed, as Temple points out, "revelation can, and in the long run must, on pain of becoming manifest as superstition, vindicate its claim by satisfying reason. . . ."[18] Theology must begin in faith but must apply reason to it in an attempt to integrate it with non-revealed knowledge. If faith seeks understanding, it can abandon neither its roots in belief nor its instrument in reason, as both Anselm and Aquinas made quite clear.

Because theology is answerable to reason, interpretations that go contrary to what we know to be true through reason cannot be accepted, and this gives us a measure we can use to judge the value and legitimacy of particular theological traditions. A religion that necessarily yields a contradictory or inadequate theology must be rejected. In some cases, it may be possible, and even easy, to reject certain theological traditions. And it may be possible, or even easy, to show that certain theological traditions make more sense than others. But it is not always possible or easy to do so. There are many cases in which the relative value and legitimacy of competing theological traditions is not readily determined. It is unacceptable to infer

from this, however, that value judgments across different theological traditions are in principle impossible. To do so would be to surrender rationality, giving up our humanity with it. It also amounts to the rejection of the
theological enterprise itself, a fact that has not escaped many of those who
favor this approach and, consequently, reject theology.

Theological Interpretations
and the Authenticity of Revelation

In chapter 1, I adopted a conception of revelation neutral with respect to authenticity. Revelation consists of texts considered to be divinely revealed by a
community of believers, and this regardless of whether the texts are in fact revealed or not. And in chapters 4–6, I argued that sociological and literary interpretations are inadequate because all revelation needs to be interpreted
within a particular theological context. This raises an important question
whose answer could undermine my thesis: If the texts regarded as revealed
turn out not to be authentic, that is, are not in fact revealed by a divinity, then
does this not invalidate my view concerning the need for their theological interpretation and the inadequacy of literary and sociological interpretations?

The answer, like most good answers to difficult questions, is not as clear-
cut as some would like. On the one hand, no, this fact does not undermine
my thesis, but on the other hand, yes, it does open the doors to non-theological interpretations, including literary and sociological ones. This is not a
contradiction. Recall that the interpretation of texts has to do with the cultural function that they have in a particular community. And the function
of texts regarded as revealed by a community of believers is to find out what
the divinity means, what it wants to convey to the community. Moreover, as
we have seen, this message can be grasped only within the theological
framework that identifies the text as revealed and provides the epistemic
norms to be followed in order to receive it. So, as argued before, the theological component of the interpretation of these texts is essential for their
understanding.

This is not all, however, for we have seen in this chapter that not all theologies are credible. Although the value of particular theological views and
interpretations of texts regarded as revealed can be judged only within particular theological traditions, theologies themselves are not epistemically independent. Theology is answerable to reason, when reason is understood in
the broad sense that I made clear earlier. This means that a particular theology can always turn out to be unacceptable, and if the theology falls, so does
the authenticity of the texts it regards as revealed.

Consider the case of the Koran and Islamic theology. The Koran is a text
that is regarded by Muslims as revealed. According to my theory, this text re-

quires an Islamic theological interpretation. That is, the text needs to be interpreted in terms of the Islamic theological framework within which it is regarded as a revelation from God. Now, let us assume for the sake of argument that it can be shown, using the criteria indicated earlier, that Islamic theology is unacceptable to reason. Then it becomes clear that the whole conceptual edifice on which the authenticity of the Koran as a revealed text rests crumbles, and that a theological interpretation of the Koran no longer provides what it is supposed to provide, namely, an understanding of God's meaning. So, under these conditions, it would appear that a theological interpretation is not necessary, and one would need to turn to non-theological interpretations, such as literary or sociological ones.

But this is not quite right. The purposes of the interpretation of texts regarded as revealed are multiple. Earlier, we identified at least six: (1) understanding what a divinity wishes believers to understand; (2) understanding what instrumental authors and particular audiences understand; (3) understanding instrumental authors and particular audiences; (4) determining sources and influences; (5) identifying causes; and (6) learning a lesson. Moreover, I argued that theological interpretations were necessary for all of these. This means that even if a revelation is not authentic, and therefore that there is no divinity that reveals a message through it, a theological interpretation is necessary for the other aims of the interpretation of texts regarded as revealed. This, of course, does not eliminate a role for sociological and literary interpretations, but neither does it undermine the claims I have made with respect to the theological interpretation of revelation.

Conclusion

My concern in this chapter has been with the questions of whether the interpretation of revealed texts is a matter of opinion; whether one interpretation is as good as another; and whether there can be legitimate contradictory interpretations of these texts. In most cases in which we consider or compare interpretations of the same specific kind, the answer to the three questions is negative. Moreover, this is also so in the case of different kinds of interpretations as long as one considers the aims of the interpreter and the function of a text within a particular society, or one is willing to accept that there are criteria by which the value of different theoretical schemes for understanding the world can be judged.

There are only two cases in which it turns out that an interpretation is a matter of opinion, that one interpretation is as good as another, and that it is possible to have legitimate contradictory interpretations: (1) when the interpreter, or interpretive community, accepts this to be the case for a particular kind of interpretation and, therefore, establishes no criteria for value or legitimacy; and (2) when one accepts that there are no ways of measuring the value of different theoretical schemes for understanding the world. The first case poses no serious difficulties insofar as it is a matter of choice, and concerns only one kind of interpretation, leaving all others subject to rules that preclude the possibility of relativism as understood here. The second is more disturbing, for although it leaves intact the non-relativity of particular kinds of interpretations, it undermines the whole idea that any interpretation can be better or more legitimate than any other, except in cases in which such value or legitimacy is measured according to personal preference or social convention. I have rejected it, both in general and in the context of theology.

Chapter 9 ❧

Conclusion:
How We Can Know
What God Means

Paradoxically, nowhere in this book have I explicitly raised the question posed by its title. Yet, everything I have said is in some sense related to, and aimed to help us answer, it. To ask about how we can know what God means is in fact to ask about the meaning of a divine text, for a divine text is what I have called revelation, or revealed text. And to ask how we can know what this divine text means is to ask how we can understand it. What are, then, the conditions under which this understanding is possible?

To say that we understand a revealed text is to say one or more of several possible things: We understand what God wishes us to understand; we understand what God understands; we understand what the instrumental author of the text understood by it; we understand what a particular audience of the text understood by it; we understand the meaning of the text considered independently of what the instrumental author and any audience understood by it; we understand the meaning of the text together with the implications of that meaning; and we understand the text or its meaning taken in relation to something the interpreter brings into play. These reflect the various kinds of interpretations that *prima facie* we can have of revealed texts.

Not all of these are possible, however, for we cannot have an understanding of all that God understands through a text he has revealed. In principle, however, the others are possible. Hence, the answer to our question is that, indeed, we can understand the meaning of a revealed text, and thus we can know what God means, as long as what we have in mind by this is one of the understandings mentioned, with the exception of God's own, full understanding. None of these makes much sense, however, considered independently of a theological framework provided by a religious tradition. Theology is at the center of the understanding of revelation, and any interpretation that ignores it, as happens with exclusively meaning, literary, or sociological ones, turns out to be inadequate.

My answer to the question How can we know what God means? is necessarily general, insofar as I claim that what a divinity means through a revealed text is to be determined only within particular theological traditions. The specific conditions for this knowledge within particular theological perspectives can be determined only within those perspectives, and is therefore outside the parameters of the general issue I address and the constraints that apply to a philosophical book.

The role that theology plays in the interpretation of revelation both explains the disagreement concerning the understanding of revelation among religious communities and points to the obstacles that need to be overcome before agreement is possible. The interpretation of revelation depends on the theology that guides it, so that different theological assumptions necessarily result in different interpretations. This does not entail that the understanding of revelation is a matter of opinion, however. Theology exercises a double control on the interpretation of revelation. One of these is, as it were, internal to the particular theological tradition within which the interpretation takes place. The other is, in a manner of speaking, external to that theological framework. The first consists of the beliefs and principles of the theology in question; the second consists of the general principles that govern all attempts to develop knowledge that goes beyond personal opinion.

Although the interpretation of revelation is not a matter of personal opinion, nonetheless the lack of agreement about it and the lack of awareness of the role of theology in it lead to conflict and frustration. The hermeneutics of religious texts must begin with the awareness of the many different kinds of textual interpretations that are possible and the variety of goals they seek, for interpretations of different kinds cannot be appropriately compared. And in particular it must take into account the all-important role of theology.

The conception of the interpretation of revelation I have provided here makes room for both faith and reason, and ought to satisfy the demands of both. The mistake of those who emphasize one of these to the exclusion of the other, when interpreting texts regarded as revealed, is that they do not do justice to the nature of revelation. They try to reduce the process of understanding revelation either to a non-rational process or to an exclusively rationalistic process that makes no room for faith. Both extremes miss an important element in the interpretation of revelation and, therefore, fail to provide an understanding of revelation that does justice to faith and reason. I hope the view I have proposed succeeds where these have failed precisely because it aims to take both faith and reason seriously. By this I do not mean that the position I take presupposes faith in general or a certain faith in particular. As noted in the preface, this is a book of philosophy, not of theology, and therefore its claims do not presuppose any beliefs except those presupposed by any serious intellectual pursuit. But I have tried, indeed, to make room as much for faith as for reason because I have taken to heart the claims made by theologians and philosophers. My aim has been to develop a view that accommodates both.

On the one hand, those who reject reason to make room for belief reject the very foundations of the theological enterprise, give up the basis for resolving disputes between different theological traditions, and open the doors to power struggles, abuse, and arbitrariness. This should be repugnant to any human being.

On the other hand, those who reject faith to make room for reason turn their backs on a phenomenon that has been with us from the beginning of human history and appears to survive all attacks brought against it. They also reject something regarded by many as the center of their lives. This seems to be as repugnant as the position of those who reject reason.

I expect readers who fall into one or the other of these two camps to be unsympathetic to this book. Regardless of their attitude, however, I hope to have given them some basis for rethinking their positions and perhaps considering an alternative to them. This is all a philosopher can aim to do.

Notes

Preface

1. For example, according to some polls, 80 percent of all Americans claim to believe in the Bible as a revelation from God. Alter, 1992, 200.
2. Bonaventure, 1955.
3. Kant, 1960, 102.
4. Brunner (1946, 20) and Macquarrie (1977, 167) claim that all religions involve revelation, but this is not an uncontested claim.

Chapter 1

1. Pannenberg, 1968, 3.
2. Wolterstorff (1995, 33) points out that communication is perlocutionary, and this does not seem to be the case with revelation.
3. I am using 'property' here in a non-Aristotelian, non-technical sense, to mean any feature or characteristic of a thing.
4. By this I do not mean to commit myself to the existence of propositions. This is a controversial topic that cannot be settled in passing. I am merely taking advantage of the notion of "proposition" because it is useful here, regardless of whether propositions exist or not. For the various issues that can be raised about propositions in the context of revelation, see Vanhoozer, 1986, 56–75.
5. Mavrodes, 1988, 99; Baillie, 1956, 64; Downing, 1964, 238.
6. Wolterstorff calls this "agentless revelation" in 1995, 23.
7. Mavrodes, 1988, 34 ff.
8. Temple, 1960, 314–15.
9. Hollaz, in Schmid, 1961, 26.
10. These come in a variety of ways, including dreams and visions. Baier, in Schmid, 1961, 27.
11. Temple, in Baillie and Martin, 1937, 96, although he restricts the notion of fact to event. Also Downing, 1964, 194–5, and 217–19; Vanhoozer, 1986, 64–5.
12. Hodge, 1878, 60; Creed, 1938, 114; McDonald, 1959, 120; Dulles, 1983, 36; Trembath, 1991, 33, 73. Some speak of "truth" or "truth claims" as well.

See: Packer 1958, 92; Pinnock, 1967, 4n; Hick, 1967, 189; Aquinas, 1967, Bk. 4, ch.1, vol. 2, p. 628. And still others of knowledge: Tyrrell, 1907, 207.

13. Suárez, 1856, Bk. 1, ch. 12, ns. 4–5, vol. 1, 571; Swinburne, 1992, 4; Packer, 1958, 92.

14. Brunner, 1946, 8, 25; Barth, 1960, I, 231, 285; Smart, 1971, 26.

15. Barth, 1960, I, 231, 285; McDonald, 1959, 63–9; Dulles, 1983, 72. Some speak of it as a process that occurs at a pre-conceptual level (Moran, 1973, and Abraham, 1982, 13).

16. Titus 1, 2; Packer, 1958. The issue of whether the Judeo-Christian God is capable of deceiving is complicated. Deception seems to go contrary to his goodness, but at the same time there are passages in the Scriptures that suggest he deceived the enemies of his people. Perhaps it is best to say that he is incapable of deceiving *his people*. I leave the matter unresolved.

17. Pannenberg, 1968, 8–9; Wolterstorff, 1995, 31–2.

18. Baillie, 1956, 28. See also: Brunner, 1946, 8, 25; Barth, 1960, I, 134; Pannenberg, 1968, 4.

19. Kelsey, 1975, 32; Baillie, 1956, 28. Often, the claim is made that revelation is the disclosure of a person and the result of a personal encounter rather than the understanding of a proposition or view. McDonald, 1963, 162.

20. Versions of the first two can be found in Swinburne, 1992, 4. For other arguments, see Packer, 1958, 92 ff.

21. Downing, 1964, 195–9.

22. The most often voiced view is that human agents understand only part of what the divinity reveals. See Swinburne, 1992, 196.

23. Indeed, many argue that an actual receiver and an actual act of reception are required. Brunner, 1946, 33; Baillie, 1956, 64; Downing, 1964, 238. The last author makes this one of the cornerstones of his argument for the view that God has not in fact already revealed himself in the Christian scriptures.

24. Brunner, 1946, 416.

25. Whence the need for metaphor and poetry to describe what is indescribable. Eriugena, 1975, II, 146–51.

26. This issue has been discussed in detail by the Lutheran scholastics and others. See, for example, Preus, 1970, 185–6; Pannenberg, 1968.

27. Swinburne, 1992, 204. But not everyone agrees. See Luther, 1984, 114–16, and Schmid, 1961, 69 and 70, on the perspicuity of Sacred Scriptures. But even these authors agree that supernatural help, i.e., assistance from the Holy Spirit, is required in order not to fall into error. See also Gerhard and Baier, in Schmid, 1961, 73–5 and 77.

28. Pannenberg, 1968, 14–15; Latourelle, 1966, 186.

29. Dulles, 1983, 84–7.

30. One exception to this occurs when the agent and the revealed fact are one and the same. This is the case with Jesus Christ, according to some theologians.

31. Wolterstorff, 1995, 23; Calov and Hollaz, in Schmid, 1961, 26; Locke, IV, 18, 1, 1959, vol. 2, 416; Downing, 1964, 216; Brunner, 1946, 32; Dulles, 1968, 54; Farrer, 1957, 99.

32. Swinburne, 1992, 3; Downing, 1964, 217; Dulles 1983, 208; Calov, Quenstedt, and Gerhard, in Schmid, 1961, 26 and 41; Brunner, 1946, 8, 33; Pannenberg, 1968, 4, 14, 16.

33. Barth, 1960, 339 ff.

34. Farmer, 1935, 85–8; Macquarrie, 1966, 7; Levinas, 1989, 209. But some theologians explicitly distinguish between the act of disclosure and the act of understanding the disclosure (Pannenberg, 1968, 9).

35. Or, as Downing, 1964, 217 and 220, puts it, "a thing which reveals." See also Leo XIII, 1973; Schmid, 1961, 38–9; McDonald, 1959, 120; Dulles, 1968, 66; Packer, 1958, 73. Some argue, contrary to this, that it is "not permissible to think of a medium of revelation that is distinct from God himself" (see Pannenberg's exposition of this position in 1968, 5).

36. Wolterstorff, 1995, 23.

37. Baillie, 1956, 19; Barth, 1960, vol. I, 362; Brunner, 1946, 23.

38. Downing, 1964, 225–9.

39. Wolterstorff, 1995, 23.

40. Although some disagree. See Brunner, 1946, 23.

41. Aquinas, 1926, I, 1, 1, p. 2.

42. The question of why have a revelation when the facts revealed are not knowable through science may also be raised, but clearly its answer is much easier and based on the supernatural end of human beings. Averroes, 1961, 49, 53; Aquinas, 1926, I, 1, 1, p. 2; Swinburne, 1992, 69–84.

43. Ibid.

44. Tillich, 1951, 110; Brunner, 1946, 22.

45. In Gracia, 1995, 4, I defend a slightly different version of this formula.

46. There is in principle no reason why they could not be gustatory or olfactory as well, although the underdeveloped and vague character of these perceptions militates against them. I discuss gustatory and olfactory texts in Gracia, 1995, 20–1.

47. This view is not accepted by everyone. For a different opinion, see Gadamer, 1975, 262 and 267.

48. The distinction between signs and the entities that constitute signs is analogous to the distinction Danto draws between a work of art and the "mere" thing of which it consists in 1981, 1 ff., and 1986, 42. Derrida appears to oppose this distinction in 1977, 183. See also chs. 1 and 4 of Gracia, 1995.

49. Not everyone accepts the distinction between texts and signs. See Goodman and Elgin, 1988, 58.

50. For the cases of compound signs like 'postman,' see Gracia, 1995, 12–13.

51. Pannenberg, 1968.

52. Bonaventure, 1955.

53. Cf. Ricoeur, 1978, 113.

54. Derrida, 1976, 249.

55. My view is that meanings are facts considered in relation to a text through which someone understands them. Nothing in my argument hinges on this

view, however, so I am not presenting it as a claim here. All the same, it is only fair that I alert the reader to it.

56. For some classic signposts of the controversy about meaning, see: Frege, 1952, 56–78; Quine, 1953, 1–19; Grice, 1989; and Putnam, 1975, 215–77. Controversies about meaning have in part motivated the claim that questions of interpretation are best addressed apart from meaning. See Stout, 1982, 1–14.

57. The theories of individuation of texts are applications of more general theories of individuation. For a taxonomy of, and reference to, these, see Gracia, 1988, ch. 4.

58. Keep in mind that a token text is spatially located in whatever place the entities that constitute it are spatially located. For example, text 1 is located where it is written. The case with universal or type texts is different; the question of their location depends on the theory adopted concerning the location of universals in general, but this is something that does not concern us here. My view on this is that to ask for the spatial location of universals of any kind, whether these happen to be texts or not, is a category mistake. Spatial location applies only to individuals, and perhaps only to certain kinds of individuals. For the defense of this view, see Gracia, 1996, 35–41, and also 1988, 104–112.

59. Often the expression used is 'ontological status' rather than 'metaphysical status.' I used to favor the first, but now I prefer the second for reasons I explain in Gracia, 1999a.

60. Gracia, 1996, chs. 1 and 2.

61. The view that texts do not have meaning makes sense only if one identifies a text with the entities that constitute it. See Vorster, 1991, 18.

62. For authors to whom this view could be attributed, or who discuss versions of it, see: Derrida, 1977, 183–4, 192–3; Shillingsburg, 1986, 49; and Goodman, 1968, 116 and 207.

63. Fish, 1980, vii.

64. Austin, 1962.

65. Grigely, 1991, 170.

66. McGann, 1991, 4.

67. Cf. Austin, 1962, 98 ff.; McLaverty, 1991, 140 and 144; and Bakhtin, 1986, 105.

68. Irwin, 1999, 63–4.

69. Wolterstorff mounted a spirited defense of divine speech acts in 1995. For an earlier defense, see Abraham, 1982.

70. See, for example, Maimonides 1963, 99, and Schneider 1991, 27. To this, Wolterstorff responds that the acts in question are not locutionary but illocutionary (see 1995). Still, some might question, first, whether locutionary acts by themselves can be considered "speech," and second, whether it is possible for there to be illocutionary acts without locutionary ones. The issue remains controversial.

71. Swinburne, 1992, 165–7.

72. Thorton, 1950, 19.
73. Averroes, 1961, 49; see also Aquinas, 1926, I, 1, 1 and 9, pp. 2 and 10; Swinburne, 1992, 76–80, and 201.

Chapter 2

1. For various senses of 'interpretation' used in the literature, see: Ricoeur, 1978a, 128; Meiland, 1978, 25; Weitz, 1964, ch. 15; Stevenson, 1962, 127; Wolterstorff, 1995, 130–3; Brown, 1990, 1147; Pannenberg, 1976, 170 *et passim;* and Gracia, 1995, 147–8.
2. Schleiermacher, 1998, 5, introduces two senses of 'hermeneutic' that parallel the two senses of 'interpretation' I have identified. One seems to correspond to interpretation$_1$, but the second is not quite the same as interpretation$_2$. He calls the latter "the presentation of understanding" and in fact rejects it.
3. See, for example, Clarembald of Arras, 1965.
4. For a discussion of various kinds of authors and audiences, see Gracia, 1996, chs. 4 and 5, 91–169. For a survey of author constructs, see Irwin, 1999, 17–33. I discuss context and give references to the pertinent literature in Gracia, 1995, 26–30, and I return to authors and audiences in chapter 3 of this book.
5. Elsewhere I have called these "textual" and "nontextual," and "textual" and "contextual." See Gracia, 1995, pp. 164–8, and 1999, 1–23. Brown uses 'contextual' and 'non-contextual' to refer to interpretations in 1990, 1159.
6. Some think this kind of interpretation is not possible, but that does not affect the point I have made. For pertinent discussions, see Nehamas, 1986, 690, and 1987, 275 ff.; Hirsch, 1967, 46–7; Irwin, 1999, 46–65; Panofsky, 1955, 14; Steiner, 1975, 26 ff.; and Gracia, 1995, 211 ff.
7. Ricoeur, 1981, 146–7, 161, 200–1, *et passim.* Those postmodernists who reject that texts have meanings must reject this function. Barthes, 1970, 11–1. Postmodernists are not the only philosophers who reject meaning, however. Cf. Quine, 1953, 11 *et passim.*
8. For earlier statements to this effect with respect to the author, see Kant, 1963, 310, and Unamuno, 1981, 974. See more recent statements in Iser, 1989, 3–10, and Fish, 1980, ch. 15.
9. Brown, 1990, 1147.
10. Some authors disagree with the distinction between the meaning of a text and the implications of that meaning, on which the notion of implicative interpretations rests. The distinction is epistemically based: It is one thing to understand a text and another to understand the implications of its meaning, even if logically one were to say that the implications of the meaning of a text are packed into its meaning. For authors who oppose the distinction, see Nehamas, 1987, 276 ff.; Horton, 1979, 7; and Irwin, 1999, 59–65.
11. Augustine, 1977, 79–80.

12. The distinction between meaning interpretations and relational ones should not be confused with Hirsch's distinction between the meaning and the significance of a text. Both significance and relational interpretations involve a relational aspect, but that is as far as they coincide. For Hirsch's distinction, see 1960, 463–79, and 1967, 62. For a defense of Hirsch's distinction, see Irwin, 1999, 46–50. I present my own view of the distinction between meaning and significance in Gracia, 1995, 18–19, 216–17.

13. This is what Alter, 1992, 133, among others, no doubt inspired by Foucault's archaeological metaphors, calls the "excavative" task. Sometimes, however, the excavation is guided by a desire to understand the text in terms of certain factors or principles to which it is related, or in terms of which the interpreter wants to understand it. When this is so, the interpretation becomes relational.

14. Cf. Hirsch, 1994, 562–6.

15. Gracia, 1992, 214–15.

Chapter 3

1. Plato, *Phaedrus* 276, 1961, 521; Aquinas, 1926, I, 1, 10, vol. 1, pp. 10–12; Eco, 1990, 14–15.

2. Schleiermacher, 1998, 8–9 and 233.

3. Hirsch, 1976, 7. Among recent defenders of versions of authorial or intentional interpretation are: Irwin, 1999; Carroll, 2000; Iseminger, 1996; and Livingston, 1998.

4. Hirsch, 1967, 170–3.

5. Hirsch, 1972, 259.

6. Ibid.

7. Hirsch, 1976, 92. For a recent defense of Hirsch's interpretive imperative, see Irwin, 1999, 50–54.

8. For a "political" reading of some of Hirsch's texts, see Crosman, 1980, 158.

9. Ricoeur, 1981, 146–7 and 200–1.

10. Hirsch, 1972, 260.

11. Hirsch, 1976, 91.

12. Many of those concerned with religious hermeneutics answer affirmatively to both of these questions. See, for example, Wolterstorff, 1995, 15, and 130–33, although Wolterstorff is concerned with discourse rather than revelation. See also Aquinas, 1926, I, 1, 10, vol. 1, p. 11.

13. Gerhard, in Schmid, 1961, 42–3.

14. Quenstedt, in Schmid, 1961, 43; Preus, 1970, 371.

15. Not everyone agrees that revealed texts have divine authors. Cf. Barth, 1960, I, 98 ff. Wolterstorff has argued that a divine author may appropriate human speech, in 1995, 51–4. If Wolterstorff is right, one could argue that a divinity may appropriate and use a text whose original author is someone else without being, strictly speaking, the author.

16. Leo XIII, 1973, 641–2.

17. For further discussion, see Swinburne, 1992, 175–6.
18. As mentioned in chapter 2, recent criticism refers to a variety of authors of a text. The literature is increasingly large. See, for example: Irwin, 1999, 17–33, and forthcoming; Nehamas, 1987, 265–71; Foucault, 1977; Currie, 1991; Morgan, 1988; Walton, 1987; Booth, 1961, 138, 273–4; McGann, 1991, 95; Shillingsburg, 1986, 39–41; Barthes, 1977; and Gracia, 1995, 91–140.
19. Clifford and Murphy, 1990, 10.
20. Brown, 1990, 1148.
21. For the notion of an unfolding revelation, see Pannenberg, 1968a, 131–5.
22. Swinburne, 1992, 170.
23. Hollaz and Calov, in Schmid, 1961, 45 and 47.
24. For descriptivism, see Russell, 1948, 303; Searle, 1984, 232–3; Quine, 1970, 223. I am not endorsing this theory, but merely using it for purposes of illustration. I have discussed the merits of a descriptive theory of proper names in Gracia, 1988, ch. 6.
25. But not everyone agrees. Gadamer, 1988, 68 ff.
26. Quine, 1987 and 1969.
27. Heidegger, 1962.
28 Vorster, 1991, 20; Wright, 1992, 55.
29. Iser, 1971 and 1980.
30. Culler, 1980, 49.
31. I have discussed these various audiences in more detail in Gracia, 1996, 141–169. The literature on the identity, nature, and function of audiences is vast. See, for example: McGann, 1991, 95; Eco, 1990, 55; Iser, 1980 and 1974; Fish, 1980; and Booth, 1961, 138.
32. Swinburne, 1992, 83.
33. Roman descriptions of Christians as cannibals certainly support this claim.
34. Although most religions hold that there are some ways in which divinities communicate directly with individual believers about issues of concern to them individually (witness Augustine's garden revelation), most acknowledge that there is also a communal dimension of revelation that goes beyond individual revelation. Schmid, 1961, 62 *et passim*.
35. This is one main criticism Reformers had of the Roman Catholic Church. Gerhard and Quenstedt, in Schmid, 1961, 59 and 61.
36. Lerins, 1985, I, 2, 5, p. 149.
37. Iser, 1989, 4 and 8; Croatto, 1987, 22; Thiselton, 1999, 164–72; see also Suleiman's discussion of "subjective criticism" in 1980, 31 ff.
38. Fish, 1980, 174 and 180.
39. Ibid.
40. This is probably what Ricoeur has in mind in 1976, 9, 29–30, 75, and 1981, 146–7, 200–1. See also Beardsley, 1992.
41. Wright, 1992, 57. Also Moo, 1986. Aquinas also accepted the view that the perfection of divine revelation is only realized in heaven. See 1926, II-II, 171, 4, ad 2 and 173, 1, vol. 3, pp. 223 and 234.

42. Not everyone agrees. Indeed, this is what the theory of "semantic autonomy" is about. Hirsch, 1992, 11.

Chapter 4

1. These are often called "contextual." See Brown, 1990, 1159–60.
2. Eagleton, 1983, ch. 5. See also Suleiman, 1980, 31n.
3. Vorster, 1991, 22.
4. For an example of this procedure, see Lowes, 1964.
5. Eagleton, 1983, 151 ff.
6. Croatto, 1987, 60–5; Domeris, 1991 and 1991a; Scheffler, 1991; and van Tilborg, 1991.
7. Cf. Kusch, 1995. See also Bartley's approach to Wittgenstein, in 1985; and Eagleton, 1983, ch. 5.
8. For Marxist interpretations, see Domeris, 1991a. To see how Marxism is used by literary interpreters, see van Aarde, 1991, 104–5.
9. Cf. Ricoeur and his notion of poetic discourse in 1980, 103–4 *et passim.* See also the introduction in Wilder, 1969, and Alter, 1992, 63–4, and Brown 1985, 10 ff. For interpreters engaged in this kind of approach, see Brown, 1990, 1158–9; Clements, 1986; van Aarde, 1991; and Wuellner, 1991.
10. Alter, 1992, 40; Frye, 1990, 1991, and 1982. The approach can be described in Frye's first sentence of 1981 with respect to the Bible: "This book attempts a study of the Bible from the point of view of a literary critic." (xi) Deconstructive approaches can perhaps be best placed here. For examples, see Hartin, 1991, and Crossan, 1980.
11. Some attempts have been made in this direction, but they seem to me quite unconvincing. See Wright, 1992, 65–9.
12. Quoted by Diether, 1997, 19.
13. For the concern with life, see Halliwell, 1993, 7, 12, and 13. For the concern with itself (the so-called Self-Referential View), see Danto's criticism of Barthes in 1987, 10 ff.
14. Innerarity defends the fictional nature of literature in 1992, 367–80; but this position is more frequently assumed than defended—see Todorov, 1980, 67. For a contrary position, see Halliwell, 1993.
15. For the controversy, see Searle, 1979, 58–75. For the basis of the non-cognitive position, see Frege, 1952. Opposing the non-cognitivists is Gabriel, 1994, 57–68.
16. See nn. 14 and 15.
17. For a defense of the institutional view of art in general, see Dickie, 1974.
18. Most recently in Anderson, 1992, 207; and earlier in Culler, 980, 65.
19. Halliwell, 1993, 6, 7, and 15–16. The position that philosophy is about universals and not about individuals goes back at least to Aristotle and the conception of science he presented in *Posterior Analytics* I.
20. For various ways in which fiction is used in philosophy, see Anderson, 1992, 204–7.

21. For other views, see: Nehamas, 1987; Barthes, 1979; Wilsmore, 1987; Currie, 1991; Goodman and Elgin, 1988; Margolis, 1974; Lamarque, 2000, 101–7.
22. A popular view today is that the work is the product of an interpreter. Iser, 1980, 106; Nehamas, 1987.
23. For suggestions, see Lamarque, 2000, 101–7, and Gracia, 1995, 59–70.
24. Hirsch, 1960, 463–79, and 1967, 62; also Gracia, 1995, 18–19.
25. For some discussions related to this issue, see Gadamer, 1980, 46 ff., and 1994, 18–19.
26. Danto, 1987, 7. Danto goes too far, however, when he argues that literature, in contrast with philosophy, is a kind of mirror, and finds its subject only when it is read. (p. 19) First of all, it is not just literary texts that require an audience, all texts do; second, that texts require audiences does not mean that they are about the audiences. For my discussion of these issues, see Gracia, 1996, ch. 4.
27. Borges, 1998, 94.
28. Indeed, some argue that it is precisely the opposition to style that distinguishes philosophy from literature. Judovitz, 1987, 24–51.
29. Plato, *Phaedrus* 276–7a.
30. Some have gone so far as to argue not only that philosophy has style, but that its style and that of literature are similar. Conley, 1983, 79.
31. Those who, like Wright (1992, 65), see the task of literary criticism as simply laying bare the view an author has presented through a text are missing an essential aspect of the procedure.
32. This is frequently the case in philosophy, for example. Anderson, 1992, 204–7.
33. For some, those that are not literary appear to be rather few. Alter, 1992, 69.
34. For a contrary opinion, see Thorton, 1950, 53.
35. Lewis, 1958, 3.

Chapter 5

1. Apart from the examples cited below, see Bréhier, 1948–51; Chartier, 1982; Febvre, 1965; Ortega y Gasset, 1942; Bartley, 1985; Levi, 1978–9; Eagleton, 1983, 151–217; and Bevir, 1999. See also my general discussion in Gracia, 1992, 226–32, and also of Bevir's position in particular in forthcoming.
2. Kusch, 2000a, 15.
3. For the sociological approach to revelation, see: Domeris, 1991 and 1987; Draper, 1991; van Tilborg, 1991; Wilson, 1984; and the sources listed in the note that follows this one.
4. Some proponents of these methods, however, do not see them as excluding theological or religious interpretations. The following are expositions or illustrations of various sociological approaches: historical, Vorster, 1991, and Räisänen, 1990; sociological/historical, Domeris, 1991; feminist, Nortjé, 1991, and Fulkerson, 1994; and Marxist, Domeris, 1991a, and Deist, 1987.

5. Elliott, 1981, 8. See also van Tilborg, 1991.
6. For example, Scheffler states: "My intention [in this article] is rather to attempt to let the Gospel of Luke *dialogue* with liberation theology." (1991, 281). My emphasis. And Deist (1984, 94) notes an interpretation from the viewpoint "of the politically and socially oppressed according to which God is by nature on the side of the oppressed (cf. the Exodus event, Is 61:1–3; Lk 1:46ff) and encourages them to liberate themselves from the oppressing powers in order to live as free human beings."
7. Peckhaus, 2000, 179.
8. Kusch, 2000, 27.
9. Vorster, 1991, 15.
10. Peckhaus, 2000, 184; Thorton, 1950, 6, 20.
11. Bloor, 2000, 4–5. My emphasis.
12. Brunner, 1946, 419–20.
13. The confusion between these two senses of faith is rampant in the religious literature and often leads to great confusion about the role of faith in the understanding of revelation.
14. Vorster, 1991, 32 ff.
15. The last point is well elaborated by Wright in 1992, 122 ff.
16. Wright presents an excellent discussion of how knowledge of history and the literary structure of a revealed text plays a role in its interpretation in 1992, 47–69 and 81–118.
17. Vorster, 1991, 22.
18. Collins, 2000, 170.
19. Peckhaus, 2000, 187.
20. Bloor, 2000, 9.
21. Chimisso, 2000.
22. Scotus, 1950, II, dist. 3, part 1, qq. 1–6. Scotus also discusses individuation elsewhere, but this is of no consequence at present.
23. For example, Scotus opposes the view that human knowledge requires supernatural agency. Scotus, 1950, I, dist. 3, q. 4.

Chapter 6

1. Childs advocates it in 1974, ix, and practices it in the rest of the book. Brown disagrees with Childs in 1985, 21–2. And Wright (1992, 121, 139, and 144) argues for its inclusion in the interpretation of revelation along with literary and historical approaches.
2. Or as it is often put, a doctrine. Muller, 1987, 103; Preus, 1970, 110–11; Wright, 1992, 14, 126, and 130.
3. Different theologians put stress on different conditions. See, for example, Macquarrie, 1966, 3; and Vanhoozer, 1986, 104.
4. Some theologians think of theology, or sacred doctrine, as a science (*scientia*), but for others it is knowledge that is not scientific (*notitia* or *cognitio*).

For the first, see Aquinas, 1926, I, 1, 2, vol. 1, p. 3; for the second, Gerhard, in Preus, 1970, 110–11.

5. Aquinas, 1926, I, 1, 3, (ad 2) and 7, vol. 1, pp. 4 and 7; Muller, 1987, 226–30; Preus, 1970, 195–6; Gerhard, in Preus, 1970, 117–18.

6. Muller, 1987, 251 ff.

7. The same could be said of metaphysics, for example. Gracia, 1999, ch. 2.

8. Boethius, 1968, II, 8.

9. Plato, *Republic* 510, 1961, 745.

10. In *Ion,* Plato is explicit about this point; see 537d, 1961, 769. But compare this text with *Republic* 346, 1961, 595, where arts seem to differ by function or aim rather than object, and also with *Theaetetus* 146e, 1961, 851, where Socrates chides Theaetetus for confusing the question concerning the objects of knowledge with the question of what knowledge is.

11. Avicenna, 1973, I, 11; Aquinas, 1963, q. 5, 4, p. 42.

12. Aquinas, 1963, q. 5, resp.

13. Ockham, 1967, 8–9; Aquinas, 1945, I, 1, 7, p. 12, and 1963, q. 5, a. 4, pp. 44–45.

14. Aristotle, *Posterior Analytics* 71b20, 1941, 112.

15. Indeed, Averroes did just that in 1961, 49, 59, and 68.

16. Aristotle, *Posterior Analytics* 71b20, 1941, 112. See also *Metaphysics* 1064a1–3, 1941, 860.

17. Aristotle, *Metaphysics* 981b, 1026a17, 1941, 690–1, 779, and *Nicomachean Ethics* 1141a20–1141b10, 1941, 1028.

18. Ockham, 1967, 15.

19. Kant, 1950, §§ 1 and 2, pp. 13–19.

20. Ayer, n.d., 102–119.

21. Aquinas, 1963, q. 5, 1, resp. and ad 1, pp. 7, 10, 16, ad 6; 5, 4, ad 7, p. 38; 6, 1, ad 4, p. 62. Also Boethius, 1968, II, p. 8.

22. Temple, 1960, 4–5. Natural theology is also sometimes called "rational" (Mavrodes, 1988, 10), and revealed theology is sometimes called "biblical theology" in Christian circles (Kant, 1960, 8; Barth, 1960, I, 3).

23. Some theologians speak also of a natural revelation, but here I am concerned only with supernatural revelation. Fries, 1969, 23.

24 Pannenberg, 1976, 297–300, and Wright, 1992, 126 and 130; or "God and divine things." Schmid, 1961, 15.

25. Ibid., and Aquinas, 1926, I, 1, 3, vol. 1, p. 4; Clarembald of Arras, 1965, 82; Pannenberg, 1970, 1.

26. Aquinas, 1926, I, 1, 8, vol. 1, p. 8; Temple, 1960, 7, 10. See also Schmid, 1961, 15.

27. Pannenberg, 1976, 297.

28. Ockham, 1967, 9.

29. Of course, even the claim that theology is composed only of a certain kind of proposition is very difficult to establish. Stead, 1958, 114–15.

30. Quenstedt, in Schmid, 1961, 27.

31. Ibid.
32. Some theologians explicitly acknowledge the impossibility of separating theology from general knowledge (Hodge, 1878, 17); others emphasize its relation to our individual and collective experience (Woods, 1958, 155–9); others claim that revelation always passes through a process of natural understanding, even if the faith it generates in some can never be reduced to this understanding (Brunner, 1946, 15–16, 415–18); and still others see very little difference in method between theology and science (see Murphy's description of Pannenberg, in 1990, 29).
33. The analyses provided are not complete by any means; they only emphasize some of the fundamental points made in the sentences.
34. This is the position often attributed to so-called secular humanists.
35. Hoffman, in Schmid, 1961, 31.
36. Calov, in Schmid, 1961, 32.
37. For discussions of this issue, see: Alston, 1989; Wolterstorff, 1995; Swinburne, 1992.
38. Aquinas, 1926, I, 1, 9 and 10, vol. 1, pp. 9–12; Averroes, 1961, 51 ff.
39. There is no agreement on this. For Augustine, for example, anything in Scripture that cannot properly refer to the truths of faith or practical matters related to a good life is to be interpreted figuratively. Augustine, 1969, 3, 10, par. 14, p. 174.
40. Brunner, 1946, 416–18.
41. Quenstedt and Gerhard, in Schmid, 1961, 27, 28, and 66.
42. Calov, in Schmid, 1961, 35, 30, and 31.
43. Brunner, 1946, 418.
44. Ibid., 421.
45. Schmid, 1961, 92.
46. Theological interpretations are also conceived in a sense different from this in the pertinent literature. For example, Wright conceives them to be understandings of the underlying theology presented in a text (1992, 8). This is not what I have in mind. A theological interpretation for me is an understanding of a text in terms of the theology the interpreter brings into the interpretive process. Wright proposes his conception in order to argue for the need to understand the theological doctrines accepted by instrumental authors and their contemporaries for the understanding of revealed texts. Still, this is not enough insofar as we must ask how subsequent interpreters can have access to them. But there are many possible answers here, depending on the theology of subsequent interpreters. So it is the theology of the interpreters that really counts when it comes to the interpretation of revelation.
47. Barr, 1986; Ferguson, 1986, 185.
48. This is in part so because revealed scriptures are considered to be the written expression of part of a larger tradition. The latter is the source and proper context of the former. See Brown, 1990, 1164; Dulles, 1968, 66, 77.
49. Schmid, 1961, 25, and Gerhard, in Schmid, 1961, 64; Packer, 1958, 106.
50. Schmid, 1961, 58 ff.

51. Some theologians explicitly acknowledge this problem and try to deal with it by distinguishing dogmatic theology (theology conceived as nothing but the understanding of the doctrines revealed in Scriptures) and predogmatic theology (theology conceived as concerned with, among other things, the procedures to be followed in order to develop dogmatic theology). Dulles, 1983, 14–15.

52. Here is what Gerhard says (in Preus, 1970, 326): "There is only one proper and legitimate sense to each Scripture passage, a sense intended by the Holy Spirit and derived from the natural meaning of the words; and only from this one literal sense can any valid argumentation be brought forth." See also Schmid, 1961, 70, and Packer, 1958, 102 ff. For a discussion of the various ways in which 'literally' is understood by different interpreters, and the problems involved, see Brown, 1990, 1148–52, and 1985, 12–23.

53. Consider Cassian's well-known distinction between four different ways of interpreting the Christian scriptures: (1) historical or literal, (2) allegorical or Christological, (3) tropological, moral, or anthropological, and (4) anagogical or eschatological. According to (1), Jerusalem is a Jewish city; according to (2), it is Christ's Church; according to (3), it is the human soul; and according to (4), it is the heavenly city. Brown, 1990, 1155.

54. Calov and Hollaz, in Schmid, 1961, 49 and 64; Packer, 1958, 74; Preus, 1970, 346–7. This principle also appears to play a role in some theological statements from authors who do not adhere to the principle of *sola Scriptura*. Cf. Leo XIII, 1973, 641–2.

55. The most one can find are statements like that of II Timothy 3:16: "All scripture is inspired by God and profitable for teaching, for reproof, for correction, and for training in righteousness. . . ." But this is a far cry from the view that the Scriptures are to be taken literally and are inerrant. Surely one can easily see that the referent of 'scriptures' is unclear, that the notion of inspiration poses problems, and that the context of the passage is moral. For someone who holds the scriptural origin of these principles, see Packer, 1958, 74 and 102.

56. Gerhard, in Schmid, 1961, 55.

57. Packer, 1958, 106.

58. Ibid.

59. This is quite evident in Luther's writings themselves, for example. He continually appeals to God conceived in a particular way. Luther, 1989, 122 *et passim*.

60. Todorov makes clear that individual sentences have a textual context in 1980, 69. In a religious context a canon is particularly important. For the formation of the Christian canon, for example, see von Campenhausen, 1972.

61. Swinburne, 1992, 169. Consider, for example, the influences of particular canons in interpretation. See Sanders, 1972, and Childs, 1979, 69–83.

62. Culler, 1980, 49.

63. Todorov, 1980, 76.

64. For a contemporary rendering of the Roman Catholic point of view, see Brown, 1990, 1149–50 and 1163–4. See also, Swinburne, 1992, ch. 5.

65. Calov, in Schmid, 1961, 69 and 70. For a contemporary twist to this position, see Pannenberg, 1968a, 135–9.

66. Luther, 1984, 103 ff.

67. Brown, 1990, 1161, calls this "exegesis for personal transformation."

68. Gerhard and Baier, in Schmid, 1961, 73–5 and 77.

69. Luther, 1984, 114–16. Among Lutherans, this view was accompanied by the doctrine that Scripture was efficacious in producing understanding. The way this was interpreted, however, varied. See Preus, 1970, 362–73.

70. The literature on this is very large. Indeed, most of the theological sources cited in the bibliography have something to say about this issue.

71. For a survey of this history, see Nineham, 1963.

72. This example was brought to my attention by Nicholas Wolterstorff at a meeting where I presented some of these ideas.

73. Muller, 1987, 232.

74. Wright (1992, 137–9) has correctly pointed out that all readings of texts take place within particular world-views, and thus in order to understand revelation we need to know the views of their authors and their contemporary readers. My claim is more radical: Revealed texts cannot be appropriately understood, as revealed, without a view about those very texts and their place within a theology accepted by the interpreter.

75. Dulles, 1983, 14–15; see also Hollaz for a slightly different formulation of the problem, in Schmid, 1961, 56.

76. Wolterstorff, 1995, 15.

77. Swinburne, 1992, 177.

78. Brunner, 1946, 7, 21. See also Niebuhr's stronger claims in 1960, 23 ff.

79. Brunner, 1946, 419–21.

Chapter 7

1. If one has understood something correctly, this entails that one's understanding is definitive in the sense of being final. Downing, 1964, 214.

2. From these statements, it should be quite clear that none of these positions coincides with what Krausz calls "singularism" in 2000, 124. As he puts it, "[s]ingularism is the view that for a given object of interpretation there must be one and only one admissible interpretation of it."

3. Among those who have challenged the view that there can be definitive interpretations of *any* texts are: Miller, 1976, 331; Foucault, 1990, 63; Peirce, 1931, vol. 6, 170; and Rée, 1988, 56. I have discussed this issue in general in Gracia, 1994, 41–51. For someone who disagrees with Foucault and other postmodernists, see Juhl, 1980, 198, and Irwin, 1999, 62–3. For theologians who believe that revelation involves a progressive or developmental understanding of the divine message, the question of definitive interpretations of revelation makes no sense, of course. For postmodernist decon-

struction techniques in the context of revelation, see Hartin, 1991, 188–9. See also Crossan, 1981.

4. This justification goes back a long way. We find it, for example, explicitly presented by Averroes in the twelfth century (1961, 68). I discuss Averroes's position in Gracia, 1997, 139–53, and in 1996a, 243–51.
5. I have argued for this point in Gracia, 1995, 168–71 and 175–6.
6. Quine, 1953 and 1970; see my answer in Gracia, 1995, ch. 6.
7. Indeed, II Peter 3:15–16 complains about the difficulties found in St. Paul's letters.
8. Iser, 1989, 3–10; Fish, 1980, ch. 15.
9. Gracia, 1995, ch. 6.
10. Nietzsche, 1969, 77–8. For arguments against historicism as more recently proposed by Gadamer in particular, see Irwin, 1999, 74–92.
11. Draper, 1991, 241.
12. Gracia, 1992, 111–14 and 121–3.
13. Pannenberg, 1968a, 131–5.
14. Schmid has collected many texts from classical authors on this topic in 1961, 51–68. See also Lerins, 1985, I, 2, 5, p. 149, and Swinburne, 1992.
15. I have discussed the role of tradition in interpretation in Gracia, 1995, 207–12.
16. Gracia 1997.

Chapter 8

1. Relativism is a topic that has received considerable attention. For two general and fairly recent collections on this topic, see: Krausz, 1989, and Meiland and Krausz, 1982. For the context of revelation, see Walhaut, 1999, 91–9, and Niebuhr, 1960, 7–38. See also Gracia, 2000a, and Margolis, 2000.
2. This is in fact the reason why some make authorial interpretations paradigmatic of all interpretations. In principle, this appears to be a good way of avoiding relativism, but as we shall see, one need not go to this extreme to avoid interpretation relativism.
3. I discuss these in Gracia, 1995, 114–27.
4. Fish 1980; Putnam, 1975, 228.
5. Cf. Pannenberg, 1976, 69 and 344–5.
6. Hollaz, in Schmid, 1961, 96.
7. Quine, 1953 and 1970; Gorgias, 1968, 295.
8. Woods, 1958, 45 ff.
9. See also Mark 3:31–2 and 6:3, and Luke 8:19–20.
10. See Brown, 1990, 1379 (81:142). Brown presents a useful schematic discussion of the position of Mary in Roman Catholic theology in 1985, 86–100.
11. Brown, 1985, 35–7.
12. Bonaventure, 1934, v. 3, d. 7.
13. Ingenieros, 1919, 79.

14. Ayer, n.d., 115–19.
15. Averroes, 1961, 49.
16. Wolff, 1963, 104.
17. The frequently neglected communitarian aspect of theology is emphasized by Macquarrie, 1966, 2.
18. Temple, 1960, 396; also Kant, 1960, 9.

Bibliography

Abraham, William J. 1982. *Divine Revelation and the Limits of Historical Criticism.* Oxford: Oxford University Press.

———. 1997. "Revelation and Scripture." In Philip L. Quinn and Charles Taliafierro, eds. *A Companion to Philosophy of Religion.* Cambridge, MA: Blackwell Publishers, 584–90.

Alston, William P. 1989. *Divine Nature and Human Language.* Ithaca, NY: Cornell University Press.

Alter, Robert. 1992. *The World of Biblical Literature.* New York: Basic Books.

Anderson, Susan L. 1992. "Philosophy and Fiction." *Metaphilosophy* 23, 3:203–13.

Aquinas, Thomas. 1963. *Commentary on "On the Trinity" of Boethius.* In *The Division and Method of the Sciences.* 3rd ed. Ed. Armand Maurer. Toronto: Pontifical Institute of Mediaeval Studies.

———. 1945. *Summa theologiae* I, 1, 7. In *The Basic Writings of Saint Thomas Aquinas.* Vol. 1. Ed. Anton Pegis. New York: Random House.

———. 1926. *Summa theologiae.* 4 vols. Ed. De Rubeis et al. Taurini: Marietti.

———. 1967. *Summa contra gentes.* 2 vols. In *Suma contra los gentiles,* bilingual edition. Ed. L. Robles Carcedo and A. Robles Sierra. Madrid: Biblioteca de Autores Cristianos.

Aristotle. 1941. *Posterior Analytics.* In *The Basic Works of Aristotle.* Ed. R. McKeon. New York: Random House, 110–87.

———. 1941. *Metaphysics.* In *The Basic Works of Aristotle.* Ed. R. McKeon. New York: Random House, 689–934.

———. 1941. *Nicomachean Ethics.* In *The Basic Works of Aristotle.* Ed. R. McKeon. New York: Random House, 935–1126.

Augustine. 1977. *Eighty-three Different Questions.* Trans. David L. Mosher. Washington, D.C.: The Catholic University of America Press.

———. 1969. *De doctrina christiana.* In *Obras de san Agustín.* Vol. 15. Ed. Balbino Martín. Madrid: Biblioteca de Autores Cristianos.

Austin, J. L. 1962. *How to Do Things with Words.* Ed. J. O. Urmson. Cambridge, MA: Harvard University Press.

Averroes. 1961. *On the Harmony of Religion and Philosophy.* Trans. G. F. Hourani. London: Luzac. This work is also known as *The Decisive Treatise.*

Avicenna. 1973. *Metaphysica* I. Trans. from Persian by P. Morewedge. New York: Columbia University Press.

Ayer, A. J. N.d. *Language, Truth and Logic.* New York: Dover.

Baillie, John. 1956. *The Idea of Revelation in Recent Thought.* New York: Columbia University Press.

Baillie, John, and Hugh Martin, eds. 1937. *Revelation.* London: Farber and Farber.

Bakhtin, Mikhail M. 1986. *Speech Genres and Other Late Essays.* Trans. Vern W. McGee; ed. Caryl Emerson and Michael Holquist. Austin: University of Texas Press.

Barr, James. 1986. "Exegesis as a Theological Discipline Reconsidered and the Shadow of the Jesus of History." In Donald G. Miller, ed., *The Hermeneutical Quest.* Allison Park, PA: Pickwick Publications, 11–45.

Barth, Karl. 1960. *Church Dogmatics.* 4 vols. Trans. G. T. Thomson et al. Edinburgh: T. Clark.

Barthes, Roland. 1979. "From Work to Text." Trans. Josué V. Harari. In Josué V. Harari, ed., *Textual Strategies: Perspectives in Post-Structuralist Criticism.* Ithaca, NY: Cornell University Press, 73–81.

———. 1977. "The Death of the Author." In *Image, Music, Text.* Trans. Stephen Heath. New York: Hill and Wang, 142–8.

———. 1970. *S/Z.* Paris: Editions du Seuil.

Bartley, W. W., III. 1985. *Wittgenstein.* 2nd rev. and enlarged ed. La Salle, IL: Open Court.

Beardsley, Monroe. 1992. "The Authority of the Text." In G. Iseminger, ed., *Intention and Interpretation.* Philadelphia: Temple University Press, 24–40.

Bevir, Mark. 1999. *The Logic of the History of Ideas.* Cambridge: Cambridge University Press.

Bloor, David. 2000. "Wittgenstein as a Conservative Thinker." In Martin Kusch, ed., *The Sociology of Philosophical Knowledge.* Dordrecht: Kluwer, 1–14.

Boethius. 1968. *On the Trinity.* In *Boethius: The Theological Tractates.* Trans. H. F. Stewart and E. K. Rand. Cambridge, MA: Harvard University Press, 2–81.

Bonaventure. 1955. *De reductione artium ad theologiam.* Trans. E. T. Healy. St. Bonaventure, NY: St. Bonaventure College.

———. 1934. *Collationes in Hexaemeron.* Ed. R. Delorme. Florence: Ad Claras Aquas.

Booth, Wayne. 1961. *The Rhetoric of Fiction.* Chicago: University of Chicago Press.

Borges, Jorge Luis. 1998. "Pierre Menard: Author of the *Quixote.*" In *Collected Fictions.* Trans. Andrew Hurley. New York: Penguin Books, 88–95.

Bréhier, Émile. 1948 - 51. *Histoire de la philosophie.* Paris: F. Alcan.

Brentano, Franz. 1963. *Geschichte der Griechischen Philosophie.* Bern and Munich: Francke Verlag.

Brown, Raymond E. 1985. *Biblical Exegesis and Church Doctrine.* New York: Paulist Press.

Brown, Raymond E., and Sandra M. Schneider. 1999. "Hermeneutics." In *The New Jerome Biblical Commentary.* Englewood Cliffs, NJ: Prentice Hall, 1146–65.

Brown, Raymond E., et al., eds. 1990. *The New Jerome Biblical Commentary.* Englewood Cliffs, NJ: Prentice Hall.

Brunner, Emil. 1946. *Revelation and Reason: The Christian Doctrine of Faith and Knowledge.* Trans. Olive Wyon. Philadelphia: Westminster Press.

Carroll, Noël. 2000. "Interpretation and Intention: The Debate Between Hypothetical and Actual Intentionalism." *Metaphilosophy* 31, 1/2:75–95.

Carson, D. A. 1986. "Recent Developments in the Doctrine of Scripture." In D. A. Carson and John D. Woodbridge, *Hermeneutics, Authority, and the Canon.* Grand Rapids, MI: Academie Books, 5–48.

———and J. D. Woodbridge, eds. 1986. *Hermeneutics, Authority, and the Canon.* Grand Rapids, MI: Academie Books.

Chartier, Roger. 1982. "Intellectual History or Sociocultural History? The French Trajectories." In Dominick La Capra and Steven L. Kaplan, eds., *Modern European Intellectual History: Reappraisals and New Perspectives.* Ithaca, NY: Cornell University Press, 13–26.

Childs, Brevard S. 1979. *Introduction to the Old Testament as Scripture.* Philadelphia: Fortress Press.

———. 1974. *The Book of Exodus: A Critical, Theological Commentary.* Philadelphia: Westminster Press.

Chimisso, Cristina. 2000. "Painting an Icon: Gaston Bachelard and the Philosophical Beard." In Martin Kusch, ed., *The Sociology of Philosophical Knowledge.* Dordrecht: Kluwer, 61–92.

Clarembald of Arras. 1965. *Tractatus super librum Boetii De Trinitate.* In Nikolaus M. Häring, *Life and Works of Clarembald of Arras: A Twelfth-Century Master of the School of Chartres.* Toronto: Pontifical Institute of Mediaeval Studies, 65–186.

Clements, Ronald S. 1986. "Prophecy as Literature: A Re-Appraisal." In Donald G. Miller, ed., *The Hermeneutical Quest.* Allison Park, PA: Pickwick Publications, 59–76.

Clifford, Richard J., and Roland E. Murphy. 1990. "Genesis." In Raymond E. Brown et al., eds., *The New Jerome Biblical Commentary.* Englewood Cliffs, NJ: Prentice Hall, 8–43.

Collins, Randall. 2000. "Reflexivity and Social Embeddedness in the History of Ethical Philosophies." In Martin Kusch, ed., *The Sociology of Philosophical Knowledge.* Dordrecht: Kluwer, 155–78.

Conley, Tom. 1983. "A Trace of Style." In Mark Krupnick, ed., *Displacement: Derrida and After.* Bloomington: Indiana University Press, 74–92.

Creed, J. M. 1938. *The Divinity of Jesus Christ: A Study in the History of Christian Doctrine since Kant.* Cambridge: Cambridge University Press.

Croatto, J. Severino. 1987. *Biblical Hermeneutics: Toward a Theory of Reading as a Production of Meaning.* Trans. from Spanish by Robert R. Barr. New York: Orbis Books.

Crosman, Robert. 1980. "Do Readers Make Meaning?" In Susan R. Suleiman and Inge Crosman, eds., *The Reader in the Text: Essays on Audience and Interpretation.* Princeton, NJ: Princeton University Press, 149–64.

Crossan, J. Dominic. 1980. *Cliffs of Fall: Paradox and Polyvalence in the Parables of Jesus.* New York: Seabury.

Culler, Jonathan. 1980. "Prolegomena to a Theory of Reading." In Susan R. Suleiman and Inge Crosman, eds., *The Reader in the Text: Essays on Audience and Interpretation*. Princeton, NJ: Princeton University Press, 46–65.

Currie, Gregory. 1991. "Work and Text." *Mind* 100:325–39.

Danto, Arthur C. 1987. "Philosophy as/and/of Literature." In Anthony J. Cascardi, ed., *Literature and the Question of Philosophy*. Baltimore: The Johns Hopkins University Press, 1–23.

———. 1986. *The Philosophical Disenfranchisement of Art*. New York: Columbia University Press.

———. 1981. *The Transfiguration of the Common Place: A Philosophy of Art*. Cambridge, MA: Harvard University Press, 1–23.

Denzinger, H., ed. 1973. *Enchiridion symbolorum definitionum et declarationum de rebus fidei et morum*. 35st ed. Rome: Herder.

Deist, F. E. 1987. "How Does a Marxist Read the Bible?" In P. G. R. de Villiers, ed., *Liberation Theology and the Bible*. Pretoria: UNISA, 15–30.

———. 1984. *A Concise Dictionary of Theological Terms*. Pretoria: Van Schaik.

Derrida, Jacques. 1981. *Positions*. Trans. and ed. Alan Bass. Chicago: University of Chicago Press.

———. 1978. *Writing and Difference*. Trans. Alan Bass. Chicago: University of Chicago Press.

———. 1977. "Signature Event Context," *Glyph* 1:172–97.

———. 1976. *Of Grammatology*. Trans. G. C. Spivak. Chicago: University of Chicago Press.

Dickie, George. 1974. *Art and the Aesthetic: An Institutional Analysis*. Ithaca, NY: Cornell University Press.

Diether, Jack. 1997. "Notes to the Program." Carnegie Hall, Tuesday evening, November 4.

Domeris, W. R. 1991. "Sociological and Social Historical Investigations." In P. J. Hartin and J. H. Petzer, eds., *Text and Interpretation: New Approaches in the Criticism of the New Testament*. Leiden: E. J. Brill, 215–34.

———. 1991a. "Historical Materialists Exegesis." In P. J. Hartin and J. H. Petzer, eds. *Text and Interpretation: New Approaches in the Criticism of the New Testament*. Leiden: E. J. Brill, 299–312.

———. 1987. *Portraits of Jesus. Matthew. A Contextual Approach to Bible Study*. London: Collins Liturgical.

Downing, F. Gerald. 1964. *Has Christianity a Revelation?* London: SCM Press.

Draper, J. A. 1991. "'For the Kingdom Is Inside of You and It Is Outside of You': Contextual Exegesis in South Africa." In P. J. Hartin and J. H. Petzer, eds., *Text and Interpretation: New Approaches in the Criticism of the New Testament*. Leiden: E. J. Brill, 225–57.

Dulles, Avery. 1983. *Models of Revelation*. Garden City, NY: Doubleday.

———. 1968. *Revelation and the Quest for Unity*. Washington, D.C.: Corpus Books.

Eagleton, Terry. 1983. *Literary Theory: An Introduction*. Minneapolis: University of Minnesota Press.

Eco, Umberto. 1990. *The Limits of Interpretation*. Bloomington: Indiana University Press.

Elliott, J. H. 1981. *A Home for the Homeless: A Sociological Exegesis of I Peter. Its Situation and Strategy.* Philadelphia: Fortress Press.

Eriugena, Iohannes Scotus. 1975. *Expositiones in Ierarchiam coelestem.* Ed. J. Barbet. Turnhout, Belgium: Brepols.

Evans, G. R. 1985. *The Language of the Bible: The Road to Reformation.* Cambridge: Cambridge University Press.

———. 1984. *The Language of the Bible: The Earlier Middle Ages.* Cambridge: Cambridge University Press.

Farmer, H. H. 1935. *The World and God: A Study of Prayer, Providence and Miracle in Christian Experience.* London: Nisbet & Co.

Farrer, A. 1957. "Revelation." In B. Mitchell, ed., *Faith and Logic.* London: Allen & Unwin, 84–107.

Febvre, Lucien. 1965. "Doctrines et sociétés." In *Combats pour l'histoire.* 2nd ed. Paris: Librarie Armand Colin, 284–8.

Ferguson, D. S. 1986. *Biblical Hermeneutics: An Introduction.* Atlanta, GA: John Knox Press.

Fish, Stanley. 1980. *Is There a Text in This Class? The Authority of Interpretive Communities.* Cambridge, MA: Harvard University Press.

Foucault, Michel. 1990. "Nietzsche, Freud, Marx." In G. L. Orminston and A. D. Schrifts, eds., *Transforming the Hermeneutic Context: From Nietzsche to Nancy.* Albany, NY: State University of New York Press, 59–68.

———. 1977. "What Is an Author?" Trans. Donald F. Bouchard and Sherry Simon. In Donald F. Bouchard, ed., *Language, Counter-Memory, Practice: Selected Essays and Interviews.* Ithaca, NY: Cornell University Press, 113–38.

Frege, Gottlob. 1952. "On Sense and Reference." In P. Geach and M. Black, eds. and trans., *Translations from the Philosophical Writings of Gottlob Frege.* Oxford: Blackwell, 56–78.

Frei, Hans. 1993. *Theology and Narrative.* Ed. G. Hunsinger and William C. Placher. New York: Oxford University Press.

———. 1992. *Types of Christian Theology.* New Haven, CT: Yale University Press.

Fries, Heinrich. 1969. *Revelation.* New York: Herder and Herder.

Frye, Northrop. 1991. *The Double Vision: Language and Meaning in Religion.* Toronto: University of Toronto Press.

———. 1990. *Words with Power: Being a Second Study of "The Bible and Literature."* New York: Harcourt Brace Jovanovich.

———. 1982. *The Great Code: The Bible and Literature.* London: Harcourt Brace Jovanovich.

Fulkerson, M. M. 1994. *Changing the Subject, Women's Discourses and Feminist Theologies.* Minneapolis, MN: Fortress Press.

Funk, Robert W. 1966. *Language, Hermeneutic, and Word of God: The Problem of Language in the New Testament and Contemporary Theology.* New York: Harper & Row.

Gabriel, G. 1994. "Sobre el significado en la literatura y el valor cognitivo de la ficción." Trans. Ma. Teresa López de la Vieja. In Ma. Teresa López de la Vieja, ed., *Figuras del Logos: Entre la filosofía y la literatura*. Mexico City: Fondo de Cultura Económica, 57–68.

Gadamer, Hans-Georg. 1994. "Goethe and Philosophy." Trans. Robert H. Paslick. In *Literature and Philosophy in Dialogue: Essays in German Literary Theory*. Albany, NY: State University of New York Press, 1–20.

———. 1988. "On the Circle of Understanding." Trans. John M. Connolly and Thomas Keutner. In John M. Connolly and Thomas Keutner, eds., *Hermeneutics versus Science? Three German Views*. Notre Dame, IN: University of Notre Dame Press, 68–78.

———. 1980. "Plato and the Poets." In *Dialogue and Dialectic: Eight Hermeneutical Studies in Plato*. Trans. P. Christopher Smith. New Haven, CT: Yale University Press.

———. 1975. *Truth and Method*. 2nd ed. Trans. Garret Barden and Robert Cumming. New York: Crossroad.

Goodman, Nelson. 1968. *Languages of Art: An Approach to the Theory of Symbols*. Oxford: Oxford University Press.

Goodman, Nelson, and Catherine Z. Elgin. 1988. "Interpretation and Identity." In *Reconceptions in Philosophy and Other Arts and Sciences*. London: Routledge, 49–65.

Gorgias. 1968. "On Not-Being." In J. M. Robinson, *An Introduction to Early Greek Philosophy: The Chief Fragments and Ancient Testimony, with Connecting Commentary*. New York: Houghton Mifflin Co., 295–8.

Gracia, Jorge J. E. Forthcoming. "The Logic of the History of Ideas or the Sociology of the History of Beliefs? *Philosophical Books*.

———. 2000. "Borges' 'Pierre Menard': Philosophy or Literature?" *Journal of Aesthetics and Art Criticism* 59, 1(2001), 45–57; rep. in Jorge J. E. Gracia et al., eds., *¿Literary Philosophers? Borges, Calvino, Eco*. New York: Routledge, 2002.

———. 2000a. "Relativism and the Interpretation of Texts." *Metaphilosophy* 31, 1/2:43–62; rep. in Joseph Margolis and Tom Rockmore, eds., *The Philosophy of Interpretation*. Masden, MA: Blackwell Publishers, 43–62.

———. 1999. "The Interpretation of Revealed Texts: Can We Know What God Means?" *Annual American Catholic Philosophical Association Proceedings* 72:1–23.

———. 1999a. *Metaphysics and Its Task: The Search for the Categorial Foundation of Knowledge*. Albany, NY: State University of New York Press.

———. 1997. "Interpretation and the Law: Averroes's Contribution to the Hermeneutics of Sacred Texts," *History of Philosophy Quarterly* 14, 1:139–53.

———. 1996. *Texts: Ontological Status, Identity, Author, Audience*. Albany, NY: State University of New York Press.

———. 1996a. "The Philosopher and the Understanding of the Law." In Mourad Wahba and Mona Abousenna, eds., *Averroes and the Enlightenment*. Buffalo, NY: Prometheus Books, 243–51.

———. 1995. *A Theory of Textuality: The Logic and Epistemology*. Albany: State University of New York Press.

———. 1994. "Can There Be Definitive Interpretations? An Interpretation of Foucault in Response to Engel." In B. Smith, ed., *European Philosophy and the American Academy*. La Salle, IL: Hegeler Institute, 41–51.

———. 1992. *Philosophy and Its History: Issues in Philosophical Historiography*. Albany: State University of New York Press.

———. 1988. *Individuality: An Essay on the Foundations of Metaphysics*. Albany, NY: State University of New York Press.

Grant, Robert M. 1972. *A Short History of the Interpretation of the Bible*. Revised Edition. New York: Macmillan Co.

Grice, H. P. 1989. *Studies in the Way of Words*. Cambridge, MA: Harvard University Press.

Grigely, Joseph. 1991. "The Textual Event." In Philip Cohen, ed., *Devils and Angels: Textual Editing and Literary Criticism*. Charlottesville and London: University Press of Virginia.

Gutiérrez, G. 1973. *A Theology of Liberation*. New York: Orbis.

Halliwell, Stephen. 1993. "Philosophy and Literature: Settling a Quarrel?" *Philosophical Investigations* 16, 1:1–17.

Hartin, P. J. 1991. "Disseminating the Word: A Deconstructive Reading of Mark 4:1–9 and Mark 4:13–20." In P. J. Hartin and J. H. Petzer, eds., *Text and Interpretation: New Approaches in the Criticism of the New Testament*. Leiden: E. J. Brill, 187–201.

Hartin, P. J., and J. H. Petzer, eds. 1991. *Text and Interpretation: New Approaches in the Criticism of the New Testament*. Leiden: E. J. Brill.

Heidegger, Martin. 1962. *Being and Time*. Trans. John Macquarrie and Edward Robinson. New York: Harper Books.

Henry, Carl F. H. 1976. *God, Revelation and Authority*. Waco, TX: Word.

Hick, John. 1967. "Revelation." In Paul Edwards, ed., *The Encyclopedia of Philosophy*. Vol. 7. New York: Macmillan, 189–91.

Hirsch, E. D., Jr. 1994. "Transhistorical Intentions and the Persistence of Allegory." *New Literary History* 25:549–67.

———. 1992. "In Defense of the Author." In G. Iseminger, ed., *Intention and Interpretation*. Philadelphia: Temple University Press, 11–23.

———. 1988. "Counterfactuals in Interpretation." In Sanford Levinson and Steven Mailloux, eds., *Interpreting Law and Literature: A Hermeneutic Reader*. Evanston, IL: Northwestern University Press, 55–68.

———. 1976. *The Aims of Interpretation*. Chicago: University of Chicago Press.

———. 1972. "Three Dimensions of Hermeneutics." *New Literary History* 3:245–61.

———. 1967. *Validity in Interpretation*. New Haven, CT: Yale University Press.

———. 1960. "Objective Interpretation." *PMLA* 75:463–79.

Hodge, Archibald Alexander. 1878. *Outlines of Theology*. Rewritten and enlarged. New York: Robert Carter and Brothers.

Horton, Susan. 1979. *Interpreting Interpreting: Interpreting Dickens' "Dombey."* Baltimore: Johns Hopkins University Press.

Ingenieros, José. 1919. *Principios de psicología*. 6th ed. Buenos Aires: L. J. Rosso.

Innerarity, Daniel. 1992. "La verdad de las mentiras: Reflexiones sobre filosofía y literatura." *Diálogo Filosófico* 24:367–80.

Irwin, William, ed. Forthcoming. *The Death and Resurrection of the Author.* Westport, CT: Greenwood Press.

———. 1999. *Intentionalist Interpretations: A Philosophical Explanation and Defense.* Westport, CT: Greenwood Press.

Iseminger, Gary. 1996. "Actual Intentionalism vs. Hypothetical Intentionalism." *Journal of Aesthetics and Art Criticism* 54:319–26.

Iser, Wolfgang. 1989. *Prospecting: From Reader-Response to Literary Anthropology.* Baltimore: Johns Hopkins University Press.

———. 1980. "Interaction between Reader and Text." In Susan R. Suleiman and Inge Crosman, eds., *The Reader in the Text: Essays on Audience and Interpretation.* Princeton, NJ: Princeton University Press, 106–119.

———. 1974. *The Implied Reader: Patterns of Communication in Prose Fiction from Bunyan to Beckett.* Baltimore: Johns Hopkins University Press.

———. 1971. "Indeterminacy and the Reader's Response in Prose Fiction." In J. Hillis Miller, ed., *Aspects of Narrative: Selected Papers from the English Institute.* New York: Columbia University Press, 1–46.

Judovitz, Dalia. 1987. "Philosophy and Poetry: The Difference between Them in Plato and Descartes." In Anthony J. Cascardi, ed., *Literature and the Question of Philosophy.* Baltimore: Johns Hopkins University Press, 24–51.

Juhl, P. D. 1980. *Interpretation: An Essay in the Philosophy of Literary Criticism.* Princeton, NJ: Princeton University Press.

Kant, Immanuel. 1963. *Critique of Pure Reason.* Ch. 1. Trans. N. K. Smith. London: Macmillan.

———. 1960. *Religion within the Limits of Reason Alone.* Trans. Theodore M. Greene and Hoyt H. Hudson. New York: Harper.

———. 1950. *Prolegomena to Any Future Metaphysics.* Ed. L. W. Beck. New York: Bobbs-Merrill Co.

Keegan, Terence J. 1985. *Interpreting the Bible: A Popular Introduction to Biblical Hermeneutics.* New York: Paulist Press.

Kelsey, David H. 1975. *The Uses of Scripture in Recent Theology.* Philadelphia: Fortress Press.

Krausz, Michael. 2000. "Interpretation and Its 'Metaphysical' Entanglements." *Metaphilosophy* 31, 1/2:124–47.

Krausz, M., ed. 1989. *Relativism: Interpretation and Confrontation.* Notre Dame, IN: University of Notre Dame Press.

Kusch, Martin, ed. 2000. *The Sociology of Philosophical Knowledge.* Dordrecht: Kluwer.

———. 2000a. "The Sociology of Philosophical Knowledge." In Martin Kusch, ed., *The Sociology of Philosophical Knowledge.* Dordrecht: Kluwer, 15–38.

———. 1995. *Psychologism: A Case Study in the Sociology of Philosophical Knowledge.* London: Routledge.

Lamarque, Peter. 2000. "Objects of Interpretation." *Metaphilosophy* 31, 1/2:96–124.

Latourelle, René. 1966. *Theology of Revelation, Including a Commentary on the Constitution "Dei Verbum" of Vatican II*. Staten Island, NY: Alba House.

Leo XIII, Pope. 1973. *"Providentissimus Deus."* In H. Denzinger, ed., *Enchiridion symbolorum definitionum et declarationum de rebus fidei et morum*. Rome: Herder, 638–43.

Lerins, Vincent of. 1985. *Commonitorium*. In Corpus Christianorum, Series Latina LXIV, 147–95. Turnhout, Belgium: Brepols.

Levi, Arthur W. 1978 - 9. "The Biographical Sources of Wittgenstein's Ethics." *Telos* 38:63–76.

Levinas, Emmanuel. 1989. "Revelation in the Jewish Tradition." In Seán Hand, ed., *The Levinas Reader*. Oxford: Basil Blackwell, 190–210.

Levinson, Sanford, and Steven Mailloux, eds. 1988. *Interpreting Law and Literature: A Hermeneutic Reader*. Evanston, IL: Northwestern University Press.

Lewis, C. S. 1958. *Reflections on the Psalms*. London: Geoffrey Bles.

Livingston, Paisley. 1998. "Intentionalism in Aesthetics." *New Literary History* 29:831–46.

Locke, John. 1959. *An Essay Concerning Human Understanding*. 2 vols. New York: Dover.

Lowes, John Livingston. 1964. *The Road to Xanadu: A Study in the Ways of the Imagination*. Boston: Houghton Mifflin Co.

Lundin, Roger, et al. 1999. *The Promise of Hermeneutics*. Grand Rapids, MI: Eerdmans.

Luther, Martin. 1989. *Basic Theological Writings*. Ed. Timothy F. Lull. Minneapolis, MN: Fortress Press.

———. 1984. *The Bondage of the Will*. Trans. Henry Cole. Grand Rapids, MI: Baker Book House.

Macquarrie, John. 1977. *Principles of Christian Theology*. 2nd ed. New York: Scribner.

———. 1966. *Principles of Christian Theology*. New York: Scribner's.

Maimonides, Moses. 1963. *The Guide of the Perplexed*. Trans. Shlomo Pines. Chicago: University of Chicago Press.

Margolis, Joseph. 2000. "Relativism and Interpretive Objectivity." In Joseph Margolis and Tom Rockmore, eds., *The Philosophy of Interpretation*. Oxford: Blackwell Publishers, 200–26.

———. 1974. "Works of Art as Physically Embodied and Culturally Emergent Entities." *British Journal of Aesthetics* 14, 3:187–96.

Mavrodes, George. 1988. *Revelation in Religious Belief*. Philadelphia: Temple University Press.

McConnell, Frank, ed. 1986. *The Biblical and the Narrative Tradition*. New York: Oxford University Press.

McDonald, H. D. 1963. *Theories of Revelation: An Historical Study 1860 - 1960*. London: Allen & Unwin.

———. 1959. *Ideas of Revelation: An Historical Study A.D. 1700 to A.D. 1860*. London: Macmillan.

McGann, Jerome. 1991. *The Textual Condition*. Princeton, NJ: Princeton University Press.

McLaverty, James. 1991. "Issues of Identity and Utterance: An Intentionalist Response to 'Textual Instability.'" In Philip Cohen, ed., *Devils and Angels: Textual Editing and Literary Criticism*. Charlottesville and London: University Press of Virginia, 134–51.

Meiland, J. W. 1978. "Interpretation as a Cognitive Discipline." *Philosophy and Literature* 2:23–45.

Meiland, J. W., and M. Krausz, eds. 1982. *Relativism: Cognitive and Moral*. Notre Dame, IN: Notre Dame University Press.

Miller, Donald G., ed. 1986. *The Hermeneutical Quest: Essays in Honor of James Luther Mays on his Sixty-Fifth Birthday*. Allison Park, PA: Pickwick Publications.

Miller, J. Hillis. 1976. "Steven's Rock and Criticism as Cure, II. " *Georgia Review* 31:330–48.

Mitchell, Basil, ed. 1957. *Faith and Logic: Oxford Essays in Philosophical Theology*. London: Allen & Unwin.

Moo, Douglas J. 1986. "The Problem of *Sensus Plenior.*" In D. A. Carson and John Woodbridge, eds., *Hermeneutics, Authority, and the Canon*. Grand Rapids, MI: Academie Books, 175–211.

Moran, Gabriel. 1973. *Theology of Revelation*. London: Search Press.

Morgan, Michael L. 1988. "Authorship and the History of Philosophy." *Review of Metaphysics* 42, 2:327–55.

Muller, Richard A. 1987 and 1993. *Post Reformation Reformed Dogmatics*. 2 vols. Grand Rapids, MI: Baker Book House.

Murphy, Nancey. 1990. *Theology in the Age of Scientific Reasoning*. Ithaca, NY: Cornell University Press.

Nehamas, Alexander. 1987. "Writer, Text, Work, Author." In Anthony J. Cascardi, ed., *Literature and the Question of Philosophy*. Baltimore: Johns Hopkins University Press, 265–91.

———. 1986. "What an Author Is." *Journal of Philosophy* 83:685–91.

Niebuhr, H. R. 1960. *The Meaning of Revelation*. New York: Macmillan.

Nietzsche, F. 1969. *On the Genealogy of Morals*. Trans. Walter Kaufman and R. J. Hollingdale. New York: Vintage Books.

Nineham, D. E., ed. 1963. *The Church's Use of the Bible: Past and Present*. London: SPCK.

Nortjé, S. J. 1991. "On the Road to Emmaus—A Woman's Experience." In P. J. Hartin and J. H. Petzer, eds., *Text and Interpretation: New Approaches in the Criticism of the New Testament*. Leiden: E. J. Brill, 271–80.

Ockham, William of. 1967. "On the Notion of Knowledge and Science" (*Expositio super viii libros Physicorum*, Prologus). In *William of Ockham: Philosophical Writings*. Ed. and trans. Philoteus Boehner. London: Nelson, 8–9.

O'Collins, Gerald. 1981. *Fundamental Theology*. New York: Paulist Press.

Oepke, Albrecht. 1964. "καλύπτω." In Gerhardt Kittel, ed., *Theological Dictionary of the New Testament*. Trans. and ed. Geoffrey W. Bromiley. Grand Rapids, MI: Eerdmans.

Ortega y Gasset, José. 1942. "Ideas para una historia de la filosofía." Preface to Émile Bréhier's *Historia de la filosofía*. Buenos Aires: Sudamericana, 379–419.

Packer, James I. 1958. *'Fundamentalism' and the Word of God: Some Evangelical Principles.* Grand Rapids, MI: Eerdmans.

Pannenberg, Wolfhart. 1976. *Theology and the Philosophy of Science.* Trans. F. McDonagh. Philadelphia: Westminster Press.

———. 1970. *Basic Questions in Theology.* Vol. 1. Trans. G. H. Kehm. London: SCM Press.

———. 1968. "Introduction." In Wolfhart Pannenberg et al., eds., *Revelation as History.* Trans. D. Granskou. New York: Macmillan, 1–21.

———. 1968a. "Dogmatic Theses on the Doctrine of Revelation." In Wolfhart Pannenberg et al., eds., *Revelation as History.* Trans. D. Granskou. New York: Macmillan, 125–58.

Panneberg, Wolfhart, et al., eds. 1968. *Revelation as History.* Trans. D. Granskou. New York: Macmillan.

Panofsky, Erwin. 1955. "The History of Art as a Humanistic Discipline." In *Meaning in the Visual Arts: Papers in and on Art History.* Garden City, NY: Doubleday, 1–25.

Peckhaus, Volker. 2000. "The Contextualism of Philosophy." In Martin Kusch, ed., *The Sociology of Philosophical Knowledge.* Dordrecht: Kluwer, 179–91.

Peirce, Charles S. 1931. *Collected Papers.* Ed. Charles Hartshorne and Paul Weiss. Cambridge, MA: Harvard University Press.

Pinnock, Clark H. 1967. *A Defense of Biblical Infallibility.* Philadelphia: Presbyterian and Reformed Publishing Co.

Plato. 1961. *Republic.* In Edith Hamilton and Huntington Cairns, eds., *The Collected Dialogues of Plato, Including the Letters.* New York: Pantheon Books, 575–844.

———. 1961. *Ion.* In Edith Hamilton and Huntington Cairns, eds., *The Collected Dialogues of Plato, Including the Letters.* New York: Pantheon Books, 215–28.

———. 1961. *Theaetetus.* In Edith Hamilton and Huntington Cairns, eds., *The Collected Dialogues of Plato, Including the Letters.* New York: Pantheon Books, 845–919.

———. 1961. *Phaedrus.* In Edith Hamilton and Huntington Cairns, eds., *The Collected Dialogues of Plato, Including the Letters.* New York: Pantheon Books, 475–525.

Preus, Robert. 1970. *Theology of Post-Reformation Lutheranism: A Study of Theological Prolegomena.* St. Louis, MO: Concordia Publishing House.

Putnam, Hilary. 1975. "The Meaning of 'Meaning.'" In *Mind, Language and Reality.* Cambridge: Cambridge University Press, 215–77.

Quine, W. V. O. 1987. "Indeterminacy of Translation Again." *Journal of Philosophy* 84:5–10.

———. 1970. "On the Reasons for Indeterminacy of Translation." *Journal of Philosophy* 67:178–83.

———. 1969. *Ontological Relativity and Other Essays.* New York: Columbia University Press.

———. 1953. "On What There Is." In *From a Logical Point of View.* Cambridge, MA: Harvard University Press, 1–19.

Rahner, Karl, and Joseph Ratzinhger. 1966. *Revelation and Tradition.* New York: Herder and Herder.

Räisänen, Heikki. 1990. *Beyond New Testament Theology: A Story and a Programme.* London: SCM Press.

Rée, Jonathan.1988. "History, Philosophy, and Interpretation: Some Reactions to Jonathan Bennett's *Study of Spinoza's 'Ethics.'"* In Peter H. Hare, ed., *Doing Philosophy Historically.* Buffalo, NY: Prometheus Books, 44–61.

Ricoeur, Paul. 1990. "Interpretative Narrative." In Regina M. Schwartz, ed. *The Book and the Text.* Oxford: Blackwell, 237–57.

———. 1981. *Hermeneutics and the Human Sciences.* Trans. J. B. Thompson. Cambridge: Cambridge University Press.

———. 1980. *Essays on Biblical Interpretation.* Philadelphia: Fortress Press.

———. 1978. "Structure, Word, Event." In Charles E. Regan and David Stewart, eds., *The Philosophy of Paul Ricoeur: An Anthology of His Work.* Boston: Beacon Press, 109–19.

———. 1978a. "Creativity in Language: Word, Polysemy, Metaphor." In Charles E. Regan and David Stewart, eds., *The Philosophy of Paul Ricoeur: An Anthology of His Work.* Boston: Beacon Press, 120–33.

———. 1976. *Interpretation Theory.* Fort Worth: Texas Christian University Press.

Russell, Bertrand. 1948. *Human Knowledge: Its Scope and Limits.* New York: Simon and Schuster.

Sanders, James A. 1972. *Torah and Canon.* Philadelphia: Fortress Press.

Scheffler, E. H. 1991. "Reading Luke from the Perspective of Liberation Theology." In P. J. Hartin and J. H. Petzer, eds., *Text and Interpretation: New Approaches in the Criticism of the New Testament.* Leiden: E. J. Brill, 281–99.

Schleiermacher, F. D. E. 1998. *Hermeneutics and Criticism and Other Writings.* Trans. and ed. Andrew Bowie. Cambridge: Cambridge University Press.

Schmid, Heinrich. 1961. *The Doctrinal Theology of the Evangelical Lutheran Church.* 3rd rev. ed. Trans. from German and Latin by Charles A. Hay and Henry E. Jacobs. Minneapolis, MN: Augsbury Publishing House. Contains texts from John Gerhard, Abraham Calov, John Andrew Quenstedt, John William Baier, David Hollaz, and Daniel Hoffman.

———. 1977. *Hermeneutics: The Handwritten Manuscripts.* Ed. Heinz Kimmerle. Trans. James Duke and Jack Forstman. Missoula, MT: Scholars Press.

Schneider, Sandra M. 1991. *The Revelatory Text.* San Francisco: Harper.

Schwartz, Regina M., ed. 1990. *The Book and the Text: The Bible and Literary Theory.* Oxford: Blackwell.

Scotus, John Duns. 1950. *Ordinatio.* Ed. Carolo Balić. In *Opera omnia.* Vatican.

Searle, John. 1984. *Intentionality: An Essay in the Philosophy of Mind.* Cambridge: Cambridge University Press.

———. 1979. "The Logical Status of Fictional Discourse." In *Expression and Meaning.* Cambridge: Cambridge University Press, 58–75.

Shillingsburg, Peter L. 1986. *Scholarly Editing in the Computer Age: Theory and Practice.* Athens: University of Georgia Press.

Shorter, Aylward. 1983. *Revelation and Its Interpretation.* London: Geoffrey Chapman.

Smaley, Beryl. 1952. *The Study of the Bible in the Middle Ages.* Oxford: Basil Blackwell.

Smart, Ninian. 1971. *The Religious Experience of Mankind.* London: Fontana.

Stead, G. C. 1958. "How Theologians Reason." In Basil Mitchell, ed., *Faith and Logic.* London: Allen & Unwin.

Steiner, George. 1975. *After Babel: Aspects of Language and Translation.* New York: Oxford University Press.

Stevenson, C. L. 1962. "On the Reasons That Can Be Given for the Interpretation of a Poem." In J. Margolis, ed., *Philosophy Looks at the Arts.* New York: Scribner, 121–39.

Stout, Jeffrey. 1982. "What Is the Meaning of a Text?" *New Literary History* 14, 1:1–14.

Stuhlmacher, Peter. 1977. *Historical Criticism and Theological Interpretation of Scripture: Toward a Hermeneutics of Consent.* Trans. Roy A. Harrisville. Philadelphia: Fortress Press.

Suárez, Francisco. 1856. *De santissimo Trinitatis mysterio.* Ed. A. D. M. André. In *Opera omnia.* Vol. 1. Paris: Vivès, 531–822.

Suleiman, Susan R. 1980. "Introduction: Varieties of Audience-Oriented Criticism." In Susan R. Suleiman and Inge Crosman, eds., *The Reader in the Text: Essays on Audience and Interpretation.* Princeton, NJ: Princeton University Press, 3–45.

Swinburne, Richard. 1992. *Revelation: From Metaphor to Analogy.* Oxford: Clarendon Press.

Temple, William. 1960. *Nature, Man and God: Being the Gifford Lectures Delivered in the University of Glasgow in the Academical Years 1932 - 33 and 1933 - 34.* London: Macmillan.

Thiselton, Anthony C. 1999. "Communicative Action and Promise in Interdisciplinary Biblical, and Theological Hermeneutics." In Roger Lundin et al., eds., *The Promise of Hermeneutics.* Grand Rapids, MI: Eerdmans, 133–239.

Thorton, L. S. 1950. *Revelation and the Modern World.* Westminster, England: Dacre Press.

Tillich, Paul. 1951. *Systematic Theology.* Vol. I. Chicago: University of Chicago Press.

Todorov, Tzvetan. 1980. "Reading as Construction." In Susan R. Suleiman and Inge Crosman, eds., *The Reader in the Text: Essays on Audience and Interpretation.* Princeton, NJ: Princeton University Press, 67–81.

Trembath, Kern Robert. 1991. *Divine Revelation: Our Moral Relation with God.* Oxford: Oxford University Press.

Tyrrell, George. 1907. *Through Scylla and Charybdis.* London: Longmans.

Unamuno, Miguel de. 1981. "On the Reading and Interpretation of *Don Quijote.*" In J. R. Jones and K. Douglas, eds., *Miguel de Cervantes, Don Quixote.* New York: W. W. Norton, 974–9.

Van Aarde, A. G. 1991. "Narrative Criticism Applied to John 4:43–54." In P. J. Hartin and J. H. Petzer, eds., *Text and Interpretation: New Approaches in the Criticism of the New Testament.* Leiden: E. J. Brill, 101–28.

Vander Goot, H. 1984. *Interpreting the Bible in Theology and the Church.* New York: Edwin Mellen Press.

Vanhoozer, Kevin J. 1986. "The Semantics of Biblical Literature: Truth and Scripture's Diverse Literary Forms." In D. A. Carson and John D. Woodbridge, eds., *Hermeneutics, Authority, and Canon.* Grand Rapids, MI: Academie Books, 49–104.

Van Riel, Gerd, Carlos Steel, and James McEvoy, eds., 1996. *Iohannes Scottus Eriugena: The Bible and Hermeneutics.* Leuven: Leuven University Press.

Van Tilborg, S. 1991. "Ideology and Text: John 15 in the Context of the Farewell Discourse." In P. J. Hartin and J. H. Petzer, eds., *Text and Interpretation: New Approaches in the Criticism of the New Testament.* Leiden: E. J. Brill, 259–71.

Von Campenhausen, Hans. 1972. *The Formation of the Christian Bible.* Trans. John Austin Baker. London: Adam & Charles Black. Philadelphia: Fortress Press.

Vorster, W. S. 1991. "Through the Eyes of the Historian." In P. J. Hartin and J. H. Petzer, eds., *Text and Interpretation: New Approaches in the Criticism of the New Testament.* Leiden: E. J. Brill, 15–46.

Walhaut, Clarence. 1999. "Narrative Hermeneutics." In Roger Lundin et al., eds., *The Promise of Hermeneutics.* Grand Rapids, MI: Eerdmans, 65–131.

Walton, Kendall L. 1987. "Style and the Products and Processes of Art." In Berel Lang, ed., *The Concept of Style.* Ithaca, NY: Cornell University Press.

Weitz, Morris. 1964. *Hamlet and the Philosophy of Literary Criticism.* Chicago: University of Chicago Press.

Wells, G. A. 1999. *The Jesus Myth.* Chicago: Open Court.

Wilder, Amos. N. 1969. *The New Voice: Religion, Literature, Hermeneutics.* Cambridge, MA: Herder and Herder.

Wilsmore, Susan. 1987. "The Literary Work Is Not Its Text." *Philosophy and Literature* 11:307–16.

Wilson, R. R. 1984. *Sociological Approaches to the Old Testament.* Philadelphia: Fortress Press.

Wimsatt, William K., and Monroe C. Beardsley. 1954. "The Intentional Fallacy." In *The Verbal Icon: Studies in the Meaning of Poetry.* Lexington: University of Kentucky Press, 3–18.

Wolff, Christian F. von. 1963. *Preliminary Discourse on Philosophy in General.* Trans. Richard J. Blackwell. Indianapolis, IN: Bobbs-Merrill Co.

Wolterstorff, Nicholas. 1995. *Divine Discourse: Philosophical Reflections on the Claim That God Speaks.* Cambridge: Cambridge University Press.

Wood, Charles M. 1981. *The Formation of Christian Understanding.* Philadelphia: Westminster Press.

Woods, G. F. 1958. *Theological Explanation: A Study of the Meaning and Means of Explaining Science, History and Theology, Based upon the Stanton Lectures Delivered in the University of Cambridge, 1953–56.* Welwyn, England: James Nisbet.

Wright, N. T. 1992. *The New Testament and the People of God.* Minneapolis, MN: Fortress Press.

———. 1992a. *Christian Origins and the Question of God.* Minneapolis, MN: Fortress Press.

Wuellner, W. 1991. "Rhetorical Criticism and Its Theory in Culture-Critical Perspective: The Narrative Rhetoric of John 11." In P. J. Hartin and J. H. Petzer, eds., *Text and Interpretation: New Approaches in the Criticism of the New Testament.* Leiden: E. J. Brill, 171–86.

Author Index

N.B.: Material in author and subject indexes is drawn from the text or notes, but not the bibliography.

Subject Index